Measuring Child Well-Being:
An Inventory of Key Indicators, Domains and Indicator Selection Criteria to Support the Development of a National Set of Child Well-Being Indicators

Anne-Marie Brooks
Sinéad Hanafin
June 2005

The National Children's Office,
1st Floor, St. Martin's House, Waterloo Road, Dublin 4
Tel: 353 1 2420000 Fax: 353 1 664 1929
Email: nco@health.gov.ie Website: www.nco.ie

Design: Penhouse Design www.penhouse.ie
Printed by: New Oceans

01

CONTENTS

02

05

07

09

INTRODUCTION

The identification of a national set of child well-being indicators to form the basis for the State of the Nation's Children report was identified as a key objective in the National Children's Strategy (2000). This objective reflected an increasing global effort to measure and monitor child well-being, which has been demonstrated by the numerous reports on child well-being that have been published in the last decade (Ben-Arieh et al., 2001). A necessary starting point, therefore, for developing the national set of child well-being indicators was to take account of existing work in this area and this, in turn, led to an examination of many different existing indicator sets. The Inventory presented here is broadly reflective of the multiplicity of indicators and their definitions, domains and categories in use and selection criteria applied to their inclusion in the indicator sets.

In the Irish context, it is important to note that although there was no agreed national set of child well-being indicators there was, nevertheless, a number of developments in different areas. These include the work of individuals (including, for example, the work of Carroll, 2002; McKeown et al., 2001, 2003), agencies (such as the Combat Poverty Agency and Best Health for Children (see, for example, Costello, 1999; Combat Poverty Agency, 2000; Nolan, 2000; New Policy Institute, 2001; and Quinlan et al., 2001), and Government Departments (Department of Health and Children, 2000, 2001, 2002a, 2002b).

This document includes more than 2,500 indicators from 80 international, national and regional reports on child well-being and outlines the way in which child well-being has been conceptualised across different reports and throughout different countries. The compilation of this Inventory helped to define priorities for the national set of child well-being indicators for Ireland.

OBJECTIVES

The main objectives for compiling this Inventory were as follows:

1. TO IDENTIFY INDICATORS CURRENTLY IN USE AND ROUTINELY PUBLISHED ACROSS DIFFERENT COUNTRIES;
2. TO IDENTIFY INDICATORS THAT ARE WELL-RECOGNISED AND ACCEPTED ACROSS DIFFERENT COUNTRIES;
3. TO IDENTIFY INDICATORS THAT HAVE BEEN RECOGNISED BY EXPERTS AND TESTED FOR SCIENTIFIC SOUNDNESS;
4. TO IDENTIFY THE KEY DOMAINS AND/OR FRAMEWORKS USED TO CONCEPTUALISE CHILD WELL-BEING ACROSS DIFFERENT COUNTRIES;
5. TO IDENTIFY THE KEY CRITERIA USED TO GUIDE THE SELECTION OF CHILD WELL-BEING INDICATORS ACROSS DIFFERENT COUNTRIES; AND
6. TO PROVIDE A RESOURCE FOR OTHERS WHO MAY BE EMBARKING ON A SIMILAR TYPE PROJECT.

METHODOLOGY

A review of indicator sets in use nationally and internationally was undertaken to compile this Inventory and Internet searches were conducted to obtain material. The review process identified recommendations from 80 international, national and regional collaborations. All reports were reviewed for content, domain, sub-domain, number of indicators used and country of origin. The criteria used for selecting the indicators were also examined when given.

The final Inventory included more than 2,500 child well-being indicators, which were drawn from:

- 6 international collaborations including *The State of the World's Children* (UNICEF, 2005) and the *Child Health Indicators of Life and Development* (Rigby and Kohler, 2002);
- 39 national indicator sets including *America's Children* (Federal Interagency Programme on Child and Family Statistics, 2002), *Australia's Children: Their Health and Well-Being* (Al-Yaman et al., 2002) and *The Well-Being of Canada's Young Children* (Government of Canada, 2002); and
- 28 regional indicator sets drawn largely on material from Canada, the United States of America and Australia.

A review of youth *'indicators in use in states'* (N = 12) compiled by the Chapin Hall Centre for Children (Reidy and Winje, 2002) was also included. According to Ben-Arieh et al. (2001), it is important that the selection of indicators should be contingent on culture and specific needs of specific populations. Therefore, in this review, particular efforts were taken to consolidate previous work undertaken in the Irish context. This included the following:

- The second annual report from the Chief Medical Officer of the Department of Health and Children *The Health of Our Children* (Department of Health and Children, 2001);
- A Mid-Western Health Board publication on *'The Health and Well-Being of Children in the Mid-West'* (Mid-Western Health Board, (2001); and
- Recommendations from the Combat Poverty Agency (2000) and those outlined in the *Literature Review of Children's Well-Being* (Costello, 1999).

A number of child well-being indicators and indicator areas recommended for use in the scientific literature were also included and this took account of, among others, the work of Hauser et al. (1997) and Ben-Arieh et al. (2001).

While the majority of the indicator sets and scientific literature from which this material was drawn relate generally to child well-being, some are more specific and concern particular aspects of children's lives, for example, perinatal health (Zeitlin and Wildman, 2003) and early childhood care and education (United Nations Educational, Scientific and Cultural Organisation, 1995), or particular periods in children's lives such as early childhood (Jensen et al., 2002; Government of Canada, 2002). A complete list of these reports and the scientific literature used in this review is presented in the Appendix.

This Inventory is not intended to be exhaustive but rather provides the reader with a general view of the current indicators of child well-being in use and those recommended for use by leading experts in the area. A short synthesis of the key findings emerging from this review is now presented.

COMMONLY USED INDICATORS

This review highlighted some of the key measures of child well-being currently in use and routinely published elsewhere, and also gave an indication of the measures that are well recognised and accepted across different countries and areas of children's lives. This ensured that indicators with the strongest association with child well-being would not be overlooked in this development. A summary of widely used measures include the following:

- Health-related measures such as infant and child mortality rates and hospitalisation. Of particular interest in these contexts are injury-related mortality rates and injury-related hospitalisation rates (both intentional and unintentional).
- Other measures of child health, in particular for the period of infancy and early childhood, include, for example, measures on birth weight, immunisation rates, infectious diseases, pre-natal care, breastfeeding rates, maternal use of tobacco, alcohol and/or drugs during pregnancy, disability and chronic health conditions.
- Mental health is also a common concern within the context of children's health. This area relates mainly to the period of adolescence where the primary focus is on the incidence of suicide, attempted suicide, suicide ideation and self-reported happiness.
- Other widely used health-related measures related to the period of adolescence focus on teenage fertility and sexual behaviour, which includes, for example, pregnancies, births and abortions among adolescents, contraceptive use, the incidence of sexually transmitted diseases and the number of those who are sexually active or sexually experienced.
- Other risk behaviours among adolescents include the use of tobacco, alcohol and drugs, in particular lifetime use and current use, the latter being defined as use within the past 30 days.
- Measures of economic well-being, in particular the number of children in poverty, which is traditionally calculated using the median family income and other non-pecuniary measures such as housing (housing conditions, overcrowding and housing costs) and social welfare dependence.
- Measures of children as perpetrators of crime, with distinctions commonly being drawn between the incidence of serious violent index crimes (which include murder, non-negligent manslaughter, forcible rape, robbery and aggravated assault) and serious non-violent or property index crimes (which include burglary, larceny and motor vehicle theft).
- Measures of children as victims of crime including abuse and neglect, which generally distinguishes between sexual abuse, physical abuse, emotional abuse and neglect (both reported and confirmed).
- Education-related measures including participation in pre-school, primary, secondary and tertiary education. This mainly includes measures on school attendance, school enrolment and school completion.
- Other education-related measures focus primarily on academic attainment or educational outcomes, particularly in reading, writing, science and mathematics.

- Children's participation in various school activities and out-of-school activities, including physical activity levels, volunteering and television viewing.
- Parental, family and community characteristics such as parental education level, parental age, parental employment/unemployment, parental mental health, family structure (two parent, mother only, father only), children placed in out-of-home care and social capital.
- Children's relationships with their parents including, for example, parental attachment, parental style, parental rules and parental time with their children. Children's relationships with teachers, peers and other significant adults in their lives also appear, albeit less frequently.

A comprehensive list of all indicators identified in this review can be found on pages 22 - 141. Indicators have been broadly categorised by subject area. The number appearing beside each indicator corresponds to the list of reports in the Appendix.

15

COMMONLY USED DOMAINS

Many of the reports in this review also described the domains or conceptual frameworks adopted for conceptualising child well-being. While there is some overlap, six relatively distinct domains are generally found, related to the following areas:

- demographic characteristics;
- economic status;
- education;
- family, school and community context;
- health and safety; and
- social, emotional and behavioural development.

A list of these domains, along with variations of them, was compiled and can be found on pages 144 - 147 of this document.

COMMONLY USED SELECTION CRITERIA

In this review, several reports also described the criteria used for selecting the indicators and in general three major types of criteria emerge, which mirror results of a similar review undertaken elsewhere (Zeitlin et al. 2003a):

- The first set of criteria assesses the importance of the indicators using terms such as 'significant', 'useful', 'relevant' and 'representative'. Importance in this context is determined both in relation to the 'significant burden' or prevalence of the problem and its amenability to 'effective action'.
- The second set of criteria for selecting indicators is that they must be practical in relation to data currently collected, with criteria such as 'feasibility', 'cost efficiency', 'data availability' and 'timeliness' routinely mentioned. The ability to disaggregate data by, for example, age, sex, gender and geographic location is also considered important in this regard.
- The third set of criteria for selecting indicators is largely technical, highlighting the importance of robust indicators that are, for example, 'valid', 'reliable', 'sensitive', 'evidence-based', 'consistent' and 'easy to understand'.

A full list of these criteria can be found on pages 149 - 150 of this document.

CHALLENGES TO INDICATOR SELECTION

In compiling this Inventory, several challenges to identifying and selecting child well-being indicators were identified and these are now described.

COMPARABILITY

Three issues emerged in respect of developing an indicator set capable of making international comparisons. First, a number of indicators identified in this review could not be used for comparison with Irish children because they reflect different situations and different circumstances. An indicator, for example, that measures the percentage of high school students who carried a weapon to school in the past 30 days or one that measures the percentage of children who were ill with fever in the last two weeks and received any appropriate anti-malarial drugs – have little relevance to the Irish context.

Likewise, because of their reference to local systems and policies, many of the indicators included in this review would not be appropriate for use in the Irish context. This included, for example, reference to specific health insurance programmes in the USA such as Medicaid and Medicare and also reference to specific social welfare assistance programmes such as Temporary Assistance for Needy Families (TANF) and Aid for Families with Dependent Children (AFDC).

Finally, because many of the indicator definitions identified in this Inventory differ across countries, the ability to identify indicators capable of drawing international comparisons is difficult since according to Lack et al. (2003) recording systems and definitions for measuring child well-being should ideally be identical to ensure perfect comparability with other countries. Examples of how definitions vary from country to country can be seen by the diversity of national immunisation schedules used or by the different poverty thresholds adopted as illustrated below:

- the proportion of households with children, that have incomes below 50% of average (median) household income (Bradshaw and Barnes, 1999);
- the percentage of children living in households with a household income below the national 60% median (Rigby and Kohler, 2002).

Zeitlin et al. (2003b) suggests, however, that despite such differences in definitions, an interface with other indicator sets can still be provided by using broad definitions of individual indicators and by adopting full distributions or thresholds. An example of how this can be achieved is found in *Trends in the Well-Being of America's Children and Youth,* as follows:

- Percentage of children in the USA under age 18 living below selected poverty thresholds: under 50% of poverty, under 100% of poverty, under 150% of poverty and under 200% of poverty (Gutmann and Hamilton, 2001).

CONSTRUCT COMPARABILITY

This review also demonstrated that even when there is broad agreement about the importance of an indicator area, many different, yet valid, indicators can be used to examine a single phenomenon of interest. All of the following, for example, were found to have been used to measure use of alcohol among youth: 1) age at first alcohol use;

2) alcohol use in the past 30 days; 3) alcohol use in the past week; 4) alcohol use in the past year; 5) approval of peer use and perception of peer acceptance of alcohol use; 6) binge-drinking and heavy drinking; 7) daily alcohol use; 8) driving after using alcohol; 9) drunkenness; 10) hospitalisation-related hospital use; 11) lifetime alcohol use; 12) parental guidance and perceived parental approval of alcohol use; 13) perception of availability of alcohol; 14) perception of harmfulness of alcohol; 15) perception of police intervention for alcohol use; 16) school attendance while using alcohol; and 17) sexual activity while using alcohol. Therefore, the challenge lies in selecting the most suitable/useful indicator from these options that reflect key priorities and the national context.

AGE-SPECIFIC INDICATORS

The final area of challenge highlighted in this review related to the extent to which children's lives at all ages can be represented. Firstly, this review demonstrated that there are many indicators in use to study older children and infants. However, a notable paucity of indicators for the middle childhood period emerged. This is due largely to the reliance on data from international studies to construct the indicators. This includes the Health Behaviour of School-aged Children (HBSC) study, which is restricted to 11, 13 and 15-year-old children only and the Programme for International Student Assessment (PISA) study, which is restricted to 15-year-olds only. In respect of infants, there is a substantial amount of administrative data to support indicator development and consequently, this area also appears commonly. The task, therefore, of finding valid indicators of child well-being that relate to children of all ages from infancy to adolescence is particularly difficult. This has been noted in similar reviews undertaken elsewhere (Pollard et al., 2002; Ben-Arieh et al., 2001).

Finally, although Ireland defines a child as under 18 years of age (United Nations Convention on the Rights of the Child, 1989); National Children's Strategy, 2000), many of the indicators identified in this review use the traditional quinquenial age bands, which are as follows: 0-4 years, 5-9 years, 10-14 years and 15-19 years. This further compounds the international comparability challenges arising in respect of this development.

CONCLUSION

The compilation of this Inventory helped to define priorities for the national set of child well-being indicators for Ireland. A number of widely used measures of child well-being were identified and these included infant and child mortality rates, mental health problems, teenage fertility and sexual behaviour, use of tobacco, alcohol and drugs, children in poverty, children as perpetrators and victims of crime, and participation rates in education. Key domains for conceptualising child well-being (demographic characteristics, economic status, education, family, school and community context, health and safety, and social, emotional and behavioural development) and key criteria used to select child well-being indicators elsewhere were also highlighted.

In addition, in this review several challenges to developing the national set of child well-being indicators were identified. These included difficulties in identifying indicators capable of drawing international comparisons (due to different situations and different circumstances, references to country-specific systems and/or policies, and the variations in indicator definitions used across countries), different understandings of, or focus on, a single phenomenon of interest and the imbalance in the availability of data for all periods of childhood from infancy to adolescence. It is intended that this document be used as a resource for others embarking on a similar type project. A full account of the broader development in this area is available through the National Children's Office website at **www.nco.ie.**

m'aime
est allé

KEY INDICATORS OF CHILD WELL-BEING

ABUSE AND NEGLECT [REPORTED AND CONFIRMED]

Related domains:

Abuse and neglect; care and support; child protection; child safety; children in strong, stable families; children live in stable, supported families; children safe in their families and communities; conditions (endangerment); education and childcare; family; family and community (family); family and community (peer relationships); family and household; family and social functioning; health; health (health conditions); health (violence); health and safety (youth engaging in risky behaviour); health conditions and health care (health conditions); health status (children); healthy children; safety (free of violence, abuse, neglect); safety and physical status; social determinants of health; social policy indicators; social well-being; victims of violence; youth engaging in risky behaviour.

Recommended measures:

- Number of children receiving services through State's Domestic Violence/Sexual Abuse shelters[1]
- Child abuse and neglect, reported and substantiated[1]
- Rate of children aged 0-14 years who are the subject of child protection substantiation[2]
- Rate of children aged 0-14 years who are the subject of care and protection orders[2]
- Rate of children aged 0-14 years who are the victim of physical and sexual assault[2]
- Prevalence of child abuse and neglect in its various forms[5]
- Children on the child protection register, rate per 1,000[6]
- Number of child protection reports[9]
- Number of reports where assessment determined abuse or neglect[9]
- Percentage of students in Grades 9-12 who reported to have ever been raped[10]
- Percentage of children who are victims of child maltreatment. Child maltreatment is defined as 'behaviour towards a child, which is: a) outside the norms of conduct and b) entails a substantial risk of causing physical or emotional harm. Behaviours included will consist of actions and omissions, ones that are intentional and ones that are unintentional'. Four types of maltreatment are generally recognised, including physical abuse, sexual abuse, neglect and emotional maltreatment. In the National Statistics System that tracks child maltreatment, children are counted as victims if an investigation classifies their case as substantiated or indicated child maltreatment. Substantiated cases are those in which an allegation of maltreatment or risk of maltreatment was supported or founded according to State law or policy. Indicated cases are those in which an allegation of maltreatment or risk of maltreatment could not be substantiated, but there was reason to suspect maltreatment or the risk of maltreatment[10]
- Percentage of students in Grades 9-12 who reported being victims of dating violence in past 12 months (hit, slapped or physically hurt on purpose by boyfriend/girlfriend)[10]
- Percentage of adults who agree that it is sometimes necessary to give a child 'a good hard spanking'[10]
- Children abused and neglected, rate per 1,000[11]

- Number of distinct children subject to child protection notification, rate per 100,000 (a matter constitutes a child protection notification when information indicates that a child has been harmed or is at risk of harm and does not have a parent or other family member both willing and able to protect the child from harm), by male, female and in total, where appropriate, by age categories <1 year, 1-3 years, 4-6 years, 7-9 years, 10-12 years, 13-15 years and 16-18 years and in total, where appropriate, and by geographic location and in total, where appropriate[13]
- Number of distinct children admitted to protective orders (a child protection notification differs from a child protection order, which is a court order made under child protection legislation), by male, female and in total, where appropriate, by age categories <1 year, 1-3 years, 4-6 years, 7-9 years, 10-12 years, 13-15 years and 16-18 years and in total, where appropriate, and by geographic location and in total, where appropriate[13]
- Number of distinct children subject to substantiated (including substantiated risk) notification, by most serious type of harm substantiated (physical, emotional, sexual, neglect), rate per 100,000, by male, female and in total, where appropriate, by age categories <1 year, 1-3 years, 4-6 years, 7-9 years, 10-12 years, 13-15 years and 16-18 years and in total, where appropriate, and by geographic location and in total, where appropriate[13]
- Proportion of children registered on the Child Protection Register[15]
- Number of child maltreatment investigations in Canada among children from birth to 5 years of age, of which, the number substantiated, suspected or unsubstantiated[19]
- Victims of child maltreatment in the USA, substantiated incidents, by type of maltreatment: a) neglect; b) physical abuse; c) sexual abuse; d) psychological or emotional; e) abuse or neglect; and f) other[20]
- Child abuse and neglect rate, reported or confirmed[21]
- Child abuse (physical, emotional, sexual) and neglect, substantiated cases[21]
- Sexually abused youth, rate per 100,000 population, ages 0-19 in Mississippi[22]
- Non-sexually abused youth, rate per 100,000 population, ages 0-19 in Mississippi[22]
- Neglected youth, rate per 100,000 population, ages 0-19 in Mississippi[22]
- Number of CPS reports that are repeat referrals[23]
- Number of substantiated cases of child abuse and neglect. Substantiated cases of child abuse and neglect are confirmed incidents of physical abuse; sexual abuse, or exploitation; negligent treatment; or maltreatment of a child by a person who is responsible for child welfare[23]
- Rate per 1,000 children of child abuse or neglect investigations ruled as 'indicated' (where credible evidence is not satisfactorily refuted) or 'unsubstantiated' (where insufficient evidence is found to support a finding as either indicated or ruled out[24]
- Sources of maltreatment reports (education, legal, social services/mental health, anonymous, other, relatives (excluding parents), medical, friends/neighbours, parents, unknown, child day care/substitute care, victims, perpetrators)[25]
- Percentage of child abuse and neglect victims, by type of maltreatment (neglect/medical neglect, physical abuse, sexual abuse, psychological maltreatment, other)[25]
- Number of referrals to the Child Protection Notification System[27]
- Number of referrals to the Child Protection Notification System, which were confirmed cases of child abuse[27]
- Number of children aged 0-16 assessed as abused (physically, emotionally, sexually) or neglected following a notification to the CYF, per 1,000 children under 17 years of age[29]
- Percentage of child protection cases with a new maltreatment finding while case is open for child protection services[30]
- Percentage of child protection cases with a new maltreatment finding within 12 months of case closure[30]
- Percentage of child maltreatment assessments initiated within 24, 48 and 72 hours of receipt of reports[30]
- Number of deaths and near deaths resulting from child abuse or neglect and child's living arrangement at time of death[30]

- Number of children assessed for maltreatment and number of children with maltreatment determined[30]
- Number of cases in which child protection services were needed and number of cases in which child protection services were provided[30]
- Substantiated victims of physical abuse, sexual abuse or neglect per 10,000 children aged 0-17[31]
- Abuse/neglect reports investigated, unduplicated[32]
- Abuse/neglect reports substantiated, unduplicated[32]
- Number of children receiving assessments for abuse and neglect[33]
- Confirmed deaths due to abuse[33]
- Number of children substantiated as victims of abuse and neglect[33]
- Number of substantiated abuse cases per 1,000 children under age 18[34]
- Number of indicated reports of child abuse and maltreatment. A report becomes 'indicated' when there is some credible evidence that a child has experienced abuse or neglect[39]
- Rate of reported child abuse and neglect cases per 1,000 children under the age of 18[41]
- Reported child abuse and neglect cases[42]
- Number and rate per 1,000 of confirmed cases of abuse to children, ages 0-17[42]
- Incidence of child abuse, neglect, exploitation and relationship violence[43]
- Number of allegations of abuse/neglect; the number of those allegations investigated by Child Protection Services; the number of allegations substantiated[45]
- Confirmed incidence of child abuse and neglect[46]
- Number of children served by child protection services[47]
- Breakdown of child maltreatment investigations, sexual abuse, physical abuse, emotional abuse and neglect[47]
- Fracture of the skull in infants and subdural haematoma[48]
- Percentage of children in the country protected by law against physical punishment, expressed as a percentage of the national child population: a) in schools and other places where children are looked after; and b) in the home or by parents and family members[48]
- Number of investigations into reported cases of abuse and neglect involving children (physical abuse, sexual abuse, mental injury, physical neglect, educational neglect, medical neglect, threat of harm for physical/sexual abuse)[51]
- Number of indicated cases of abuse and neglect involving children (physical abuse, sexual abuse, mental injury, physical neglect, educational neglect, medical neglect, threat of harm for physical/sexual abuse)[51]
- Number of new cases of abuse detected each year in children 0-14 years of age, per 1,000 children 0-14[52]
- Number of new cases of sexual abuse detected each year in children 0-14 years of age, per 1,000 children 0-14[52]
- Female genital mutilation/cutting: a) women - the percentage of women aged 15-49 years of age that have been mutilated/cut; b) daughters - the percentage of women aged 15-49 with at least one mutilated/cut daughter. Female genital mutilation/cutting (FGM/C) involves the cutting or alteration of the female genitalia for social reasons. Generally, there are three recognised types of FGM/C: clitoridectomy, excision and infibulations. Clitoridectomy is the removal of the prepuce with or without excision of all or part of the clitoris. Excision is the removal of the prepuce and clitoris along with all or part of the labia minora. Infibulation is the most severe form and consists of removal of all or part of external genitalia, followed by joining together of the two sides of the labia minora using threads, thorns or other materials to narrow the vaginal opening. A more detailed analysis of this data can be found at www.measuredhs.com and www.prb.org[56]

ACADEMIC ATTAINMENT, AT, ABOVE AND BEHIND GRADE FOR AGE

Related domains:
Academic achievement; children's academic experiences; education and childcare (enrolment); readiness and early school performance.

Recommended measures:

- Children not graduating on time[11]
- Percentage of students aged 7-17 who are behind age-for-grade[21]
- Children aged 12-17 who are 'on track' academically, by marital status and work status of parents[49]
- Percentage of children overage in Grade 3[51]
- Percentage of children aged 12-17 on track academically for their age. Enrolled in school at or above the modal grade level for their age, as reported by parents[54]

ACADEMIC ATTAINMENT, LANGUAGE

Related domains:

Academic performance; children succeed in school; children successful in school; culture and identity; education; educational achievement; educational attainment; family and community context.

Recommended measures:

- Percentage achieving Key Stage 2 in English[6]
- New Standards English/Language Arts assessment scores[31]
- Percentage of 11-year-olds achieving Level 4 or above in the Key Stage 2 tests for English[15]
- Percentage of high school graduates who completed high-level coursework in English[18]
- Percentage of high school graduates who completed high-level coursework in a foreign language[18]
- Percentage of students in Grades 3, 5 and 8 scoring satisfactory or excellent levels on curriculum-based assessments in language usage[24]
- Top 10 languages, other than English spoken at home[38]
- Population by knowledge of official language (English only, French only, both, neither)[38]
- Proportion of Maori children under 15 years and Maori young people aged 15-24 who can speak te reo Maori, as recorded in the New Zealand census of Population and Dwellings 2001. The ability to speak te reo Maori is defined in the census as being able to hold a conversation about a lot of everyday things in Maori language[29]

ACADEMIC ATTAINMENT, MATHEMATICS

Related domains:

Academic performance; access to developmental opportunities (childhood learning and care); achievement; child health and development (developmental); children succeed in school; children succeeding in school; children successful in school; education; education and achievement (achievement and proficiency); education and childcare; education and childcare (achievement and proficiency); education and skills (learning assessments); education outcome; educational achievement; educational attainment; educational development; educational well-being; personal life skills; readiness to learn; school (outcomes); social determinants of health (development).

Recommended measures:

- Number of students who are proficient in mathematics at the end of 3rd Grade[1]
- Percentage of a) 4th and b) 8th Grade public school students failing to reach the basic proficiency level in mathematics, as measured by the National Assessment of Educational Progress (NAEP)[4]
- Numeracy level[5]
- Percentage achieving Key Stage 2 in Maths[6]
- Maths scores at various ages[7]
- Percentage of children registered in Grade 3 mean math scores, by region[8]
- National Assessment of Educational Progress (NAEP) mathematics scale scores for Grades 4, 8 and 12[10]

- The mean number score at 3, 5 and 7, by male, female and in total, where appropriate, by age categories <1 year, 1-3 years, 4-6 years, 7-9 years, 10-12 years, 13-15 years and 16-18 years and in total, where appropriate, and by geographic location and in total, where appropriate[13]
- Percentage of 11-year-olds achieving Level 4 or above in the Key Stage 2 tests for mathematics[15]
- Average mathematics scale scores for students ages 9, 13 and 17[18]
- Percentage of high school graduates who completed high-level coursework in mathematics[18]
- Average mathematics proficiency for children ages 9, 13 and 17 in the USA[20]
- Math achievement for 4th, 8th and 12th Graders, percentage of children demonstrating proficient or advanced achievement in these areas[21]
- Math achievement ages 5-12[21]
- Percentage of public school students demonstrating basic skills in mathematics at the passing level at the end of Grade 11[24]
- Percentage of students in Grades 3, 5 and 8 scoring satisfactory or excellent levels on curriculum-based assessments in math[24]
- Mean scores for 15-year-old New Zealand students based on the international mathematics literacy scales set by the PISA study 2000[29]
- Percentage of children ages 3 to 5 who pass the 3rd Grade math test by the time of case closing[30]
- Percentage of children age 13 and older who pass the 8th Grade math tests by the time of case closing[30]
- New Standards Math assessment scores[31]
- End of Grade math tests, 3rd Grade proficiency[32]
- End of Grade math tests, 8th Grade proficiency[32]
- Percentage of 5th Graders scoring below proficient in math[34]
- Percentage of children at Grade 3 (indicative of high achievement) in the area of maths[36]
- Percentage of English as a second language (ESL) students vs. non-ESL students in Grades 3 and 6 who attained Level 3 or 4 in the EQAO assessment (math)[47]
- Percentage of all schools within low income areas with more than 70% of students achieving Level 3 or 4 in at least one of the EQAO assessments (reading, writing, math)[47]
- Percentage of all schools with more than 70% of students achieving Level 3 or 4 in at least one of the EQAO assessments (reading, writing, math)[47]
- Scores on international mathematics assessments of 13- and 14-year-olds in selected countries[50]
- Mathematics proficiency, by age (9, 13, and 17-years) sex, race, television watched per day (0-2 hours, 3-5 hours, 6 or more hours), reading material in the home (0-2 items, 3 items, 4 items), language other than English (often, sometimes, never) and type of school (public, private)[50]
- Test results of students (below basic, basic, proficient, advanced) on PACT math[51]
- Percentage of students in Grades 3 and 8 scoring below basic in math[51]

ACADEMIC ATTAINMENT, OTHER

Related domains:
Academic performance; children successful in school; education and childcare (achievement and proficiency); educational attainment.

Recommended measures:
- Proportion of 7-year-olds achieving Level 2 or above in the Key Stage 1 test/task in schools in Sure Start areas[15]
- Average music and visual arts proficiency for children in Grade 8 in the USA[20]
- US history and geography achievement for 4th, 8th and 12th Graders, percentage of children demonstrating proficient or advanced achievement in these areas[21]
- Percentage of students in Grades 3, 5 and 8 scoring satisfactory or excellent levels on curriculum-based assessments in social studies[24]

ACADEMIC ATTAINMENT, READING

Related domains:

Academic performance; access to developmental opportunities (childhood learning and care); achievement; child health and development (developmental); children succeed in school; children succeeding in school; children successful in school; education; education and achievement (achievement and proficiency); education and childcare; education and childcare (achievement and proficiency); education and skills (learning assessments); education outcome; educational benchmarks; educational development; educational well-being; personal life skills; readiness to learn; school (outcomes); student achievement.

Recommended measures:

- Number of children who are independent readers by end of 3rd Grade[1]
- Number of students who are proficient in reading at end of 3rd Grade[1]
- Percentage of children in years 3, 5 and 7 meeting national literacy (reading and writing) and numeracy benchmarks[2]
- Literacy level[5]
- Reading scores at various ages[7]
- National Assessment of Educational Progress (NAEP) reading scale scores for Grades 4, 8 and 12[10]
- Mean reading score in years 3, 5 and 7, by male, female and in total, where appropriate, by age categories <1 year, 1-3 years, 4-6 years, 7-9 years, 10-12 years, 13-15 years and 16-18 years and in total, where appropriate, and by geographic location and in total, where appropriate[13]
- Average reading scale scores for students ages 9, 13 and 17[18]
- Average reading proficiency for children ages 9, 13 and 17 in the USA[20]
- Reading achievement for 4th, 8th and 12th Graders, percentage of children demonstrating proficient or advanced achievement in this area[21]
- Reading achievement ages 5-12[21]
- Percentage of public school students demonstrating basic skills in reading at the passing level at the end of Grade 11[24]
- Percentage of students in Grades 3, 5 and 8 scoring satisfactory or excellent levels on curriculum-based assessments in reading[24]
- Mean score in reading literacy achievement for New Zealand Year 5 students (aged around 9-10 years) who took part in the 2001 Progress in International Reading Literacy Study (PILRS-01)[29]
- Mean scores for 15-year-old New Zealand students based on the international reading literacy scales set by the PISA study 2000[29]
- Percentage of children ages 3 to 5 who pass the 3rd Grade basic reading test by the time of case closing[30]
- Percentage of children age 13 and older who pass the 8th Grade reading test by the time of case closing[30]
- Percentage of 2nd Graders meeting reading standards[31]
- End of Grade reading, 3rd Grade proficiency[32]
- End of Grade reading, 8th Grade proficiency[32]
- Percentage of 5th Graders scoring below proficient in reading[34]
- Percentage of children at Grade 3 (indicative of high achievement) in the areas of reading[36]
- Percentage of all schools within low income areas with more than 70% of students achieving Level 3 or 4 in at least one of the EQAO assessments (reading, writing, math)[47]
- Percentage of all schools with more than 70% of students achieving Level 3 or 4 in at least one of the EQAO assessments (reading, writing, math)[47]
- Percentage of English as a second language (ESL) students vs. non-ESL students in Grades 3 and 6 who attained Level 3 or 4 in the EQAO assessment (reading)[47]
- Scores on international reading assessments of 13- and 14-year-olds in selected countries[50]

- Student proficiency in reading, by age (9, 13, and 17-years), sex, race, parental education as reported by students (not high school graduate, graduated high school, some college, graduated college), reading materials in the home (less than 3 items, 3 items, 4 items) and type of school (public, private)[50]
- Test results of students (below basic, basic, proficient, advanced) in reading[51]
- Percentage of students in Grades 3 and 8 scoring below basic in reading[51]

ACADEMIC ATTAINMENT, SCHOLASTIC ASSESSMENT TEST (SAT)

Related domains:
Children succeed in school; education and childcare (achievement and proficiency); educational well-being.

Recommended measures:
- Average SAT scores for college-bound high school seniors (math and verbal)[21]
- SAT scores[31]
- Percentage of graduating seniors taking test and average SAT scores[32]

ACADEMIC ATTAINMENT, SCIENCE

Related domains:
Children successful in school; education; education and achievement (achievement and proficiency); education and childcare (achievement and proficiency); education and skills (learning assessments); education outcome; educational achievement; school (outcomes).

Recommended measures:
- Percentage achieving Key Stage 2 in Science[6]
- Science scores at various ages[7]
- National Assessment of Educational Progress (NAEP) science scale scores for Grades 4, 8 and 12[10]
- Percentage of high school graduates who completed high-level coursework in science[18]
- Average science proficiency for children ages 9, 13 and 17 in the USA[20]
- Science achievement for 4th, 8th, and 12th Graders, percentage of children demonstrating proficient or advanced achievement in these areas[21]
- Percentage of students in Grades 3, 5 and 8 scoring satisfactory or excellent levels on curriculum-based assessments in science[24]
- Mean scores for 15-year-old New Zealand students based on the international scientific literacy scales set by the PISA study 2000[29]
- Science proficiency, by age (9, 13, and 17-years), sex, race, region, parental education as reported by students (not high school graduate, graduated high school, some college, graduated college) and type of school (public, private)[50]
- Scores on international science assessments of 13- and 14-year-olds in selected countries[50]

ACADEMIC ATTAINMENT, WRITING

Related domains:
Academic performance; access to developmental opportunities (childhood learning and care); child health and development (developmental); children succeeding in school; children successful in school; education and childcare (achievement and proficiency); education and skills (learning assessments); education outcome; educational benchmarks; educational development (student achievement); personal life skills; readiness to learn; school (outcomes).

Recommended measures:
- Number of students who are proficient in writing at the end of 3rd Grade[1]
- Percentage of children in years 3, 5 and 7 meeting national literacy (reading and writing) and numeracy benchmarks[2]

- Literacy level[5]
- Written language scores at various ages[7]
- National Assessment of Educational Progress (NAEP) writing scale scores for Grades 4, 8 and 12[10]
- Writing achievement for 4th, 8th, and 12th Graders, percentage of children demonstrating proficient or advanced achievement in these areas[21]
- Percentage of students in Grades 3, 5 and 8 scoring satisfactory or excellent levels on curriculum-based assessments in writing[24]
- Percentage of public school students demonstrating basic skills in writing at the passing level at the end of Grade 11[24]
- Percentage of children ages 3 to 5 who pass the 3rd Grade basic writing test by the time of case closing[30]
- Percentage of children age 13 and older who pass the 8th Grade writing test by the time of case closing[30]
- Percentage of children at Grade 3 (indicative of high achievement) in the areas of writing[36]
- Percentage of all schools within low income areas with more than 70% of students achieving Level 3 or 4 in at least one of the EQAO assessments (reading, writing, math)[47]
- Percentage of all schools with more than 70% of students achieving Level 3 or 4 in at least one of the EQAO assessments (reading, writing, math)[47]
- Percentage of English as a second language (ESL) students vs. non-ESL students in Grades 3 and 6 who attained Level 3 or 4 in the EQAO assessment (writing)[47]
- Average writing proficiency scores, by Grade (4th, 8th, 11th), sex and race/ethnicity[50]

29

ACADEMIC COMMITMENT

Related domains:
Education and childcare (behavioural characteristic); pro-social behaviour; social development, behavioural health and teen fertility (social development).

Recommended measures:
- Percentage of 8th, 10th, and 12th Grade students in the USA reporting that good grades have great or very great importance to peers[20]
- Percentage of 8th, 10th and 12th Grade students in the USA reporting peer disapproval of intentionally angering a teacher in school[20]
- Percentage of students with positive attitudes towards mathematics, sciences (4th, 8th, 12th Grade)[21]
- Percentage of children in Grades 6-12 reporting peer approval of hard work and good behaviour[21]

ACCESS TO HEALTHCARE SERVICES, AVAILABILITY:

Related domains:
Communities which support family life; community and school environment strengths (effective services: other); health.

Recommended measures:
- Number of licensed healthcare professionals per 1,000 population, especially paediatricians, gynaecologists/obstetricians, and family practice/general practice physicians[24]
- Population to primary care physician ratio – calculated ratio that divides the estimated mid-year population of the total full-time equivalency (FTE) of the primary care physicians in the county. One FTE equals 40 hours (those physicians engaged solely in administration, research or teaching were excluded)[42]
- Healthcare providers, rate of the following per 1,000 children: paediatricians/family practitioners/general practitioners (MDs and DOEs); general practice dentists and core mental health professionals[45]
- Ratio of students to school nurses[51]

ACCESS TO HEALTHCARE SERVICES, PHYSICIAN VISITS

Related domains:

Deprivation (other); health (health service utilisation); health (healthcare); health services utilisation.

Recommended measures:

- Rate per 1,000 at which children, ages 0-19, visit physicians, by income, by region[8]
- Attendance at a doctor when a child is ill and access to health and medical care needed[12]
- Percentage of children with no physician visits in last 12 months[21]
- Percentage of children with a usual source of healthcare (doctor's office, clinic)[21]
- Number of physician visits per year[21]
- Physician utilisation (no visits, 1 - 3 visits, 4 - 9 visits, 10 or more visits), by children with activity limitations, by age (under 5 years, over 5 years)[25]
- Percentage of children with no physician visits in the past year, by age and race/ethnicity[25]
- Usual source of acute care (clinic or health centre, doctor's office or HMO, hospital emergency room, hospital out-patient department), by age (under 5 years, 5-12 years, 13-17 years)[25]

ACCESS TO HEALTHCARE SERVICES, WAITING TIMES AND WAITING LISTS

Related domains:

Access to developmental opportunities (inclusive services for children); community; economic resources and contribution; health; health and survival; health systems policy.

Recommended measures:

- Access to various social, educational and health services regardless of economic status[5]
- Children on hospital waiting lists[12]
- Percentage of children who have access to healthcare during the time a service case is open[30]
- Waiting times[47]
- Is it national policy that children in all ages in the following groups have access to both immunisation and to non-emergency diagnostic investigations comparable to that offered to the general resident child population: a) asylum seekers; b) children of illegal immigrants/illegal residents; c) homeless children; and d) culturally itinerant children (e.g. gypsies)[48]
- Access to healthcare services[57]

ACUTE ILLNESSES (DIARRHOEA, PNEUMONIA, MALARIA) AND ACUTE RESPIRATORY INFECTION (ARI)

Related domains:

Health

Recommended measures:

- Percentage of mothers who offered more fluids and continued feeding to their children during diarrhoeal episodes[17]
- Percentage of children under 5 who had diarrhoea in the two weeks preceding the survey[17]
- Percentage of mothers and caretakers who have Oral Rehydration Solution (ORS) at home or who know where they can get ORS[17]
- Percentage of diarrhoeal episodes treated with ORS[17]
- Percentage of mothers of children under 5 who know the signs of pneumonia[17]
- Percentage of children under 5 who had signs of pneumonia in the two weeks preceding the survey[17]
- Percentage of children under 5 who had signs of pneumonia in the two weeks preceding the survey and were seen at a health facility and treated with antibiotics[17]
- Percentage of children (0-4 years) who slept under a mosquito net[56]
- Percentage of children (0-4 years) who slept under an insecticide-impregnated mosquito net[56]

- Percentage of children (0-4 years) who were ill with fever in the two weeks preceding the survey and received any appropriate (locally defined) anti-malarial drugs[56]
- Percentage of children (0-4 years) with diarrhoea (in the two weeks preceding the survey) who received either oral rehydration therapy (Oral Rehydration Solution or recommended home-made fluids) or increased fluids, with continued feeding[56]
- Percentage of children (0-4 years) with an Acute Respiratory Infection (ARI) in the two weeks preceding the survey[56]
- Percentage of children (0-4 years) with ARI in the two weeks preceding the survey taken to a health provider[56]

ALCOHOL USE AMONG ADULTS (INCLUDING PARENTS)

Related domains:
Children in strong, stable families; community and school environment deficits (negative adult behaviour); family and community (family); family environment (family health and safety); family well-being; health (drugs, alcohol, tobacco).

Recommended measures:
- Parental alcohol and substance abuse[1]
- Percentage of parents who reported drinking heavily. Heavy drinking is defined as drinking five or more alcoholic drinks in a row at least once a) per month; b) per week[10]
- Percentage of adult care-givers whose illicit drug or alcohol use within the last three months is affecting their ability to raise their children during the time a service case is open[30]
- Percentage of adults aged 18 or more who report they consumed five or more alcoholic drinks on one occasion at least once in the past 30 days (binge-drinkers)[31]
- Family history of alcohol and/or drug abuse, percentage of students in Grades 6, 8, 10 and 12 who answered 'yes' to the question 'has anyone in your family ever had a severe alcohol and/or drug problem?'[41]
- Number of adults in drug or alcohol treatment[42]

ALCOHOL USE AMONG YOUTH, AGE OF FIRST ALCOHOL USE AND EARLY INITIATION

Related domains:
Adolescent risk behaviours; health and safety (youth engaging in risky behaviour: youth use of alcohol/illicit drugs); safety and physical status.

Recommended measures:
- Substance (tobacco, alcohol and drugs) abuse, by age[5]
- Average age students (Grades 6, 8, 10 and 12) first drank alcohol, as reported by students[41]
- Early initiation of alcohol, tobacco and other drugs among students in Grades 6, 8 and 11[42]
- Percentage of high school students who reported first drinking alcohol at ages 11, 13, 15[51]

ALCOHOL USE AMONG YOUTH, ALCOHOL USE IN THE PAST 30 DAYS

Related domains:
Adolescent risk behaviours; child health and lifestyle behaviours; health; health (health-related behaviour); health and safety (youth engaging in risky behaviour: youth use of alcohol/illicit drugs); health status (adolescents); healthy children; youth choose healthy behaviour.

Recommended measures:
- Proportion of 16-year-old boys and girls who reported alcohol consumption 10 times or more in the previous 30 days, by sex and rank among participating countries between 1995 and 1999[16]
- Proportion of 16-year-old boys and girls reporting drunkenness 3 times or more in the previous 30 days, by sex and rank among participating countries between 1995 and 1999[16]

- Percentage of teens who drink alcohol (daily, in previous month)[21]
- Percentage of public school students who report using alcohol, tobacco or illegal drugs in the last 30 days by type of substance (cigarettes, alcohol, marijuana, heroin, ecstasy, LSD) and by age/Grade (6th, 8th, 10th and 12th)[24]
- 30-day prevalence of drug use (alcohol, marijuana, cocaine) among adolescents aged 12-17[25]
- Percentage of children who are current drinkers[27]
- Percentage of students in Grades 8 and 12 reporting they had one or more drinks of alcohol within the past 30 days[31]
- Percentage of students in Grades 9-12 who reported using the following in the past 30 days: cigarettes, smokeless tobacco, marijuana, alcohol (beer), cocaine[33]
- Teen alcohol use within the past 30 days among students in Grades 9-12[40]
- Percentage of students in Grades 6, 8, 10 and 12 reporting to have consumed at least one alcoholic drink in the last 30 days[41]
- Percentage of students in Grades 6, 8, 10 and 12 reporting drinking alcohol at least once within the past 30 days[42]
- Percentage of youth in Grades 9-12 consuming at least one alcoholic drink in the past 30 days[45]
- Percentage of seniors reporting cigarette, alcohol and drug use, by substance (cigarettes, alcohol, marijuana/hashish, cocaine) and frequency of use (ever used, used in the previous 30 days)[50]
- Percentage of high school students who reported drinking alcohol in past month[51]

ALCOHOL USE AMONG YOUTH, ALCOHOL USE IN THE PAST WEEK

Related domains:

Condition manifested in childhood; health; substance misuse; tobacco, alcohol and drug use.

Recommended measures:

- Percentage of children aged 15 drinking alcohol at least weekly, by male, female and in total[6]
- Alcohol use in last week[7]
- Percentage who have drank alcohol in the past week[9]
- Percentage of children by age (11, 13, 15) and gender who report weekly consumption of beer, wine and spirits[16]
- Percentage of current drinkers, children aged 12-19 reporting to consume 15 or more drinks per week[38]

ALCOHOL USE AMONG YOUTH, ALCOHOL USE IN THE PAST YEAR

Related domains:

Health; tobacco, alcohol and drug use.

Recommended measures:

- Percentage of 16-year-olds who reported having had alcohol in previous 12 months[16]
- Percentage of 16-year-olds who reported being drunk in previous 12 months[16]
- Proportion of current drinkers (consumed alcohol in the past 12 months) by sex, children aged 12-19 years[38]

ALCOHOL USE AMONG YOUTH, APPROVAL OF PEER USE AND PERCEPTION OF PEER ACCEPTANCE OF ALCOHOL USE

Related domains:

Health and safety (youth engaging in risky behaviour: youth use of alcohol/illicit drugs); problem behaviour; social development, behavioural health and teen fertility (smoking, alcohol and substance abuse); substance misuse.

Recommended measures:

- Attitudes towards smoking, alcohol and illegal substances[7]
- Percentage of 12th Grade students in the USA who report that peers would not approve of their using alcohol, marijuana, cocaine or cigarettes[20]
- Percentage of teens who report peer approval of smoking tobacco, drinking alcohol[21]
- Percentage of students in Grades 6, 8, 10 and 12 who answered 'not wrong at all' to the question 'how wrong do you think it is for someone your age to drink beer, wine or hard liquor regularly?'[41]

ALCOHOL USE AMONG YOUTH, BINGE-DRINKING AND HEAVY DRINKING

Related domains:

Adolescent risk behaviours; behaviour and social environment; condition manifested in childhood; development and behaviour measures; health; health (drugs, alcohol, tobacco); health and safety (youth engaging in risky behaviour: youth use of alcohol/illicit drugs); health status (adolescents); problem behaviour; social and emotional development (delinquency and crime); social development, behavioural health and teen fertility (smoking, alcohol and substance abuse); substance misuse; tobacco and alcohol use; tobacco, alcohol and drug use.

Recommended measures:

- Proportion of children aged 12-14 who have engaged in high-risk (five or more drinks in a row) drinking at least once in the last two weeks[2]
- 5 or more drinks in one session (binge-drinking)[7]
- Percentage who have indulged in binge-drinking during the previous two weeks (five or more drinks)[9]
- Percentage of students in Grades 8, 10 and 12 who reported drinking five or more alcoholic drinks in a row at least once in the past two weeks[10]
- Percentage of 8th, 10th and 12th Grade students who reported having five or more alcoholic beverages in a row in the last two weeks[18]
- Percentage of 8th, 10th and 12th Grade students in the USA who reported binge-drinking. Binge-drinking means having five or more drinks in a row in the previous 2 weeks[20]
- Percentage of youth aged 12 through 17 in the USA reporting illicit drug use and/or binge-drinking in the past month. Illicit drugs include marijuana, cocaine (including crack), heroin, hallucinogens (including PCP), inhalants and non-medical use of psychotherapeutics[20]
- Problem-drinking, percentage of teens who have had five or more drinks in a single evening in the last 30 days[21]
- Current drinkers, binge-drinkers, heavy drinkers, perception of risk and access to drug, approached by someone selling drugs in the month prior to the survey[25]
- Quantity of alcohol consumed on typical occasion[29]
- Percentage of current drinkers, children aged 12-19 reporting to have drunk five or more drinks on one occasion, once or more per month[38]
- Percentage of youth in Grades 9-12 consuming at least five or more alcoholic drinks on one occasion[40]
- Percentage of high school students in Grade 7 and 8 who reported drinking five or more alcoholic drinks in a row in past month[51]

ALCOHOL USE AMONG YOUTH, DAILY ALCOHOL USE

Related domains:

Health (health-related behaviour)

Recommended measures:

- Percentage of teens who drink alcohol (daily, in previous month)[21]

ALCOHOL USE AMONG YOUTH, DRIVING AFTER USING ALCOHOL

Related domains:
Adolescent risk behaviours; health (drugs, alcohol, tobacco); health (health-related behaviour); health and safety (youth health: good health and health habits among youth); social and emotional development (social community relationships: behaviour problems: delinquent or criminal activity: alcohol/illicit drug-related offence arrests); social development, behavioural health and teen fertility (smoking, alcohol and substance abuse); substance misuse; tobacco, alcohol and drug use.

Recommended measures:

- Exposure to drunk driving by self/others[7]
- Percentage of students in Grades 9-12 who reported driving after drinking alcohol or riding with a driver who had been drinking alcohol one or more times during the past 30 days[10]
- Percentage of students in Grades 9 through 12 in the USA who reported driving after drinking alcohol or riding with a driver who had been drinking alcohol within the last 30 days[20]
- Percentage of 9th-12th Graders who have driven drunk (or with a drunk driver) in the past 30 days[21]
- Percentage of drivers aged 16-19 reporting to have driven under the influence of alcohol once or more in the past 12 months[38]
- Driving while intoxicated: data collected as part of this indicator: driving while intoxicated and intoxicated youth in auto accidents. (Driving while intoxicated: Arrest rate per 10,000 youth and youth who were intoxicated and involved in an automobile accident (as a driver, passenger or pedestrian) per 10,000 youth aged 16-20 years)[39]
- Percentage of youth in Grades 9-12 who rode with a driver who had been drinking alcohol[40]
- Drinking alcohol and driving among children in Grades 9-12[40]
- Drunken driving arrests[42]
- Percentage of high school students who reported riding with a drunk driver[51]
- Percentage of high school students who reported driving after drinking alcohol[51]

ALCOHOL USE AMONG YOUTH, DRUNKENNESS

Related domains:
Child health and lifestyle behaviours; child lifestyle determinants of child health, risk and protective factors; health.

Recommended measures:

- Proportion of 16-year-old boys and girls reporting drunkenness three times or more in the previous 30 days, by sex and rank among participating countries between 1995 and 1999[16]
- Percentage of children who have been drunk at least once[27]
- Percentage of children age 15 reporting that they have been drunk from alcohol consumption on two or more occasions, by male, female and in total, and by socio-economic group when available[48]

ALCOHOL USE AMONG YOUTH, HOSPITALISATION-RELATED ALCOHOL USE

Related domains:
Health and safety (youth engaging in risky behaviour)

Recommended measures:

- Rate per 100,000 of alcohol dependency hospitalisations, by the estimated mid-year population[41]

ALCOHOL USE AMONG YOUTH, LIFETIME ALCOHOL USE

Related domains:

Child health and lifestyle behaviours; condition manifested in childhood; health; health and survival; social development, behavioural health and teen fertility (smoking, alcohol and substance abuse); substance misuse.

Recommended measures:

- Alcohol use subdivided by whether spirits/other[7]
- Percentage who have ever drunk alcohol[9]
- Children using alcohol or drugs[12]
- Percentage of 8th, 10th and 12th Grade students in the USA who reported drinking alcohol on one or more occasions[20]
- Percentage of children who have drunk alcohol at least once in their lifetime[27]
- Percentage of children using drugs or alcohol during the time a service case is open[30]
- Percentage of seniors reporting cigarette, alcohol and drug use, by substance (cigarettes, alcohol, marijuana/hashish, cocaine) and frequency of use (ever used, used in the previous 30 days)[50]

ALCOHOL USE AMONG YOUTH, PARENTAL GUIDANCE AND PERCEIVED PARENTAL APPROVAL OF ALCOHOL USE

Related domains:

Health and safety (youth engaging in risky behaviour: youth use of alcohol/illicit drugs)

Recommended measures:

- Percentage of students in Grades 6, 8, 10 and 12 who answered 'not wrong at all' to the question 'how wrong do your parents feel it would be for you to drink beer, wine or other hard liquor regularly?'[41]
- Percentage of youth in Grades 8, 10 and 12 whose parents/guardians have talked to them about not using alcohol[43]

ALCOHOL USE AMONG YOUTH, PERCEPTION OF AVAILABILITY OF ALCOHOL

Related domains:

Adolescent risk behaviours; community and school environment deficits; health and safety (youth engaging in risky behaviour: youth use of alcohol/illicit drugs).

Recommended measures:

- Percentage of students in Grades 6, 8, 10 and 12 who answered 'very easy' to the question 'if you wanted to get some beer, wine or hard liquor, how easy would it be for you to get some?'[41]
- Alcohol access by youth[43]
- Percentage of high school students who reported that beer is easy to get[51]

ALCOHOL USE AMONG YOUTH, PERCEPTION OF HARMFULNESS OF ALCOHOL USE

Related domains:

Adolescent risk behaviours; health and safety (youth engaging in risky behaviour: youth use of alcohol/illicit drugs).

Recommended measures:

- Percentage of students in Grades 6, 8, 10 and 12 who answered 'no risk' to the question 'how much do you think people risk harming themselves (physically or other ways) if they take two drinks of an alcoholic beverage (beer, wine, liquor) nearly every day?'[41]

- Perceived harmfulness of alcohol, tobacco and other drugs among students in Grades 6, 8 and 11[42]
- Percentage of high school students who report that it is not a great risk to drink two alcoholic drinks a day[51]
- Percentage of high school students who report that it is not a great risk to drink five alcoholic drinks every weekend[51]

ALCOHOL USE AMONG YOUTH, PERCEPTION OF POLICE INTERVENTION FOR ALCOHOL USE

Related domains:
Health and safety (youth engaging in risky behaviour: youth use of alcohol/illicit drugs)

Recommended measures:
- Percentage of students in Grades 6, 8, 10 and 12 who answered 'no' to the question 'if a kid drank some beer, wine or hard liquor in your neighbourhood or in the area around where you live, would he or she be caught by the police?'[41]

ALCOHOL USE AMONG YOUTH, SCHOOL ATTENDANCE WHILE USING ALCOHOL

Related domains:
Health and safety (youth engaging in risky behaviour: youth use of alcohol/illicit drugs)

Recommended measures:
- Percentage of students who reported attending school drunk or high in the past 12 months[41]

ALCOHOL USE AMONG YOUTH, SEXUAL ACTIVITY WHILE USING ALCOHOL

Related domains:
Health and safety (youth engaging in risky behaviour: sexual activities while using alcohol/illicit drugs)

Recommended measures:
- Percentage of students in Grades 9-12 who reported using alcohol or drugs at last sexual intercourse[40]

ALCOHOL USE DURING PREGNANCY

Related domains:
Health; health (health conditions); health and safety (youth engaging in risky behaviour: youth use of alcohol/illicit drugs); healthy children; pre-natal period (healthy babies).

Recommended measures:
- Percentage of women who drink pre-natally[1]
- Number of children born with foetal alcohol syndrome[1]
- Percentage of women who reported drinking alcohol throughout their pregnancies[8]
- Percentage of mothers who continued to consume alcohol during pregnancy[19]
- Maternal use of tobacco, alcohol and other drug use during pregnancy[21]
- Percentage of women who used drugs during pregnancy. This includes women who reported that they had used alcohol and illegal drugs during some part of their pregnancy[23]
- Percentage of alcohol use in women who visited the pre-natal clinic[36]
- Number of pregnant women receiving alcohol, tobacco and other drug treatment from State-supported treatment centres, per 1,000 live births[41]
- Number of live births to mothers who reported consuming any alcohol during pregnancy by the total number of live births[42]

- Percentage of mothers (broken down by age 0-65+) who drank during pregnancy[42]
- Number of infants born to mothers who did not drink or smoke during pregnancy[46]

APGAR SCORE

Related domains:

Health (health conditions); maternal and neo-natal conditions; neo-natal health; pre-natal period (healthy babies).

Recommended measures:

- APGAR score[9]
- Proportion of births with low APGAR scores[21]
- Percentage of babies with APGAR scores (0-5, 6-8, 9-10) at one and five minutes after birth[36]
- Distribution of APGAR score at five minutes (0-10)[58]

BASIC DEMOGRAPHICS, ABORTION

Related domains:

Natality

Recommended measures:

- Abortions, per 100 live births[55]

BASIC DEMOGRAPHICS, BIRTH RATE

Related domains:

Child population and population projections; children in strong, stable families; demographic indicators; home (demographics and family composition); maternal and neo-natal conditions; natality; population, family and neighbourhood (child population characteristics); pre-natal period (demographics).

Recommended measures:

- Percentage of unintended births[1]
- Total births, number[9]
- Total number of births in the USA[20]
- Number of live births per 1,000[27]
- Birth rates for all women 15 to 44 years old, by age (15-19, 20-24, 25-29, 30-34, 35-39, 40-44) and marital status[36]
- Crude birth rates, per 1,000 population[38]
- Birth rates for all women 15 to 44 years old, by age (15-19, 20-24, 25-29, 30-34, 35-39, 40-44) and race[50]
- Live births, per 1,000 population[55]
- Annual number of births, per 1,000 population[56]

BASIC DEMOGRAPHICS, CHILD AND ADULT POPULATION [INCLUDING DEPENDENCY RATIOS]

Related domains:

Child population and population projections; demographic characteristics; demographics; demographics (basic); entry (pregnancy, birth); family; family and household; home (demographics and family composition); population; population and family characteristics; population characteristics; population, family and neighbourhood (child population characteristics).

Recommended measures:

- Alaska population by age (number, % and % change)[1]
- Percentage of children, by age (0-4, 5-9, 10-14, 15-19) and gender of total population[8]

- Number of children under age 18 as a percentage of the population[10]
- Children under age 18 and adults aged 65 and older as a percentage of the USA population[18]
- Number of children under age 18 in the USA (in millions)[18]
- Number (in millions) of children under age 18 in the USA[20]
- Children under age 18 as a percentage of the USA population[20]
- Children under age 18 and adults aged 65 and over as a percentage of the USA population[20]
- Number of children[21]
- Children as a percentage of the total population[21]
- Adult/child or parent/child ratio[21]
- Mississippi population, by age group (0-4, 5-9, 10-14, 15-19) [22]
- US resident population, by age group (under 5, 5-9, 10-14, 1-19, 20-21, 22-64, 65 and over)[25]
- Young dependency ratio, the ratio of the population aged less than 15 expressed as a percentage of those aged 15-64[27]
- Projected population among children aged 0-18 years[27]
- Number of children and young people, expressed as a proportion of the total population[29]
- Total population, ages 0-17[32]
- Number and proportion of children aged 0-19 years, by age group (0-4, 5-9, 10-14, 15-19) and municipality[38]
- Projections of the population, birth to age 24, by race/ethnicity and age[50]
- Population, by selected age groups (14-17, 18-19, 20-21, 22-24)[50]
- Ratio of adults to children and youth[51]
- Population, ages 0-17[51]
- Ratio of 0-14 population to 15-59 population, percentage[55]
- Population, age 0-4 (beginning of year, 1,000)[55]
- Population age 0-17 (beginning of year, 1,000)[55]
- Ratio of 60+ population to 15-59 population, percentage[55]
- Total population (beginning of year de facto population, thousands)[55]
- Birth rate minus death rate, per thousand population, excludes changes due to migration[55]
- Immigrants minus emigrants, thousands[55]
- Percentage of children less than 5 years of age who were registered at the moment of the survey. The numerator of this indicator includes children whose birth certificate was seen by the interviewer or whose mother or caretaker says the birth has been registered[56]
- Number of children under 5 years[57]

BASIC DEMOGRAPHICS, DIVORCE

Related domains:

Children in strong, stable families; conditions (divorce); demographic characteristics; family; family environment (household structure: parental marital status); family formation; home (demographics and family composition); risk and enabling factors (transience).

Recommended measures:

- Divorce rate[1]
- Risk of experiencing poverty/family break-up in any given year[7]
- Divorce rate (per 1,000 population) in Mississippi[22]
- Proportion of children under 18 years whose parents divorce[29]
- Percentage whose parents divorce[37]
- Percentage of all divorces in which one or more children are involved[41]
- Divorce - a court decree dissolving a legal union of individuals[42]
- Number and rate of divorces and number and per cent of children under 18 involved annually in divorces[50]
- Divorce ratios in selected countries[50]
- Number of children under age 18 in families involved in divorce[51]

- Divorces per thousand mid-year population[55]
- Divorces per hundred marriages[55]
- Children involved in divorce, per thousand 0-17 population[55]

BASIC DEMOGRAPHICS, FAMILIES WITH CHILDREN

Related domains:
Children in strong, stable families; family and household; population, family and neighbourhood (family structure).

Recommended measures:
- Parent/child ratio in the household[1]
- Percentage of families in the USA with no children, and with four or more resident children[20]
- Percentage distribution of families in the USA by number of own children under age 18[20]
- Percentage of households with children[21]
- Number of children in household[21]

BASIC DEMOGRAPHICS, FERTILITY

Related domains:
Adolescents (reproductive health); child health and development (health); demographic indicators; demographics; family; natality; population, family and neighbourhood (child population characteristics); pre-natal period (demographics); the rate of progress.

Recommended measures:
- 'Total fertility rate' interprets as 'the number of children who would be born to an average woman who experiences each of the age-specific fertility rates of a population in a given year as she progresses through her reproductive lifetime'[8]
- 'General fertility rate' calculates the number of births per 1,000 women age 15-44 years old[8]
- Percentage of females who report menstruation (ages 10-11; 12-13 years old)[8]
- Percentage of pregnant women among married women of reproductive age[17]
- Birth rates in the USA (per 1,000 women in each age group: 10-14, 15-19, 20-24, 25-29, 30-34, 35-39, 40-44)[20]
- Average number of live births to mothers of child-bearing age by age, martial status and by year[36]
- Births per woman[55]
- Number of children that would be born per woman if she were to live to the end of her child-bearing years and bear children at each age in accordance with prevailing age-specific fertility rates[56]
- Total fertility rate[57]

BASIC DEMOGRAPHICS, LIFE EXPECTANCY

Related domains:
Basic indicators; demographic indicators; demographics (birth and related outcomes); demographics (death); life expectancy and adult mortality; women.

Recommended measures:
- Estimated life expectancy of newborns by year of birth[10]
- Life expectancy (years) at birth, by male, female and in total[55]
- Number of years newborn children would live if subject to the mortality risks prevailing for the cross-section of population at the time of their birth[56]

BASIC DEMOGRAPHICS, MARRIAGE

Related domains:
Child protection; family formation; home (demographics and family composition).

Recommended measures:

- Number and rate of marriages and median age at first marriage[50]
- Marriage ratios in selected countries[50]
- Percentage of women 20-24 years of age that were married or in union before they were 18 years old[56]
- Marriages per thousand mid-year population[55]
- Average age at first marriage (years), by male, female and in total[55]

BASIC DEMOGRAPHICS, MORTALITY

Related domains:

Life expectancy and adult mortality

Recommended measures:

- Deaths per thousand population[55]
- Adult mortality rate at ages 20-24, 25-39, 40-59, 60+, by male, female and in total[55]

BASIC DEMOGRAPHICS, RACIAL AND ETHNIC COMPOSITION OF CHILDREN

Related domains:

Access to developmental opportunities (inclusive services for children: diversity of children); demographic and socio-economic determinants of child health; demographic characteristics; demographic indicators; demographics; demographics (basic); population; population and family characteristics; population characteristics; population, family and neighbourhood (child population characteristics); school (description).

Recommended measures:

- Children by race (number, % and % change)[1]
- Percentage distribution of children under 18, by race and ethnicity[10]
- Percentage of children under age 18 by race and Hispanic origin[18]
- Percentage of children under age 18 by nativity of child and parents[18]
- Number (in millions) and percentage distribution of children under age 18 in the USA, by race and Hispanic origin[20]
- Percentage of children under age 20 in the USA who were foreign-born. This includes both immigrants (citizens and non-citizens) and illegal aliens[20]
- Percentage of children under age 18 in the USA who were foreign-born. This includes both immigrants (citizens and non-citizens) and illegal aliens[20]
- Percentage of children who are immigrants[21]
- Percentage of children in major race/ethnicity groups[21]
- Percentage of children under 18 by poverty status (below 100%, 100%-199%, 200% and above) and the nativity of child and parents (native child and parent, native child and foreign-born parent, foreign-born child and foreign-born parent)[25]
- Ethnic distribution of children under 18[29]
- Number of children living in New Zealand who were born overseas[29]
- Percentage of children in Toronto's public and elementary schools who were born in a country other than Canada[47]
- Percentage of children in subsidised childcare with at least one parent who was a recent immigrant[47]
- Rate of children seeking asylum, alone or as part of a family, per 1,000 resident children, by male, female and in total, in age groups 0-4, 5-9, 10-14, 15-17[48]
- Percentage of students 3 to 34 years old, by race/ethnicity and level of enrolment (elementary school, high school, colleges)[50]
- Annual number of deaths per 1,000 population[56]

BIRTH DEFECTS

Related domains:

Health (health conditions); healthy children; infant health - the first year of life; maternal and neo-natal conditions (disability); neo-natal health.

Recommended measures:

- Rate of neural tube defects[1]
- Birth defect rates[1]
- Birth defect rate, per 1,000 births (birth defects are structural defects detected during pregnancy or at birth, excluding firth injuries and minor anomalies)[9]
- Proportion of births with congenital anomalies[21]
- Number of cases of neural tube defects, per 10,000 total births[38]
- Number of cases of congenital anomalies, per 10,000 total births[38]
- Total birth defects detected at birth, per 1,000 live births[52]
- Neural tube defects at birth, per 1,000 live births[52]
- Cleft lip and palate at birth, per 1,000 live births[52]
- Prevalence of cerebral palsy[58]
- Prevalence of hypoxic-ischemic encephalopathy[58]
- Number of live births, foetal deaths and induced abortions with neural tube defects or Down's Syndrome as a proportion of all live births, foetal deaths and induced abortions[58]

BIRTH FACTORS, MISCELLANEOUS

Related domains:

Health (health conditions); healthcare services; maternal and neo-natal conditions; population characteristics or risk factors.

Recommended measures:

- Percentage of un-booked confinements[9]
- Pregnancy complications (e.g. gestational diabetes, pre-eclampsia)[21]
- Number of caesarean births, per 100 births[52]
- Number of women with a multiple gestation pregnancy at delivery expressed as a proportion of all women delivering live or stillborn babies[58]
- Distribution of parity (number of previous live or still births) of women delivering a live or stillbirth[58]
- For a population of women giving birth in a given year, the number of deliveries associated with each of the following modes: a) spontaneous vaginal; b) instrument assisted vaginal (subdivided into forceps and ventouse); c) caesarean undertaken before onset of labour; d) caesarean undertaken during labour, each expressed as a proportion of total annual births[58]
- Number of women delivering live or stillborn babies after fertility treatment as a percentage of all women delivering live or stillborn babies. Fertility treatments are identified as: a) induction of ovulation only; b) artificial insemination only (sperm fresh/frozen); c) artificial insemination any (sperm fresh/frozen); and d) implantation of ovum/ova[58]
- Number of deliveries associated with each of the following modes of labour onset, as a proportion of deliveries resulting in a live or stillbirth: a) spontaneous onset; b) caesarean section prior to the onset of labour; and c) labour induction (initiation of uterine contractions) by surgical or pharmacological means prior to the onset of labour[58]
- Number of births occurring at home or in maternity units defined by the total number of births in the same year, with the following groups: home, < 300, 300-499, 500-999, 1,000-1,499, 1,500-1,999, 2,000-3,999, 4,000+. The number of units in each category should also be provided[58]
- Distribution of mother's country of origin[58]
- Indicator of support to women[58]
- Indicator of maternal satisfaction[58]
- Births without medical intervention[58]

BIRTH WEIGHT

Related domains:

Babies born healthy; children's health well-being; demographics (birth/related outcomes); health; health (children born healthy); health (health conditions); health (health status and disability); health conditions and health care (health conditions); health status (infant); healthy children; infant health - the first year of life; infant, child and teen health indicators; infant well-being; maternal and neo-natal conditions; natality; neo-natal health; nutrition; physical health; pregnant women and young children thrive; pre-natal period (healthy babies); reproductive health.

Recommended measures:

- Low birth weight[1]
- Percentage of very low birth weight live births[1]
- Percentage of very low birth weight infants delivered at facilities for high-risk deliveries and neonates[1]
- Proportion of infants weighing less than 2,500 grams at birth[2]
- Share of live births weighing less than 2,500 grams (5.5 pounds)[4]
- Low or very low birth rate[7]
- Percentage of births by birth weight (very low less than 1,500grams; low: 1,500-less than 2,500 grams; intermediate: 2,500-less than 4,000 grams; high: 4,000-4,500 grams; very high more than 4500 grams)[8]
- Percentage weighing less than 2,500 grams[9]
- Percentage of infants born at low (weighing less than 2,500 grams) and very low (weighing less than 1,500 grams) birth weight[10]
- Children born at low birth weight[11]
- Percentage of low birth weight (infants weighing less than 2,000 grams) and very low birth weight (infants weighing less than 1,000 grams), by male, female and in total, where appropriate, by age categories <1 year, 1-3 years, 4-6 years, 7-9 years, 10-12 years, 13-15 years and 16-18 years and in total, where appropriate, and by geographic location and in total, where appropriate[13]
- Average/above average weight of child at birth[14]
- Percentage of infants born of low birth weight (weighing less than 2,500 grams or 5.5 pounds at birth)[18]
- Percentage of children born at a healthy birth weight (between 2,500 and 4,000 grams), low birth weight (less than 2,500 grams) and high birth weight (more than 4,000 grams)[19]
- Low birth weight (less than 2,500 grams) and very low birth weight (less than 1,500 grams) infants as a percentage of all infants born in the USA[20]
- Low birth rate (less than 5.5 lbs) and very low birth rate (less than 3.3 lbs)[21]
- Percentage of all births, births in various racial and ethnic groups, and births to mothers in various age groups with birth weights less than 2,500 grams (low birth weight) and less than 1,500 grams (very low birth weight)[24]
- Percentage of infants born at very low birth weight, weighing less than 1,500 grams or 3 pounds 3 ounces, by race[25]
- Percentage of infants born at low birth weight, weighing less than 2,500 grams or 5 pounds 8 ounces, by race[25]
- Percentage of live births with a weight of less than 2,500 grams[28]
- Percentage of live births with a weight of more than 4,000 grams[28]
- Number of children who weighed less than 2,500 grams at birth, per 100 live births[29]
- Percentage low birth weight[31]
- Low birth weight babies (weighing less than 2,500 grams)[32]
- Percentage of infants born weighing 5 pounds 8 ounces or less[33]
- Percentage of children born at low birth weight, per 100 births[34]
- Babies born with birth weight less than 2.5kg (2,500g or 5.5lb)[36]

- Percentage low birth weight[37]
- Number of low birth weight babies, per 100 live births[38]
- Percentage of births weighing less than 2,500 grams among total singleton live births[47]
- Percentage of births weighing less than 2,500 grams among total live births[47]
- Number of babies born with low birth weight (less than 5.5 pounds) and very low birth weight (less than 3.3 pounds)[51]
- Newborn babies with birth weight less than 2,500 grams, per 1,000 live births[52]
- Low birth weight babies, per 1,000 live births[53]
- Births under 2,500 grams as a percentage of total live births to mothers under age 20[55]
- Births under 2,500 grams as a percentage of total live births[55]
- Infants that weigh less than 2,500 grams[56]
- Number of births within each 500 gram-weight interval, expressed as a proportion of all registered live and stillbirths[58]

BIRTHS ATTENDED

Related domains:
Development indicators; health; healthcare services; women.

Recommended measures:

- Number of births attended by a skilled health worker over one year as a percentage of total number of births during the same period. Skilled health workers are doctors (specialist and non-specialist) and/or persons with midwifery skills who can manage normal deliveries and diagnose, manage or refer obstetric complications[35]
- Births attended by skilled personnel, percentage of all births[55]
- Percentage of births attended by skilled health personnel (doctors, nurses or midwives)[56]
- Percentage of women aged 15-49 years attended by skilled health personnel (doctors, nurses or midwives)[56]
- Births attended by a midwife[58]

BIRTHS TO UNMARRIED MOTHERS

Related domains:
Demographics (birth and related outcomes); demographics (family structure and living arrangements); entry (pregnancy, birth); family; family and community (family); family/household; health and safety (youth engaging in risky behaviour: youth sexual activities); home (demographics and family composition); maternal and neo-natal conditions; natality; population and family characteristics; population, family and neighbourhood (child population characteristics).

Recommended measures:

- Marital status of women who give birth[9]
- Percentage never married[9]
- Percentage of births to unmarried women[10]
- Birth rates for unmarried women, per 1,000, for ages 15-17, 18-19, 20-24, 25-29, 30-34, 35-39 and 40-44[18]
- Percentage of all births to unmarried women in the USA[20]
- Percentage of all births to unmarried women ages 15 through 19 in the USA[20]
- Percentage of births to unmarried women[21]
- Percentage of teen births to unmarried teen females[21]
- Percentage of all registered births to single teen mothers[22]
- Rate of out-of-wedlock live births, per 1,000 live births to women aged 10-17[41]
- Number of births per 1,000 unmarried women 15 to 44 years old, by age (15-19, 20-24, 25-29, 30-34, 35-39, 40-44) and race[50]
- Births to unmarried women as a percentage of all live births in selected countries[50]

- Number of babies recorded as born to single mothers. This includes paternity acknowledged babies[51]
- Share of non-marital births to mothers under age 20, expressed as a percentage of live births to mothers under age 20[55]
- Share of non-marital births, expressed as a percentage of total live births[55]

BREASTFEEDING

Related domains:

Child health; child health and lifestyle behaviours; health; health (postpartum period); healthcare services; health status (infant); healthy children; infant health - the first year of life; maternal and neo-natal conditions; parental determinants of child health, risk and protective factors; physical health.

Recommended measures:

- Percentage of mothers who breastfed their infants at hospital discharge[1]
- Proportion of infants exclusively breastfed at ages 3 and 6 months[2]
- Breastfeeding as a percentage of all births[6]
- Percentage of women who report breastfeeding (initially, at 3 months, at 6 months and at one year)[8]
- Percentage of breastfeeding initiation rate[8]
- Percentage of mothers breastfeeding at 8 weeks or more[9]
- Percentage of mothers breastfeeding at 26 weeks or more[9]
- Percentage of children under 4 months who are exclusively breastfed[17]
- Percentage of children aged 6-9 months receiving breast milk and supplementary feeding[17]
- Percentage of children from birth to 3 years of age who were ever breastfed[19]
- Number of women who initiated breastfeeding. Historically, breastfeeding initiation has been defined as women who have attempted to breastfeed their infants, whether successful or not, at least once during the first hours or days of the infant's life. In the study cited, a woman was recorded as having initiated breastfeeding if she successfully breastfed her infant within two hours of the child's birth[23]
- Number of women who breastfeed their infants until 6 months and 11 months of age[23]
- Number of women who initiated breastfeeding[23]
- Number of women who breastfed their infants until 6 months of age[23]
- Number of women who breastfed their infants until one year of age[23]
- Breastfeeding in hospital and at 6 months (includes exclusive and supplemented breastfeeding), by race[25]
- Duration of breastfeeding in Ireland (birth, 2 weeks, 6 weeks, 4 months and 6 months)[27]
- Percentage of children ever breastfed[27]
- Proportion of children aged 0-3 years who are currently being or have ever been breastfed[28]
- Length of time children aged 0-3 years were breastfed[28]
- Percentage of mothers breastfeeding at 6 months and one year[36]
- Proportion of mothers initiating breastfeeding and breastfeeding to 6 months, by age of mother (15-24, 25-29, 30-34, 35+)[38]
- Percentage of: a) newborn children exclusively breastfed at hospital discharge or immediately after birth; b) all 6-month-old children breastfeeding; and c) all 12-month-old children breastfeeding at 12 months[48]
- Number of 4-month-old infants exclusively breastfed in the last 24 hours, per 100 4-month-old infants[52]
- Number of newborn babies who are breastfed (baby receives breast milk and is allowed any food or liquid including non-human milk) and who are exclusively breastfed (baby receives breast milk and is allowed to receive drops and syrups) throughout the first 48 hours of age as a proportion of all newborn babies[58]

CHILD MORTALITY, AGE-SPECIFIC DEATHS

Related domains:

Adolescent risk behaviours; basic indicators; child and maternal mortality; child and teen well-being indicators; child health and development (health); child health status and well-being; children's health well-being; deaths; demographics (death); development indicators; exit (deaths); health and survival; health conditions and health care (mortality); health; health and safety (youth engaging in risky behaviour: youth death); healthy children; mortality; pregnant women and young children thrive; the rate of progress.

Recommended measures:

- Child death rate from all causes[1]
- Death rate for children aged 1-14 years[2]
- Number of deaths to children between ages 1 and 14, from all causes, per 100,000 in this age range[4]
- Rate of child deaths, by age and cause[5]
- Age-specific mortality[7]
- Age-specific mortality, by age category, gender, and geographical location[8]
- Total child mortality rate, expressed per 1,000 in age brackets (1-4, 5-9, 10-14, 15-19)[8]
- Children and adolescent (0-24 years) mortality rate, per 100,000[9]
- Childhood (1-17 years) mortality rate, per 100,000[9]
- Death rate, per 100,000 for: a) infants (less than 1 year); b) children (ages 1-14 years); and c) youth (ages 15-19 years)[10]
- Mortality rate for children under 5 years[12]
- Mortality rates for children aged 0-18, by male, female and in total, where appropriate, by age categories <1 year, 1-3 years, 4-6 years, 7-9 years, 10-12 years, 13-15 years and 16-18 years and in total, where appropriate, and by geographic location and in total, where appropriate[13]
- Death rates per 100,000 among children ages 1 to 4[18]
- Death rates per 100,000 among children ages 5 to 14[18]
- Death rates per 100,000 among adolescents ages 15 to 19[18]
- Youth death rates per 100,000 population in the USA for ages 15-19[20]
- Child and youth death rates per 100,000 population in the USA, by age (1-4, 5-9, 10-14, 15-19)[20]
- Child/youth death rate per 1,000 population, ages 0–19[22]
- Rate per 100,000 of deaths among children one year of age and older, by age (1-9, 10-19) and race/ethnicity[24]
- Child mortality rates for all causes[21]
- Child mortality rate per 1,000 population, aged 1-14[31]
- Child deaths per 100,000 children, aged 1-17, all causes[32]
- Number of deaths per 100,000 children aged 0-17 [33]
- Number of deaths per 100,000 children aged 1-19[34]
- Number of children who have died between birth and their 5th birthday, expressed per 1,000 live births[35]
- Deaths per 1,000 of child population 0-9 years[36]
- Number of deaths from all causes to children between ages 1-14, per 1,000 children of those ages[41]
- Total under 20 years mortality rate per 100,000 population, by male, female and in total, and by socio-economic group when available[48]
- Total mortality rate between birth and exactly 5 years of age (U5MR), expressed per 1,000 live births, by male, female and in total, and by socio-economic group when available[48]
- Number of deaths per 100,000 persons 5 to 34 years old, by sex, age, and race[50]
- Child mortality rate 1-14 years[51]
- Number of deaths among children aged 15-19[51]
- Number of deaths 1-14 years of age per 100,000 population 1-14 years[52]

- Number of deaths 15-24 years of age per 100,000 population 15-24 years[52]
- Child deaths per 100,000 children ages 1-14[53]
- Teen deaths per 10,000 teens ages 15-19[53]
- Under-5 mortality rate, per 1,000 population, by male, female and in total[55]
- Age 5-14 mortality rate per 100,000 population, by male, female and in total[55]
- Probability of dying between birth and exactly 5 years of age, expressed per 1,000 live births[56]
- Percentage reduction in the under-5 mortality rate (U5MR) from 1990 to 2003[56]
- Under-5 mortality rate[57]

CHILD MORTALITY, CAUSE SPECIFIC-DEATHS

Related domains:

Child and maternal mortality; child health and development (health); child health status and well-being; health; health (mortality); health and safety (youth engaging in risky behaviour); health status (adolescents); health status (children); healthy children; mortality; safety and physical status; youth successfully transition to adulthood.

Recommended measures:

- Child death rate from all causes[1]
- Rate of child death, by age and cause[5]
- Causes of children's mortality in ages 1-4, 5-9, 10-14, & 15-19 (injury, neoplasm's, congenital anomalies, respiratory, nervous, circulatory systems...)[8]
- Cancer-related mortality rate, per 100,000[9]
- Ten most frequent causes of death resulting in mortality among children[9]
- Mortality rates for children aged 0-18, by cause of death, by male, female and in total, where appropriate, by age categories <1 year, 1-3 years, 4-6 years, 7-9 years, 10-12 years, 13-15 years and 16-18 years and in total, where appropriate, and by geographic location and in total, where appropriate[13]
- Child mortality rates for all causes[21]
- Mortality rate, by cause of death (including medical vs. accidental)[21]
- Leading causes of death in children ages 1-14 (1-4, 5-14)[25]
- Leading causes of death in adolescents in ages 15-19, per 100,000 population[25]
- Teen non-violent deaths ages 15-19 for all causes, except for injuries, suicides and homicides, per 1,000[31]
- Top five causes of death for children 0-9 years[36]
- Number, proportion and crude death rates per 100,000, by leading cause for children aged 1-9 and 10-19 years (injury and poisoning, cancer, congenital anomalies, nervous system and sense organ disorders, respiratory system, circulatory system, all other causes)[38]
- Five leading causes of death, by age group (ages 1-4, 5-9, 10-14 and 15-19) (e.g. motor vehicle-related fatalities, AIDS and AIDS-related conditions, congenital anomalies, homicides, suicides, etc)[39]
- Number of deaths from all causes to children between ages 1-14, per 1,000 children of those ages[41]
- Cause-specific mortality rates, per 100,000 population for: a) infectious diseases; b) congenital malformations; c) malignant neoplasms (cancers); d) unintentional injuries (burns, poisoning, transport accidents, drowning); e) suicide; f) assault and homicide; and g) perinatal causes, by male, female and in total, in age groups under 1, 1-4, 5-9, 10-14, 15-17 and by socio-economic group when available[48]
- Number of deaths per 100,000 persons 5 to 24 years old, by age and cause of death (motor vehicle accidents, homicide, cancer, suicide, all other accidents)[50]
- Under-5 mortality rate, per 1,000 live births, due to respiratory diseases. Codes of respiratory diseases are J00-J98 (according to ICD-10)[55]
- Under-5 mortality rate, per 1,000 live births, due to infectious diseases. Codes of infectious diseases are A00-B99 (according to ICD-10)[55]

- Under-5 mortality rate, per 1,000 live births, due to congenital malformations. Codes for congenital malformations are Q00-Q99 (according to ICD-10)[55]
- Age 15-19 mortality rate per 100,000 population, due to natural causes, by male, female and in total. Total causes of death less external causes of death (V01-Y89)[55]

CHILD MORTALITY, INJURY-RELATED DEATHS [INTENTIONAL AND UNINTENTIONAL]

Related domains:

Abuse; abuse and neglect; accidents in childhood; adolescent risk behaviours; child and maternal mortality; child health and development (health); children safe in their families and communities; deaths; demographics (death); health; health (injuries); health (mortality); health (violence); health and safety (youth engaging in risky behaviour: youth death); health and survival; health conditions and health care (mortality); health status (adolescents); health status (children); healthy children; injuries and violence (intentional injuries); injuries and violence (unintentional injuries); injuries to children; mortality (injury); safety; safety and security; youth successfully transition to adulthood.

Recommended measures:

- Injury rates and deaths by drowning, fire, ATVs, snowmobile, vehicle crashes[1]
- Injury death rate for children ages 0-14 years[2]
- Road transport accident death rate for children ages 0-14 years[2]
- Accidental drowning death rate for children ages 0-14 years[2]
- Assault death rate for children ages 0-14 years[2]
- Number of deaths from: a) accidents; b) homicide; and c) suicide to teens between ages 15 and 19, per 100,000 teens[4]
- Cause-specific mortality (accidents, traffic deaths, homicides, suicides)[7]
- Injury mortality rates, per 100,000, by age (<1, 1-4, 5-9, 10-14, 15-19) and gender[8]
- Percentage mortality, by cause of injury in children aged 0-19 (motor vehicle, violence by others, suffocation/choking, drowning, fire, violence by self, falls, natural environment, poisoning, other vehicle and late effects), by income quintile and region[8]
- Injury-related mortality rate, per 100,000[9]
- Homicide rate, per 100,000, for infants under one year. Infant homicides are classified as deaths purposefully inflicted by other persons on children less than one year[10]
- Motor vehicle death rate, per 100,000, among teens ages 15-19[10]
- Death rate, per 100,000, of youth ages 15-19 for homicide, suicide and firearm-related deaths[10]
- Children dying from homicide, suicide and injuries[11]
- Child pedestrian/bicycle deaths[12]
- Injury death rates, per 100,000, among adolescents ages 15-19[18]
- Injury mortality rate, per 1,000[19]
- Youth motor vehicle crash deaths, rate per 100,000, in the USA, by ages 10-14, 15-19[20]
- Youth homicides for males 15 through 19, rate per 100,000, in the USA. Homicide includes death by legal intervention[20]
- Youth homicides due to firearms, rate per 100,000, in the USA. Includes assault by handguns and all other and unspecified firearms[20]
- Teen violent death rate (accident, suicide, homicide) ages 15-19, together and by type of death[21]
- Rate per 100,000 of injury-related deaths to children ages 0-9, 10-19, in three broad injury categories: accidents (motor vehicle or other), homicide or suicide[24]
- Motor vehicle crashes and firearms mortality among adolescents ages 15-19[25]
- Childhood deaths due to external cause, by cause (motor vehicle crashes, drowning, fires and burns, firearms) and age (1-4, 5-14)[25]
- Teen violent death rate, per 1,000, ages 15-19. Deaths from injuries, suicides and homicides[21]
- Standardised death rate from motor vehicle accidents[27]
- Proportion of children aged 0-5 years who die as a result of injury[28]

- Number of children under 15 years of age who have died as a result of an unintentional injury, per 100,000 children under 15 years[29]
- Number of children under 15 years of age who have died as a result of an intentional injury, per 100,000 children under 15 years[29]
- Number of children and young people under 25 years who died or were injured in motor vehicle crashes, as a proportion (per 100,000) of all children and young people under 25[29]
- Number of deaths ages 0-18: motor vehicle-related, drowning, fire/burn, bicycle, suicide, homicide, firearm[33]
- Causes of death due to injury, by percentage[36]
- Number of accidental child deaths[37]
- Unintentional injury-related death rate per 100,000, by age group (less than 1, 1-4, 5-9, 10-14, 15-19)[38]
- Selected leading causes of death, per 100,000, for unintentional injury, by age group (less than 1, 1-4, 5-9, 10-14, 15-19)[38]
- Intentional injury-related death rate, per 100,000, by age group (less than 1, 1-4, 5-9, 10-14, 15-19)[38]
- Homicides[42]
- The rate of deaths from unintentional injuries per 100,000 persons ages 0-19. Deaths may be caused by motor vehicle accidents, fire/burns, falls, drowning, poisoning and firearms[45]
- Teenage homicide rate[46]
- Number of homicides among children aged 15-19[51]
- Number of automobile-related deaths among children aged 15-19[51]
- Number of deaths among children from unintentional injuries[51]
- Number of deaths under one year of age due to accidents, per 1,000 live births[52]
- Number of deaths 1-14 years of age due to accidents, per 100,000 population 1-14 years[52]
- Number of deaths 15-24 years of age due to accidents, per 100,000 population 15-24 years[52]
- Number of deaths 15-24 years of age due to suicide, per 100,000 population 15-24 years[52]
- Age 15-19 mortality rate, per 100,000 population, due to injuries, by male, female and in total. Includes suicides[55]
- Under-5 mortality rate, per 1,000 live births, due to poisoning and violence. Codes of accidents, poisoning and violence are V01-Y89 (according to ICD-10)[55]

CHILD OUTCOMES, GENERAL

Related domains:
Civic life skills; education and childcare (achievement and proficiency); personal life skills; pro-social behaviour; risk and enabling factors (parenting and cultural resources).

Recommended measures:
- Perceived self-efficacy[5]
- Level of 'general' knowledge[5]
- Behaviour among and within peer groups[5]
- Conflict resolution skills[5]
- Communication skills[5]
- Belief in one's ability to bring about change[5]
- Technological knowledge level[5]
- Child's own locus of control – 'can do' factor – itself highly dependent on parenting style[7]
- Percentage of children with good conflict resolution and interpersonal problem-solving skills[21]
- Percentage of children with a sense of basic security (0-3)[21]
- Percentage of children who are suitably flexible in adjusting to new environments[21]
- Citizenship knowledge[21]
- Percentage of children who are self-regulating (ages 4-7 [21]
- Percentage of children who are actively curious, exploratory and inquisitive (ages 2-5)[21]
- Knowledge and skills for making choices about responsible parenthood[21]
- Approaches to learning (e.g. task persistence, impulse control, attentiveness, curiosity, creativity, co-operativeness and independence)[21]

CHILD SUPPORT

Related domains:
Children in strong, stable families; children live in stable, supported families; economic security (financial support); economic security (poverty and income); family environment (family socio-economic status); home (family income).

Recommended measures:
- Percentage of children entitled to child support who are receiving child support[1]
- Percentage of families headed by an unmarried woman (living with one or more of her own children under age 18) receiving child support or alimony payments during the previous calendar year[4]
- Percentage of eligible women in the USA who are not receiving child support[20]
- Percentage of mother-headed families receiving child support or alimony[21]
- Percentage of eligible families not receiving child support payments[21]
- Percentage of child support paid, annual total amount of payments received, as a per cent of annual total amount payable for cases with current or arrears obligations[31]
- Women receiving court-ordered child support payments from absent fathers[50]

CHILDREN WITH SPECIAL NEEDS, GENERAL

Related domains:
Child health and development (developmental); demographic characteristics; disability; disability in childhood; health.

Recommended measures:
- Proportion of children aged 0-14 years with severe or profound core activity restrictions[2]
- Disability (limitation of activity)[7]
- Estimated number of children with a disability[9]
- Primary disability of children under 18 years of age, by male, female and in total, where appropriate, by age categories <1 year, 1-3 years, 4-6 years, 7-9 years, 10-12 years, 13-15 years and 16-18 years and in total, where appropriate, and by geographic location and in total, where appropriate[13]
- Number of children aged 0-18 years registered as having a disability, by male, female and in total, where appropriate, by age categories <1 year, 1-3 years, 4-6 years, 7-9 years, 10-12 years, 13-15 years and 16-18 years and in total, where appropriate, and by geographic location and in total, where appropriate[13]
- Percentage of children aged 5-14 years with any disability[17]
- Prevalence rates of childhood physical and sensory disability by age groups (0-4, 5-9, 10-14, 15-19 and in total)[27]
- Disability rate, children aged under 15 years[29]
- Percentages of severity of disabilities in children ages 0-19[36]
- Number of children aged 0-9 years with the following disabilities and special needs: allergies, asthma, bronchitis, heart condition, epilepsy, cerebral palsy, kidney disease, mental handicap, other condition, other activity limitation in age-appropriate activities, learning disabilities, emotional problems, chronic pain or discomfort, visual impairments, hearing impairments and mobility impairments[36]
- Number of children and youth under age 18 currently affected by disabilities[51]
- Number of children 0-4 years of age with a disability, per 1,000 children 0-4 years[52]
- Number of children 5-14 years of age with a disability, per 1,000 children 5-14 years[52]
- Number of infants <2 years of age with cerebral palsy, per 1,000 infants <2 years[52]

CHILDREN WITH SPECIAL NEEDS, HEARING AND VISION [INCLUDING SCREENING]

Related domains:
Access to developmental opportunities (inclusive services for children); children are ready for

school; condition manifested in childhood; developmental measures; health; healthy children; youth health (access to services: pregnancy and early childhood services).

Recommended measures:

- Percentage of newborns who have been screened for hearing impairment before hospital discharge[1]
- Upper respiratory and middle ear infections[1]
- Hearing impairments by age of fitting[9]
- Percentage of 5-year-old children failing the school entry hearing screening test[29]
- Percentage of children screened by 1st Grade for vision and hearing problems[31]
- Number of babies who have had their hearing screened and the number of whom were found to be deaf or hard of hearing[47]

CHILDREN WITH SPECIAL NEEDS, LEARNING/BEHAVIOURAL DISABILITIES AND DEVELOPMENTAL DELAYS

Related domains:

Child health and development (developmental); civic life skills; education and childcare (achievement and proficiency, education and childcare (behavioural characteristics); education and skills (behaviour affecting learning); health; health (health status and disability); personal life skills; problem behaviour; pro-social behaviour; risk and enabling factors (parenting and cultural resources).

Recommended measures:

- Percentage of children with developmental disabilities[1]
- School behaviour problems[5]
- Percentage of children entering kindergarten who exhibit positive social behaviours when interacting with their peers: a) often or very often (positive social development); or b) never or sometimes (poor social development). This is measured using Social Skills Rating System[10]
- Percentage of children ages 3 to 17 who have been diagnosed by a doctor or health professional as having Attention Deficit Hyperactivity Disorder (ADHD)[10]
- Percentage of children ages 3 to 17 reported to have ever been diagnosed by a school or health professional as having a learning disability[10]
- Percentage of young children showing signs of behavioural problems, by category, emotional problems, anxiety, hyperactivity, inattention, physical aggression, conduct problem, low pro-social behaviour[19]
- Distribution of children from birth to 3 years of age by score on the Motor and Social Development Scale[19]
- Percentage of children with developmental delays[21]
- Percentage of children ever experiencing a delay in growth or development[21]
- Motor skills acquisition during infancy[21]
- Cognitive development during infancy[21]
- Percentage of children with high rates of behaviour problems, as measured by the Behaviour Problems Index (BPI)[21]
- Percentage of children ages 3+ who ever had learning disabilities[21]
- Percentage of children with learning disabilities[21]
- Prevalence rates of childhood intellectual disability, by age groups (0-4, 5-9, 10-14, 15-19 and in total) and by grade of disability (mild, moderate, severe and profound) [27]
- Standard score for PPVT-R (Peabody Picture and Vocabulary Test - Revised) reflects the proportion of children aged 4-5 years who have delayed, average and advanced levels of receptive hearing or vocabulary[28]
- Motor and social development – the proportion of children aged 0-3 years who have delayed, average and advanced levels of motor and social development[28]
- Emotional health and social knowledge and competence: a) emotional problem - anxiety score is the proportion of children aged 2-5 years who exhibit high levels of emotional

and/or anxiety problems; b) hyperactivity – inattention score is the proportion of children aged 2-5 years who exhibit high levels of hyperactivity and/or inattention; c) physical aggression score is the proportion of children aged 2-5 years who exhibit high levels of physical aggression, opposition and/or conduct disorder; and d) pro-social behaviour score is the proportion of children aged 2-5 years who exhibit low levels of pro-social behaviour[28]

- Rate of children ages 0-4 who have one or more serious emotional, behavioural or learning disabilities[36]
- Percentage of children ages 0-11 who experience a learning or behavioural disability[36]
- Learning disorders/intellectual disability[48]
- Childhood behaviour disorders: hyperactivity; conduct disorder, adolescent depression, adolescent anxiety[48]
- Number of students in Grades 1-12 with a learning disability[51]

CHILDREN WITH SPECIAL NEEDS, SERVICES AND SUPPORT

Related domains:

Academic achievement; access to developmental opportunities (inclusive services for children); child well-being within education; children succeed in school; children succeeding in school; education and childcare (childcare); education and personal development; education indicators; education outcome; family and social functioning; healthy children; readiness and early school performance.

Recommended measures:

- Percentage of infants/children with appropriate referral to childhood development programmes[1]
- Percentage of State SSI beneficiaries less than 16 years old receiving rehabilitative services from the State Children with Special Health Care Needs Program[1]
- Percentage of Children with Special Health Care Needs in the State who have a medical/ health home[1]
- Degree to which the State Children with Special Health Care Needs Program provides or pays for speciality and subspecialty services, including care co-ordination, not otherwise accessible or affordable to its clients[1]
- Number of children receiving special education services[1]
- Percentage requiring special assistance at school[7]
- Child disability allowance, payments related to persons under 25 years of age, last quarter[9]
- Children with disabilities attending mainstream schools[12]
- Ability of the school to address particular needs of the pupil[14]
- Proportion of eligible children in early intervention programmes[21]
- Number of vendors providing respite services for families with children aged 0-5. Respite refers to short-term, temporary care provided to children with disabilities[23]
- Percentage of students with special education IEPs[31]
- Number of children (0-3) enrolled in early intervention services to reduce effects of developmental delay, emotional disturbance and/or chronic illness[33]
- Special education expenditures per pupil[34]
- Students with disabilities as a percentage of all students[34]
- Percentage of children aged 0-9 with a special need who would benefit from specialised support services[47]
- Number of children with special needs currently waiting for subsidised childcare[47]
- Percentage of children enrolled in licensed childcare receiving specialised services to support their development, and in some instances to assist in securing their childcare placement[47]
- Percentage of children aged 0-9 living in Toronto receiving specialised supports in licensed childcare[47]
- Assessment of children with special needs[48]

- Children and young people in long-term receipt of practical or financial assistance because of permanent or severe disability[48]
- Integration of children with special needs[48]
- Percentage of children aged 6-7 and 7-8, placed in special education classes[51]
- Students receiving special education (per cent for ages 6-21)[53]
- Percentage of children aged 6-11 and 12-17 who were in a special class for gifted students or did advance work in any subjects, as reported by parents[54]

CHILDREN WITH SPECIAL NEEDS, SPEECH AND LANGUAGE

Related domains:
Access to developmental opportunities (inclusive services for children); child health and development (developmental); health.

Recommended measures:
- Percentage of children aged 0-4 identified and receiving assistance for speech and language disorders[36]
- Number of children identified with speech and language problems, who received services[47]
- Number of children assessed for speech and language problems[47]
- Age at which children with speech and language problems are identified and referred for treatment[47]
- Number of students in Grades 1-12 with a speech/language deficit[51]

CHILDREN'S TIME

Related domains:
Children's activities

Recommended measures:
- Percentage of time spent in productive activities (school, paid work, household work and contributing to the community)[5]
- Percentage of time spent in places not designated specifically for children[5]
- Percentage of time spent in obligatory versus voluntary activities[5]
- Distribution of children's time with different participants (with family, alone, with other children, with other adults or other adults and children)[5]
- Distribution of children's time by satisfaction levels[5]
- Distribution of children's time across types of activities[5]

CHRONIC HEALTH, ANAEMIA-RELATED

Related domains:
Health (health conditions); healthy children.

Recommended measures:
- Iron deficiency anaemia[1]
- Rates of iron deficiency anaemia[21]
- Number of reported cases of children aged 0 to 5 who were anaemic. Anaemia is a low haemoglobin (Hb) concentration or a low haematocrit (Hct) or red blood cell level that indicates an iron deficiency. For children aged 1 to 2 years, anaemia is defined as an Hb concentration less than 11.0 g/dL or an Hct level less than 33% of whole blood. For children aged 2 through 4, anaemia is defined as an Hb concentration less than 11.2 g/dL or an Hct level less than 34%[23]

CHRONIC HEALTH, ASTHMA-RELATED

Related domains:
Child health status and well-being (child morbidity); childhood morbidity and mortality; disability; health; health (acute and chronic conditions); health (health status and disability); healthy children; morbidity.

Recommended measures:

- Asthma morbidity[1]
- Proportion of children aged 0-14 years with asthma as a long-term condition[2]
- Rate per 1,000 of children with at least one healthcare contact or prescription drug for asthma by age (5-9, 10-14, 15-19) and by geographical location[8]
- Asthma interference rating: percentage extreme; percentage moderate/quite a lot; percentage a little bit[9]
- Asthma prevalence, percentage of children diagnosed with asthma[9]
- Percentage of children aged 0-17 reported to have asthma[10]
- Prevalence of diagnosed asthma among young children[19]
- Rates of admission in children, aged 1-15 years, who have spent more than 72 hours in hospital because of asthma[27]
- Hospital admissions in Ireland for asthma in children under 16 years[27]
- Percentage of children (Grades 7-8) who have: a) reported asthma symptoms; and b) diagnosed asthma[33]
- Asthma-related hospital discharges per 100,000 children aged 0-14[33]
- Prevalence of childhood asthma, by male, female and in total, in age groups 0-4, 5-9, 10-14, 15-17, by socio-economic group[48]

CHRONIC HEALTH, CANCER-RELATED

Related domains:

Child health status and well-being (child morbidity); childhood morbidity and mortality; disability; health system quality; morbidity; mortality.

Recommended measures:

- New cases of cancer per 100,000 children aged 0-14 years[2]
- Five-year relative survival rate for leukaemia in children aged 0-14 years[2]
- Cancer-related mortality rate per 100,000[9]
- Cancer-related hospital separation rates[9]
- Cancer incidence among children[9]
- Incidence of childhood cancer among children aged 0-18, by male, female and in total[27]
- Five-year survival rate for acute lymphatic leukaemia, in age groups at diagnosis, 0-4, 5-9, 10-14, 15-19[48]
- Annual incidence of childhood cancer per 100,000 population for: a) leukaemia; b) malignant brain/CNS tumours; and c) other malignant tumours, in age groups 0-14, 15-17 and in total[48]

CHRONIC HEALTH, CYSTIC FIBROSIS-RELATED

Related domains:

Disability in childhood

Recommended measures:

- Number of children with cystic fibrosis availing of services among children aged 0-19[27]

CHRONIC HEALTH, DIABETES-RELATED

Related domains:

Child health status and well-being (child morbidity); health (acute and chronic conditions); morbidity.

Recommended measures:

- New cases of children aged 0-14 years receiving insulin on the National Diabetes Register, rate per 100,000 children[2]
- Treatment prevalence rate per 1,000 of cardiovascular conditions, seizure disorders and Type 1 diabetes in children (ages 5-9, 10-14, 15-19), by region and neighbourhood income[8]

- Age-specific annual incidence of Type I insulin-dependent diabetes per 100,000 population, in age groups 0-4, 5-9, 10-14, 15-17 and in total[48]

CHRONIC HEALTH, GENERAL

Related domains:
Children with limitations; health; health (acute and chronic conditions); health (disability); health (health conditions); health (health status and disability); health conditions and health care (health conditions); healthy children.

Recommended measures:
- Child is able to take part in usual play activities[1]
- Chronic health conditions (e.g. eczema, asthma)[7]
- Percentage of children hospitalised for lower respiratory tract infections (including pneumonia, bronchitis and asthma) by age groups (<1, 1-4, 5-9, 10-14, 15-19) and geographical location[8]
- Percentage of children aged 5-17 reported to have at least one limitation. A child is defined as having a limitation if the child exhibits at least one of the following: a) difficulty seeing even when wearing glasses or contact lenses; b) difficulty hearing without a hearing aid; c) an impairment or health problem that limits his or her ability to crawl, walk, run or play; d) has been identified by a school representative or health professional as having a learning disability; e) has been identified by a school representative or health professional as having ADD/ADHD; or f) needs the help of other persons with bathing or showering[10]
- Percentage of children aged 5 to 17 with any limitation in activity resulting from chronic conditions[18]
- Selected chronic health conditions for children under age 18 (rate per 1,000 children) in the USA[20]
- Percentage of children under age 18 in the USA with any activity limitation due to a chronic condition[20]
- Play limited by health condition[21]
- Percentage of children who are limited by chronic health conditions[21]
- Number of children and youth under age 18 with a chronic health condition[51]

COMMUNITY CRIME

Related domains:
Community and school environment deficits (community crime); crime; crime indicators; risk and enabling factors.

Recommended measures:
- Local crime rate[7]
- Levels of criminal behaviour in immediate neighbourhood[7]
- Repeated/escalating criminal behaviour[7]
- Violent/non-violent crimes[7]
- Violent crime – incidents of homicide, rape, aggravated assault and robbery reported by local law enforcement agencies[31]
- Sexual assaults – reported rapes and other sexual offences (offenders and victims may be of any age)[31]
- Property and violent index crimes known to police. Violent index crimes include murder, non-negligent manslaughter, forcible rape, robbery and aggravated assault. Property index crimes include burglary, larceny and motor vehicle theft[39]
- Firearm-related index crimes – track whether a firearm was present during the commission of a murder, forcible rape, robbery or aggravated assault[39]
- Prisoners in State and local correctional facilities – the unduplicated number of new admissions to State and local prisons, by prisoner's county of residence per 1,000 population[41]
- Narcotics arrests[42]

- Adult violent crime rate[42]
- Adult alcohol-related arrests[42]
- Quantity of drugs seized (meth)[43]
- Rates of crime against property (burglary, theft and motor vehicle theft)[44]
- Rate of crimes against the person (murder, forcible rape, robbery, aggravated assault)[44]
- Hate crimes – the number of hate crimes incidents (i.e. criminal incidents motivated by bias against persons based on their race, religion, disability, sexual orientation or ethnicity/ national origin)[45]
- Crime rate per 1,000 people[45]
- Total sentencing rate (sentences per 100,000 population)[55]
- Registered total crime (crimes per 100,000 population)[55]

COMMUNITY RESOURCES AND SOCIAL CAPITAL

Related domains:
Access to developmental opportunities (recreation and skill development opportunities); child well-being within community; communities which support family life; community and school environment strengths (community economic and geographic stability: business support of the community); community and school environment strengths (community economic safety); community-related indicators (neighbourhood satisfaction, safety and cohesion); deprivation (other); neighbourhood; risk and enabling factors (connectedness); risk and enabling factors (geographic concentration); social and emotional development (social community relationships: civic engagement).

Recommended measures:
- Degree to which the State assures family participation in programme and policy activities in the State CSHCN Program[1]
- Satisfaction with area of residence[7]
- Multiple risk factors/behaviours[7]
- Level of social contact and support from neighbours[7]
- Closeness (geographic/emotional) to other relatives[7]
- 'Neighbourhood stress'[7]
- Tenure patterns[7]
- Census Z scores[7]
- Access to safe play and recreation facilities[12]
- Proximity of community resources to family home[14]
- Level of social capital within the community[14]
- Level of geographic mobility of child[14]
- Availability of quality play space and a clean environment[14]
- Access to preferred leisure/play areas[14]
- Neighbourhood physical infrastructure (e.g. quality of housing, per cent rentals, presence of graffiti)[21]
- Neighbourhood institutions (e.g. Outside: availability of police, social welfare, health clinics, libraries. Inside: local business, churches, community centres)[21]
- Neighbourhood demographic composition (e.g. family structure, education levels, income, welfare use, mobility status, employment rates)[21]
- Degree of social organisation: social capital (e.g. shared norms, reciprocal obligation networks), dysfunctional organisation (deviant culture, gangs)[21]
- Number of parks, gyms and other health-enhancing recreational spaces and programmes[23]
- Number of parks and public spaces available for family activities[23]
- Number of free or reduced price entrance fees to cultural arts programmes[23]
- Number of community offerings of affordable and accessible activities that promote physical activity for families with young children[23]
- Number of booster swings and other equipment suitable for toddlers available in parks and recreational facilities[23]

- Adult education and training programmes[24]
- Parent education and support programmes[24]
- Recreational facilities and enrichment programmes for families, young children, school-age children and adolescents[24]
- Proportion of children aged 0-5 living in neighbourhoods with low neighbourhood cohesion, as judged by the Primary Caregiver[28]
- Extent to which areas important for conserving biodiversity, cultural heritage, recreation, natural resource maintenance and other values are protected from incompatible uses[35]
- Percentage of countries who have completed or who are preparing national sustainable development strategies[35]
- Net migration, number of new residents moved into an area minus the number of residents moved out of an area per 1,000 population[41]
- Perception of communities as a good place to raise children: asked respondents, 'how would you rate your community as a place to raise children?', analysed by income[45]
- Business' need to provide training: asked business executives if their company needs to provide basic education in math, writing/spelling, reading, computer skills and people skills to entry-level positions[45]
- Business involvement with community: asked business executives 'how well does the following statement describe your company: our company takes an interest and gets involved in local school and civic events', by size of business[45]
- Percentage of businesses applying for recognition of parental programmes, such as paid paternal leave policies[45]
- Parental satisfaction with youth recreational programmes: asked adults with children under 19 at home how much they agree/disagree with the following, 'I'm satisfied with youth recreational programmes in my community'[45]
- Percentage of parks and recreation programme registrations for children's programmes and services[47]
- Number of registration opportunities for children aged 0-12 living in communities with a high percentage of low-income families provided by Toronto Parks and Recreation[47]
- Percentage of children whose parents reported the availability of a free access safe outdoor play space within 100 metres, 400 metres of the home, by gender and 5 year age group[48]

COMPUTER USE AND ACCESS TO THE INTERNET

Related domains:
Education and achievement (related behaviours and characteristics); education and skills (education-related asset); school (description); social connectedness.

Recommended measures:
- Percentage of children aged 3-17 who: a) have access to computers at home; and b) who use the Internet at home[10]
- Percentage of students who reported using a computer at school or at home[20]
- Percentage of students who reported using a computer for schoolwork[20]
- Percentage of students in Grades 7-12 who reported using a computer at home[20]
- Number of children under 18 years and young people aged 18-24 years living in households with access to the Internet, as a proportion of all children and young people[29]
- Percentage of students (Grades 1-8, Grades 9-12, 1st to 4th year of college, 5th or later year of college) using a computer at school and at home[50]

CONTRACEPTIVE USE

Related domains:
Adolescents (reproductive health); development indicators; entry (pregnancy, birth); health (health-related behaviour); health status (adolescents: sexual activity and condom use); HIV/AIDS; problem behaviour; sexual health; social and emotional development (sexual activity

and teen child-bearing); social development, behavioural health and teen fertility (sexual activity and fertility); teenage fertility; women.

Recommended measures:

- Use of contraception at last intercourse[7]
- Prevalence of birth control pill use by age (15-19), gender, geographical location, income and parental status[8]
- Percentage of 15-19-year-olds who reported using a condom the last time they had sexual intercourse by age, gender, geographical location, income and parental status[8]
- Percentage of students in Grades 9-12 who reported using a condom at most recent sexual intercourse[10]
- Percentage of sexually active students in Grades 9-12 who reported using birth control pills at most recent sexual intercourse[10]
- Contraceptive prevalence among married women of reproductive age[17]
- Percentage of currently sexually active high school students in the USA who reported using a condom during last sexual intercourse. Currently sexually active is defined as having sexual intercourse during the three months preceding the survey[20]
- Percentage of currently sexually active high school students in the USA who reported birth control use during last sexual intercourse. Currently sexually active is defined as having sexual intercourse during the three months preceding the survey[20]
- Percentage of currently sexually active high school students in the USA who reported using a contraceptive during last sexual intercourse. Currently sexually active is defined as having sexual intercourse during the three months preceding the survey[20]
- Rate of birth control use, by type, among 9th to 12th Graders[21]
- Percentage of teens who have had unprotected intercourse within the last year[21]
- Percentage of teens who have had unprotected intercourse at last episode[21]
- Sexual behaviour (condom use during last sexual intercourse) of Mississippi youth, by sex[22]
- Sexual behaviour (birth control pill use during last intercourse) of Mississippi youth, by sex[22]
- Condom use (at last sexual intercourse) by high school students, by Grade (9th, 10th, 11th, 12th)[25]
- Percentage currently using contraception, both traditional and modern methods, among currently married women of reproductive age, including, where possible, those in consensual unions[35]
- Proportion of teens aged 15-19 years who reported always using a condom in the past 12 months[38]
- Percentage of women in union aged 15-49 years currently using contraception[56]
- Percentage of young men and women (15-24 years) who say they used a condom the last time they had sex with a non-marital, non-cohabiting partner, of those who have had sex with such a partner in the last 12 months[56]

CRIMES COMMITTED BY YOUTH, OFFENCES, ARRESTS AND DETENTION

Related domains:

Adolescent risk behaviours; behaviour and social environment; children safe in their families and communities; citizenship and values; conditions (juvenile delinquency); crime; crime indicators; development and behaviour measures; education and childcare; involvement in the juvenile justice system; justice; participation, quality of life and inclusion; problem behaviour; social adjustment; social and emotional development (social community relationships: behaviour problems: delinquent or criminal activity); social determinants of child health; social development, behavioural health and teen fertility (social development); social well-being; youth choose healthy behaviour.

Recommended measures:

- Rate of children aged 10-14 years who are in detention in juvenile justice facilities[2]
- Numbers of children and young people in custody[7]

- Involvement in behaviour likely to lead to crime (e.g. truancy, association with those who have already committed crimes, staying out all night without permission)[7]
- Crimes committed by children according to official statistics[7]
- Attitudes towards crime[7]
- Contact with police not resulting in prosecution[7]
- Behaviour by children too young to be classified as criminal[7]
- Number of crimes committed by children[9]
- Children arrested for serious crimes, rate per 1,000[11]
- Children involved with the law[12]
- Number of distinct children appearing in court for offences, by male, female and in total, where appropriate, by age categories <1 year, 1-3 years, 4-6 years, 7-9 years, 10-12 years, 13-15 years and 16-18 years and in total, where appropriate, and by geographic location and in total, where appropriate[13]
- Reported offences by children by type (offences against the person, offences against property, other), by male, female and in total, where appropriate, by age categories <1 year, 1-3 years, 4-6 years, 7-9 years, 10-12 years, 13-15 years and 16-18 years and in total, where appropriate, and by geographic location and in total, where appropriate[13]
- Drug offences among children, by male, female and in total, where appropriate, by age categories <1 year, 1-3 years, 4-6 years, 7-9 years, 10-12 years, 13-15 years and 16-18 years and in total, where appropriate, and by geographic location and in total, where appropriate[13]
- Serious violent crime offending rate (per 1,000) by youth ages 12 to 17[18]
- Violent crime arrest rates for youth ages 10 through 17 in the USA. Violent crime includes murder, forcible rape, robbery and aggravated assault[20]
- Percentage of youth ages 10-17 arrested for violent crimes in the past year[21]
- Juvenile and adult violent crime rate (per 100,000 population) in Mississippi[22]
- Juvenile and adult property crime rate (per 100,000 population) in Mississippi[22]
- Rate per 100,000 of arrests of youth ages 10-17 for violent criminal offences: murder, forcible rape, robbery and aggravated assault[24]
- Rate per 100,000 of arrests of youth ages 10-17 for serious non-violent criminal offences: breaking or entering, larceny, motor vehicle theft[24]
- Percentage of offences within the following categories (criminal damage, larceny, burglary, public order, vehicle offences, drink offences, other) involving juvenile offenders[27]
- Age distribution (<10 years, 10, 11, 12, 13, 14, 15, 16 and 17) and number of offences committed by juvenile offenders[27]
- Number of cautions and prosecutions among juvenile offenders[27]
- Number of police apprehensions of 14-16-year-olds for all offences except non-prisonable traffic offences, as a proportion of all 14-16-year-olds[29]
- Number of cases proved in the Youth Court, excluding cases involving non-prisonable traffic offences, as a proportion of all 14-16-year-olds[29]
- Percentage of children ages 11 through 18 arrested for a serious crime during the time a case is open[30]
- Rate of court dispositions for delinquency (ages 10-17) – delinquency problems filed in Family Court per 10,000 children[31]
- Custody rate for children deemed delinquent – the average daily number of delinquent children in Social and Rehabilitation Services custody, rate per 10,000 children ages 10-17[31]
- Custody rate for children deemed 'unmanageable' – the average daily number of 'Children in Social Need of Supervision' in Social and Rehabilitation Services custody, rate per 10,000 children ages 10-17[31]
- Youth, ages 10-17, in juvenile justice system[32]
- Number of placements by juvenile court per 1,000 children ages 10-17[34]
- Number of young offenders' institutions[37]

- Persons in Need of Supervision (PINS) cases opened for services (ages 10-15). PINS are juveniles less than 16 for whom complaints were filed with local probation departments because of non-criminal misconduct, such as truancy from school, incorrigibility, ungovernability or habitual disobedience[39]
- Number and rate (per 10,000 youth, ages 10-20) of arrests for drug use/possession/sale/driving under the influence (DUI)[39]
- Adolescent arrests – violent index crimes (ages 10-12, 13-15 and 16-19). Violent index crimes include murder, non-negligent manslaughter, forcible rape, robbery, aggravated assault[39]
- Adolescent arrests – property index crimes (ages 10-12, 13-15 and 16-19). Property index crimes include burglary, larceny and motor vehicle theft[39]
- Annual student rate of selling illegal drugs – the percentage of students in Grades 6, 8, 10 and 12 who reported having sold illegal drugs at least once in the past 12 months[41]
- Average age students in Grades 6, 8, 10 and 12 were first arrested, as reported by students[41]
- Annual student arrest rate – the percentage of students in Grades 6, 8, 10 and 12 who reported having been arrested at least once in the past 12 months[41]
- Adolescents in juvenile detention[42]
- Juvenile arrest rate (any offence)[42]
- Juvenile arrest for violent crime[42]
- Juvenile arrest for vandalism[42]
- Juvenile arrest for alcohol and drug violations[42]
- Rate of youth recidivism[43]
- Arrests per 1,000 youth ages 0-17 for any of the following: manslaughter, rape, robbery, aggravated assault, burglary, larceny, motor vehicle theft, forgery and counterfeiting, fraud, stolen property, vandalism, possession of a weapon, prostitution, sex offences, drug and alcohol-related offences, violation of liquor laws, driving under the influence, drunkenness, disorderly conduct and curfew and loitering law violations[45]
- Juvenile arrests – the percentage of youth arrested[46]
- Persons arrested, by type of charge and age[50]
- Number of arrests per 1,000 persons, by age[50]
- Percentage of youth ages 15-17 referred to family courts who had at least one prior referral[51]
- Number of youth ages 15-17 referred to family courts[51]
- Number of individual juvenile offenders less than 12, 13 or 14 years, and 15 and older referred to the Solicitor for delinquency[51]
- Number of crimes committed by or with participation of juveniles (thousands)[55]
- Registered juvenile crime rate (juvenile crimes per 100,000 population, ages 14-17)[55]
- Juveniles sentenced for criminal activity (thousands)[55]
- Juvenile sentencing rate (juvenile sentences per 100,000 population, ages 14-17)[55]
- Homicides committed by or with participation of juveniles (absolute number)[55]

CRIMES COMMITTED BY YOUTH, YOUTH PERCEPTION OF PARENTAL/PEER ACCEPTANCE OF STEALING

Related domains:

Social and emotional development (social community relationships: behaviour problems: delinquent or criminal activity).

Recommended measures:

- Perceived parental approval of stealing by youth – the percentage of students in Grades 6, 8, 10 and 12 who answered 'not wrong at all' to the question 'how wrong do your parents feel it would be for you to steal anything worth more than $5?'[41]
- Approval of stealing by peers – the percentage of students in Grades 6, 8, 10, 12 who answered 'not wrong at all' to the question 'how wrong do you think it is for someone your age to steal anything worth more than $5?'[41]

CRIMES COMMITTED ON YOUTH

[*SEE ALSO* ABUSE AND NEGLECT, REPORTED AND CONFIRMED]

Related domains:

Behaviour and social environment; conditions (endangerment); crime; education and childcare; health; health (health conditions); health (health-related behaviour); health (violence); health conditions and health care (health conditions); safety; safety (free of violence, abuse, neglect).

Recommended measures:

- Children and young people as victims of crime (including rape, child abuse and child murders)[7]
- Number of crimes committed on children[9]
- Violent crime victimisation rate (per 1,000) of youth ages 12-19. Violent crime includes robbery, simple assault, aggravated assault and rape/sexual assault[10]
- Reported offences against children aged 0-18 by type (homicide, assault, sexual offences, robbery, kidnapping and abduction, other), by male, female and in total, where appropriate, by age categories <1 year, 1-3 years, 4-6 years, 7-9 years, 10-12 years, 13-15 years and 16-18 years and in total, where appropriate, and by geographic location and in total, where appropriate[13]
- Rate of serious violent crime victimisations (per 1,000) of youth ages 12-17[18]
- Serious violent victimisation of youth ages 12 through 17 in the USA (rates per 1,000). Serious violent victimisation is defined as being a victim of violent crime, including aggravated assaults, rape and robbery (stealing by force or threat of violence)[20]
- Criminal victimisation of youth ages 12-20[21]
- Annual victimisation rate among youth ages 12-17 from violent crime[21]
- Child endangerment rates (per 100,000 population) in Mississippi[22]
- Proportion of the population aged 15-24 who have been the victim of one or more incidents of offending as measured by the 2001 National Survey of Crime Victims[29]
- Offences (sexual assault, non-sexual assault, robbery, other) against victims 0-11 years by sex[47]
- Number and percentage of offences (sexual assault, non-sexual assault, robbery, other) against victims 0-11 years by sex[47]
- Number of violent crime victims per 1,000 persons, by type of crime (robbery, assault, rape), age (12-15, 16-19, 20-24, 25 and over), sex and race[50]

DATING

Related domains:

Adolescents (reproductive health: onset of sexual activity); family and community (peer relationships); fertility (sexual activity and fertility); social and emotional development (sexual activity and teen child-bearing); teenage fertility.

Recommended measures:

- Percentage and frequency of dating activity reported by 12-13 year-olds. Activities include holding hands, hugging, kissing, petting above the waist, petting below the waist, sexual intercourse and touching someone who was unwilling[8]
- Percentage of students in Grades 8, 10 and 12 who reported that they a) never date and b) date frequently. Frequent dating is going out on one or more dates each week[10]

DENTAL HEALTH

Related domains:

Child health and development (health: oral health); child health status and well-being (child morbidity: child dental morbidity); childhood morbidity and mortality; condition manifested in childhood (oral health); dental health; health; health (children stay healthy: dental and oral health); health (dental health); health (healthcare); health conditions and health care (health conditions); health services utilisation (dental health); healthy children.

Recommended measures:

- Untreated caries, sealant usage, dental access[1]
- Proportion of children decay-free at age 6 and at age 12[2]
- Mean decayed, missing or filled teeth scores at age 6 and at age 12[2]
- Dental caries[7]
- Oral health, percentage screened[9]
- Oral health, percentage needing care[9]
- Percentage of children ages 2 through 14 in the USA with untreated dental caries[20]
- Percentage of pre-school children who have not seen a dentist in the past year[21]
- Number of children receiving early dental assessments in Shasta County. Early dental assessments mean children who have visited a dentist for a routine check-up in the last 6 months[23]
- Number of children receiving early dental services[23]
- Dental caries and diseases for children entering kindergarten[23]
- Percentage of children with dental care needs and those receiving dental care (unmet dental needs, no dental visits, fewer than two dental visits) in the last 12 months by income (below 200% FPL, above 200% FPL)[25]
- Percentage of children receiving an EPSDT preventative dental service[25]
- Dental treatment among children aged 0-18 years by type (permanent teeth extractions, deciduous (baby) teeth extractions, permanent teeth fillings and deciduous teeth fillings, number of teeth fissure sealed and in total)[27]
- Oral health at school entry[29]
- Percentage of children with one or more sealants (Grade 5)[33]
- Percentage of population on fluoridated water systems[33]
- Percentage of Medicaid-eligible children ages 1-5, 6-14 and 15-20 who received dental services[33]
- Percentage of children in families with no medical insurance in need of urgent dental treatment[36]
- Percentage of children ages 0-4 affected by early childhood tooth decay[36]
- Average number of teeth affected by decay in children ages 5, 7, 9 and 5-13[36]
- Percentage of children with untreated decay for children aged 4, 5, 6, 11 and 12[38]
- Percentage of children with bleeding gums for children aged 4, 5, 6, 11 and 12[38]
- Percentage of children who ever had caries for children aged 4, 5, 6, 11 and 12[38]
- Percentage of children requiring urgent treatment for children aged 4, 5, 6, 11 and 12[38]
- Mean DMFT/deft for children aged 4, 5, 6, 11 and 12[38]
- Percentage of children aged 5 with two or more untreated cavities[47]
- Percentage of children aged 5 with early childhood tooth decay[47]
- Mean DMFT index for 5-year-old children and mean DMFT index for 12-year-old children respectively, by socio-economic group when available[48]

DOMESTIC VIOLENCE

Related domains:

Children in strong, stable families; children safe in their families and communities; family (family violence); family environment (family health and safety); family well-being; healthy children.

Recommended measures:

- Number of children receiving services through State's domestic violence/sexual abuse shelters[1]
- Percentage of women experiencing physical abuse by husbands/partners surrounding pre-natal period[1]
- Percentage of all injuries from domestic violence[1]

- Number of families reporting domestic violence incidents[1]
- Number of children who are victims of or witness to domestic violence[1]
- Number of domestic violence calls for Shasta County and California[23]
- Number of domestic violence reports involving young children aged 0-5 years[23]
- Rate of victims (adults and minor children) receiving domestic violence services through community-based programmes funded by the Department of Human Resources[24]
- Percentage of families experiencing domestic abuse issues during the time a service case is open[30]
- Court petitions filed for Relief from Domestic Abuse[31]
- Domestic violence reports[42, 45]
- Number of domestic assaults recorded by law enforcement officials[51]

DRUG USE AMONG ADULTS (INCLUDING PARENTS)

Related domains:
Children in strong, stable families; community and school environment deficits (negative adult behaviour); family environment (family health and safety); family well-being.

Recommended measures:
- Parental alcohol and substance abuse[1]
- Percentage of adult caregivers whose illicit drug or alcohol use within the last 3 months is affecting their ability to raise their children during the time a service case is open[30]
- Family history of alcohol and/or drug abuse (Grades 6, 8, 10 and 12) – the percentage of students in Grades 6, 8, 10 and 12 who answered 'yes' to the question 'has anyone in your family ever had a severe alcohol and/or drug problem?'[41]
- Number of adults in drug or alcohol treatment[42]

DRUG USE AMONG YOUTH, AGE OF FIRST DRUG USE

Related domains:
Health and safety (youth engaging in risky behaviour); safety and physical status.

Recommended measures:
- Substance (tobacco, alcohol and drugs) abuse by age[5]
- Average age at which students in Grades 6, 8, 10 and 12 first used marijuana as reported by the students[41]
- Early initiation of alcohol, tobacco and other drugs among students in Grades 6, 8 and 11[42]

DRUG USE AMONG YOUTH, APPROVAL OF PEER USE AND PERCEPTION OF PEER ACCEPTANCE OF DRUG USE

Related domains:
Health and safety (youth engaging in risky behaviour); problem behaviour; social development, behavioural health and teen fertility (smoking, alcohol and substance abuse); substance misuse.

Recommended measures:
- Attitudes towards smoking, alcohol and illegal substances[7]
- Percentage of 12th Grade students in the USA who report that peers would not approve of their using alcohol, marijuana, cocaine or cigarettes[20]
- Percentage of teens who report peer approval of smoking tobacco, drinking alcohol[21]
- Percentage of students in Grades 6, 8, 10 and 12 who answered 'not wrong at all' to the question 'how wrong do you think it is for someone your age to smoke marijuana?'[41]
- Percentage of students in Grades 6, 8, 10 and 12 who answered 'very good chance' to the question 'what are the chances you would be seen as cool if you smoked marijuana?'[41]

DRUG USE AMONG YOUTH, CRIME RELATED TO DRUG USE

Related domains:

Substance misuse

Recommended measures:

- Crime figures related to misuse of drugs[7]

DRUG USE AMONG YOUTH, DRIVING AFTER USING DRUGS

Related domains:

Adolescent risk behaviours

Recommended measures:

- Percentage of high school students who reported driving after using drugs[51]

DRUG USE AMONG YOUTH, DRUG ADDICTION

Related domains:

Adolescent risk behaviours

Recommended measures:

- Number of new cases of drug addicts in population less than 19 years of age per 1,000 population less than 19 years[52]

DRUG USE AMONG YOUTH, DRUG USE IN THE PAST 30 DAYS

Related domains:

Adolescent risk behaviours; behaviour and social environment; child health and lifestyle behaviours; child lifestyle determinants of child health, risk and protective factors; health; health (drugs, alcohol, tobacco); health status (adolescents); healthy children; health and safety (youth engaging in risky behaviour); social and emotional development (delinquency and crime); youth choose healthy behaviour.

Recommended measures:

- Percentage of children aged 15 using drugs in the last month, by male, female and in total[6]
- Percentage of students in Grades 8, 10 and 12 who reported using any illicit drugs other than marijuana at least once in the past 30 days[10]
- Percentage of students in Grades 8, 10 and 12 who reported using marijuana at least once in the past 30 days[10]
- Percentage of 8th, 10th and 12th Grade students who reported using illicit drugs in the previous 30 days[18]
- Percentage of youth ages 12 through 17 in the USA reporting illicit drug use and/or binge drinking in the past month. Illicit drugs include marijuana, cocaine (including crack), heroin, hallucinogens (including PCP), inhalants, and non-medical use of psychotherapeutics[20]
- Percentage of 8th, 10th and 12th Grade students in the USA who report having used any illicit drugs within the previous 30 days. For 12th Graders only: use of 'any illicit drug' includes any use of marijuana, LSD, other hallucinogens, crack, other cocaine, heroin or other opiates, stimulants, barbiturates or tranquillisers not under a doctor's orders. For 8th and 10th Graders only: the use of other opiates and barbiturates has been excluded because these younger respondents appear to over-report use[20]
- Percentage of 8th, 10th and 12th Grade students in the USA who report having used marijuana within the previous 30 days[20]
- Percentage of 8th, 10th and 12th Grade students in the USA who report having used specified drugs (marijuana, inhalants, hallucinogens, cocaine) within the previous 30 days[20]
- Percentage of public school students who report using alcohol, tobacco or illegal drugs in the last 30 days by type of substance (cigarettes, alcohol, marijuana, heroin, ecstasy, LSD) and by age/Grade (6th, 8th, 10th and 12th)[24]

- 30-day prevalence of drug use (alcohol, marijuana, cocaine) among adolescents ages 12-17[25]
- Percentage of children who are current drug users[27]
- Prevalence of regular marijuana use[29]
- Percentage of students using marijuana within the last 30 days[31]
- Percentage of students in Grades 9-12 who reported using the following in the past 30 days: cigarettes, smokeless tobacco, marijuana, alcohol (beer), cocaine[33]
- Percentage of children aged 15 reporting that they have a) used cannabis more than twice during the last 30 days, b) ever used heroin, and c) ever used ecstasy, by male, female and in total, and by socio-economic group when available[48]
- Percentage seniors reporting cigarette, alcohol and drug use by substance (cigarettes, alcohol, marijuana/hashish, cocaine) and frequency of use (ever used, used in the previous 30 days)[50]
- Percentage of high school students who reported first using illicit drugs at ages 11, 13, 15[51]
- Percentage of high school students in Grades 7 and 8 who reported using illegal drugs in the last month[51]

DRUG USE AMONG YOUTH, DRUG USE IN THE PAST YEAR

Related domains:
Development and behaviour measures; tobacco, alcohol and drug use.

Recommended measures:
- Drug use in the past 12 months among students in Grades 7-13, by type of drug used (cannabis, hallucinogens, NM stimulants, ecstasy, solvents, LSD, cocaine, NM barbiturates, methamphetamine, glue, rohypnol, PCP, NM tranquillisers, crack, GHB, heroin, ice)[38]

DRUG USE AMONG YOUTH, HOSPITALISATION-RELATED DRUG USE

Related domains:
Substance misuse

Recommended measures:
- Hospitalisations related to misuse of drugs[7]

DRUG USE AMONG YOUTH, LIFETIME DRUG USE

Related domains:
Child health and lifestyle behaviours; child lifestyle determinants of child health, risk and protective factors; health; health and survival; problem behaviour; substance misuse.

Recommended measures:
- Use of marijuana[7]
- Use of inhalants/hallucinogens/cocaine[7]
- Children using alcohol or drugs[12]
- Percentage of 16-year-olds who reported use of cannabis[16]
- Percentage of 16-year-olds who reported use of any drug other than cannabis[16]
- Proportion of 16-year-old boys and girls who reported ever using an illicit drug, by sex and rank among participating countries between 1995 and 1999[16]
- Percentage of 16-year-olds who reported use of inhalants in their lifetime[16]
- Percentage of teens who have used illicit drugs (e.g. marijuana, cocaine, crack, LSD, PCP, ecstasy, mushrooms, speed, ice, heroin or pills)[21]
- Percentage of children who used at least one illicit drug in their lifetime[27]
- Percentage of children aged 15 reporting that they have a) used cannabis more than twice during the last 30 days, b) ever used heroin, and c) ever used ecstasy, by male, female and in total, and by socio-economic group when available[48]

- Percentage of seniors reporting cigarette, alcohol and drug use by substance (cigarettes, alcohol, marijuana/hashish, cocaine) and frequency of use (ever used, used in the previous 30 days)[50]

DRUG USE AMONG YOUTH, PARENTAL GUIDANCE AND PERCEIVED PARENTAL APPROVAL OF DRUG USE

Related domains:
Health and safety (youth engaging in risky behaviour); social and emotional development (social community relationships: positive parent-child relationships: communication between parents and children: provision of parental guidance around acceptable behaviour); substance misuse.

Recommended measures:
- Attitudes towards smoking, alcohol and illegal substances[7]
- Percentage of students in Grades 6, 8, 10 and 12 who answered 'not wrong at all' to the question 'how wrong do your parents feel it would be for you to smoke marijuana?'[41]
- Percentage of youths in Grades 8, 10 and 12 whose parents/guardians have talked to them about not using marijuana and other illegal drugs[43]

DRUG USE AMONG YOUTH, PERCEPTION OF AVAILABILITY OF DRUGS

Related domains:
Adolescent risk behaviours; health; health and safety (youth engaging in risky behaviour); health status (adolescents); substance misuse.

Recommended measures:
- Price of common illegal drugs/whether initially supplied free[7]
- Proportion of 16-year-old boys and girls who perceive marijuana or hashish 'very easy' or 'fairly easy' to obtain, by sex and rank among participating countries between 1995 and 1999[16]
- Proportion of 16-year-old boys and girls who perceive LSD or other hallucinogens 'very easy' or 'fairly easy' to obtain, by sex and rank among participating countries between 1995 and 1999[16]
- Current drinkers, binge-drinkers, heavy drinkers, perception of risk and access to drugs, approached by someone selling drugs in the month prior to the survey[25]
- Percentage of students in Grades 6, 8, 10 and 12 who answered 'very easy' to the question 'if you wanted to get some marijuana, how easy would it be for you to get some?'[41]
- Percentage of high school students in Grade 8 who reported that it is easy to get marijuana[51]
- Percentage of high school students in Grade 8 who reported that it is easy to get cocaine or crack[51]

DRUG USE AMONG YOUTH, PERCEPTION OF HARMFULNESS OF DRUG USE

Related domains:
Health and safety (youth engaging in risky behaviour); health status (adolescents); substance misuse.

Recommended measures:
- Attitudes towards smoking, alcohol and illegal substances[7]
- Current drinkers, binge-drinkers, heavy drinkers, perception of risk and access to drugs, approached by someone selling drugs in the month prior to the survey[25]
- Percentage of students in Grades 6, 8, 10 and 12 who answered 'no risk' to the question – 'how much do you think people risk harming themselves (physically or other ways) if they smoke marijuana regularly?'[41]

- Perceived harmfulness of alcohol, tobacco and other drugs among students in Grades 6, 8 and 11[42]

DRUG USE AMONG YOUTH, PERCEPTION OF POLICE INTERVENTION FOR DRUG USE

Related domains:
Health and safety (youth engaging in risky behaviour)

Recommended measures:
- Percentage of students in Grades 6, 8, 10 and 12 who answered 'no' to the question 'if a kid smoked marijuana in your neighbourhood or in the area around where you live, would he or she be caught by the police?'[41]

DRUG USE AMONG YOUTH, SCHOOL ATTENDANCE WHILE USING DRUGS

Related domains:
Health and safety (youth engaging in risky behaviour)

Recommended measures:
- Percentage of students who reported attending school drunk or high in the past 12 months[41]

DRUG USE AMONG YOUTH, SEXUAL ACTIVITY WHILE USING DRUGS

Related domains:
Health and safety (youth engaging in risky behaviour)

Recommended measures:
- Percentage of students in Grades 9-12 who reported using alcohol or drugs at last sexual intercourse[40]

DRUG USE DURING PREGNANCY

Related domains:
Health (health conditions); health and safety (youth engaging in risky behaviour: youth use of alcohol/illicit drugs); pre-natal period (healthy babies).

Recommended measures:
- Maternal use of tobacco, alcohol and other drug use during pregnancy[21]
- Percentage of women who used drugs during pregnancy. This includes women who reported that they had used alcohol and illegal drugs during some part of their pregnancy[23]
- Number of infants whose mothers used drugs during their pregnancy[23]
- Percentage of street drug use in women who visited the pre-natal clinic[36]
- Number of pregnant women receiving alcohol, tobacco and other drug treatment from State-supported treatment centres, per 1,000 live births[41]

EARLY CHILDHOOD CARE AND EDUCATION, AVAILABILITY

Related domains:
Child health and development (developmental); children in strong, stable families; communities provide safety and support for families and individuals; communities which support family life; community and school environment strengths (effective services); early learning and school readiness; economic security (parental supports); education and childcare (childcare); education indicators; family; social determinants of health (development).

Recommended measures:
- Childcare slots available per 100 children ages 0-12[1]
- Number and capacity of licensed childcare facilities[1]

- Availability of childcare[1]
- Proportion of children aged 3-4 years enrolled at pre-school[2]
- Number of regulated child day care spaces available per 1,000 children ages 0-1[28]
- Type and mix of childcare[21]
- Number of available accredited childcare homes and early care education centres[23]
- Percentage of early care and education facilities that offer care for children in families with non-traditional work hours. Non traditional work hours apply to childcare facilities that provide services outside the regular hours of 08:00am to 17:00pm and on weekends[23]
- Number of providers of early care and education services who will care for mildly ill (i.e. cold, flus) children. Most childcare facilities will not provide services for such children because of the risk of spreading disease or infection[23]
- Number of unlicensed providers who become licensed[23]
- Number of licensed infant centres available for children 0-24 months[23]
- Pre-school programmes, public and private[24]
- Number of slots of licensed centres and regulated family childcare homes compared to the number of families with children in which the mother works[24]
- Estimated percentage met need for childcare – number of regulated childcare slots as a percentage of need for childcare (slots are estimated by capacity figures as of summer of the named year)[31]
- Number of spaces available in childcare programmes (infants 0-18 months, toddlers 18 months-2.5 years; pre-school 2.6-5 years; school age 5 years>) [36]
- Childcare availability – the childcare capacity for children under 13 including the number of registered day care homes, licensed day care homes, group day care homes and childcare centres per 100 children under 13[41]
- Number of affordable, accessible quality childcare options from births through pre-kindergarten[43]
- On-site before or after school programming – the number of school administrative units that offer on-site before and/or after school programmes[45]
- Opportunities for expanded-day kindergarten – the percentage of all public kindergarten students in schools offering all-day or expanded-day kindergarten (excluding Head Start Programmes) [45]
- Number of licensed, centre-based childcare spaces[47]
- Number of spaces in State-regulated childcare[51]
- Regulated childcare spaces (number)[53]

EARLY CHILDHOOD CARE AND EDUCATION PROGRAMMES, COSTS

Related domains:
Access to developmental opportunities (childhood learning and care); children in strong, stable families; community and school environment strengths (effective services); economic security (parental supports); education and childcare (childcare); family.

Recommended measures:

- Percentage of families that spend less than 20% of their income on childcare[1]
- Average ratio of childcare costs to family income less than 10%[1]
- Ratio of childcare costs to family income[21]
- Number of childcare centres receiving funding for subsidised children and wages subsidies or pay equity payments[47]
- Average annual salary for a full-time trained Early Childhood Educator working in a childcare centre with a purchase of service contract[47]
- Average weekly wage of State-regulated childcare providers[51]
- Average weekly charge for State-regulated childcare[51]

- Access to childcare (parents of children under 18) – asked parents with children under 18 how much they agreed or disagreed with the statement: 'I have access to high quality, affordable childcare in my community', by income[45]

EARLY CHILDHOOD CARE AND EDUCATION, TYPE OF EARLY CHILDHOOD CARE AND EDUCATION ARRANGEMENTS

Related domains:

Child health and development (developmental); children in strong, stable families; children ready for school and vice versa; children's economic well-being; community and school environment strengths (effective services); early childhood experience; economic security (parental employment); education; education and achievement (enrolment and attendance); education and childcare; education and childcare (childcare); education and childcare (enrolment); education and personal development; education and skills (attendance and attainment); educational well-being; infant well-being; other determinant factors of child health, risk and protective factors; participation; population; population and family characteristics; population characteristics; pre-primary education; social and emotional development (early development).

Recommended measures:

- Kindergarten students who participated in pre-school or childcare programmes[1]
- Number of children under age 13 in 'latch key' situations[1]
- Percentage of low-income students in Head Start or pre-kindergarten programmes[1]
- Number of children participating in certified pre-school programmes[1]
- Average number of moves within childcare system[1]
- Share of children ages 3 to 5 enrolled in nursery school or kindergarten during the fall school term[4]
- Percentage of children under age 6 who spent some time during the calendar year in paid childcare while their parents worked. This measure includes children in pre-school and nursery school, but not those in kindergarten or elementary school[4]
- Estimated percentage of children attending early education[6]
- Percentage of children aged 3-5, not yet in kindergarten, who attend early childhood care and education programmes (day care centres, Head Start programmes, nursery schools, pre-schools, pre-kindergartens and other early childhood programmes)[10]
- Percentage of children from birth through age 6, who are not yet in kindergarten, in various childcare arrangements: a) parental care only; b) total in non-parental care; c) care in a home by a relative; d) care in a home by a non-relative; and e) centre-based care[10]
- Attendance at pre-school[12]
- Number of children attending licensed childcare services by type of childcare service, family day care, kindergarten, long day care, limited hours day care (by male, female and in total, where appropriate, by age categories <1 year, 1-3 years, 4-6 years, 7-9 years, 10-12 years, 13-15 years and 16-18 years and in total, where appropriate, and by geographic location and in total, where appropriate) [13]
- Receipt of maternal and paternal care-giving in first two years of the child's life[14]
- Receipt of early education[14]
- Percentage of children in kindergarten through 8th Grade by weekday care and activities (parental care only, home-based care, centre-based care, self-care)[18]
- Percentage of children ages 3 to 5 who are enrolled in centre-based early childhood care and education programmes[18]
- Percentage of children from birth through age 6, not yet in kindergarten, by type of care arrangement (parental care only, care in home by a relative, care in home by a non-relative, centre-based programmes)[18]
- Percentage distribution of childcare arrangements of children under age 5 in the USA with employed mothers (day care centre or pre-school, non-relative care in provider's home,

grandparent/other relative in relative's home, father in child's home, other care in child's home, other care outside child's home)[20]

- Percentage of 3- and 4-year-olds (not yet in kindergarten) in the USA enrolled in centre-based programmes. Centre-based programmes include day-care centres, Head Start programmes, pre-schools, pre-kindergartens, and other early childhood programmes[20]
- Percentage of 3- and 4-year-olds (not yet in kindergarten) in the USA enrolled in nursery school[20]
- Stability of care[21]
- HOME environment scale[21]
- Pre-school enrolment rate of 3-4-year-olds[21]
- Percentage of pre-kindergarten 3-5-year-olds enrolled in centre-based programmes[21]
- Percentage of eligible children enrolled in Head Start[21]
- Proportion of children under age 13 in 'latch key' situations[21]
- Percentage of children under 5 in childcare[21]
- Number of families accessing early care and education through a co-ordinated, centralised service[23]
- Number of 4-year-old children enrolled in Head Start. Head Start is a partial-day comprehensive child development programme for children 3 to 5 years of age from low-income families[23]
- Number of 4-year-old children eligible for Head Start who are enrolled in Head Start[23]
- Hours per week in childcare for children under 3 with mothers employed full-time (no hours, 1-20 hours, 21-40 hours, 41 or more hours)[25]
- Number of enrolments of children aged 3-4 in early childhood education services, as a proportion of all 3-4-year-olds[29]
- Children in publicly subsidised childcare[32]
- Children enrolled in childcare[32]
- Percentage of 5-year-olds in kindergarten attending full-day programmes[34]
- Percentage of children in non-parental childcare arrangements while their parents go to school[36]
- Percentage of children prepared for kindergarten[44]
- Percentage of low-income students in Head Start or pre-kindergarten programmes[46]
- Percentage of kindergarten students in pre-school or childcare programmes[46]
- Percentage of children aged 3 and under 5 years enrolled in a Level 0 (pre-primary) education or kindergarten programme, by male, female and in total, and by socio-economic group when available[48]
- Weekly hours spent in first childcare arrangement among 3-5-year-olds[49]
- Children ever in childcare by poverty status and age group[49]
- Age at first childcare experience among 3-5-year-olds by education level of designated parent[49]
- Pre-primary enrolments (net rates, per cent of 3-6 population)[55]
- Pre-primary gross enrolment ratio[57]
- Age group enrolled in pre-primary education[57]

EARLY CHILDHOOD CARE AND EDUCATION, QUALITY
[INCL. PARENTAL SATISFACTION, ADULT-CHILD RATIO AND QUALIFICATION OF CARE-GIVERS]

Related domains:

Access to developmental opportunities (childhood learning and care); children in strong, stable families; children ready for school and vice versa; community and school environment strengths (effective services); education and childcare (childcare); family; infant well-being.

Recommended measures:

- Adult/child ratio in childcare programme[1]
- Percentage of teachers in Grades K-3 with early childhood endorsement or early childhood degree[1]

- Childcare providers' educational background[1]
- Alaska childcare rating by *Working Mother* magazine[1]
- Size at which regulation of childcare begins in Alaska[1]
- Percentage of children in care who receive quality childcare[1]
- Number of parents satisfied with childcare arrangements[1]
- Receipt of high quality childcare[14]
- Adult/child ratio in childcare setting[21]
- Childcare givers' education background[21]
- Quality of care[21]
- Proportion of parents who are satisfied with their childcare arrangements[21]
- Number and diversity of early childhood care and education college courses and programmes available in Shasta County[23]
- Number of care-givers who have had their jobs for more than 12 months[23]
- Number of care-givers who leave the early care and education profession in a 12-month period[23]
- Average number of years of experience working in early care and education per provider[23]
- Average class size (Grades K-4)[42]
- Availability of service learning opportunities[43]
- Number of elementary school teachers with Early Childhood Education Certificates[45]
- Satisfaction with childcare (parents of children under 18) – asked parents with children under 18 how satisfied they are with the quality of their childcare, by income[45]
- Access to childcare (parents of children under 18) – asked parents with children under 18 how much they agreed or disagreed with the statement: 'I have access to high quality, affordable childcare in my community', by income[45]
- Number of full-time and part-time teaching staff in childcare centres[47]
- Ratio of trained to untrained staff in childcare centres[47]
- Percentage of childcare providers who have attained more than high school degree[51]

ECONOMIC INDICATORS, GENERAL

Related domains:

Basic indicators; community; economic indicators; general economic well-being; the rate of progress.

Recommended measures:

- Per capita income[32]
- a) State revenues and b) local taxes as a percentage of total revenue[34]
- Real GDP growth (index)[55]
- General government balance (per cent of GDP)[55]
- Distribution of income: Gini co-efficient[55]
- Real wages (index)[55]
- Annual inflation rate (annual average per change on consumer prices)[55]
- Distribution of earnings: Gini co-efficient[55]
- Gross domestic product (GDP) is the sum of money added by all resident producers plus any product taxes (less subsidies) not included in the valuation of output. GDP per capita is gross domestic product divided by mid-year population. Growth is calculated from constant price GDP data in local currency[56]
- The sum of interest payments and repayment of principal on external public and publicly guaranteed long-term debts[56]
- Net official development assistance[56]
- Gross national income (GNI) is the sum of value added by all resident producers plus any product taxes (less subsidies) not included in the valuation of output plus net receipts of primary income (compensation of employees and property income) from abroad. GNI per capita is gross national income divided by mid-year population. GNI per capita in US dollars is converted using the World Bank Atlas method[56]
- GNP per capita[57]

EMPLOYMENT/UNEMPLOYMENT

Related domains:

Community and school environment strengths (community economic and geographic stability); economic indicators; family environment (family socio-economic status); general economic well-being; risk and enabling factors; social determinants of child health.

Recommended measures:

- Local unemployment/poverty rates[7]
- Number of people unemployed expressed as a percentage of the total labour force[27]
- Rate of job creation, the percentage change from the previous year in the total number of private sector jobs covered by unemployment compensation[31]
- Employment/unemployment[31, 39, 41, 42, 44, 45, 46]
- Unemployment rate[32]
- Percentage of workers unemployed (per 100 persons in labour force)[34]
- Employment rates of the disabled – the percentage of non-institutionalised disabled persons who are employed (persons in the labour force only), 1994-2000[45]
- Percentage of non-institutionalised disabled persons who are employed (persons in the labour force only), 1994-2000[45]
- Rate of growth in employment[46]
- Employment ratio (number employed as a per cent of 15-59 population)[55]
- Annual registered unemployment rate (average per cent of labour force), by male, female and in total[55]

EXPOSURE TO ENVIRONMENTAL HAZARDS, AIR POLLUTION

Related domains:

Air quality and respiratory health; development indicators; other determinant factors of child health, risk and protective factors; population and family characteristics (children's environments); safety (free of violence, abuse, neglect).

Recommended measures:

- Percentage of children under age 18 living in areas that do not meet one or more of the Primary National Ambient Air Quality Standards[18]
- Emissions of carbon dioxide from industrial processes and land use change[35]
- Number of smog advisory days[47]
- Percentage of children aged 0-14 living in localities with an annual mean concentration of >40ppm of PM10[48]

EXPOSURE TO ENVIRONMENTAL HAZARDS, ENVIRONMENTAL TOBACCO SMOKE

Related domains:

Air quality and respiratory health; child health and development (health); exposure to tobacco smoke; family and community (family); health (drugs, alcohol, tobacco); parental determinants of child health, risk and protective factors; physical protection policy; safety (free of violence, abuse, neglect); safety and physical status; social determinants of health; tobacco, alcohol and drug use.

Recommended measures:

- Proportion of households with children aged 0-14 years where adults smoke inside[2]
- Exposure of children to environmental hazards[5]
- Percentage of children aged 12-19 exposed to second-hand smoke regularly at home, by region[8]
- Percentage of parents who are current smokers. Current smokers are defined as those who have ever smoked 100 cigarettes and currently smoke every day or some days[10]
- Percentage of persons most knowledgeable about the child and the percentage of their spouses who are non-smokers[19]

- Number of children aged 0 to 5 who are exposed to second-hand smoke in their homes[23]
- Percentage of homes with total, partial or no restriction on smoking in the home[36]
- Proportion of non-smoking residents, aged 12-19, living in smoke-free homes, by sex[38]
- Percentage of households with children aged 0-14 that are completely smoke-free. No household member smokes regularly inside the home and visitors are not allowed to smoke[47]
- Existence and enforcement of laws aimed at protecting children from exposure to environmental tobacco smoke in public places[48]
- Percentage of children aged 0-4 living in households where any member of the household smokes, by socio-economic group when available[48]

EXPOSURE TO ENVIRONMENTAL HAZARDS, LEAD

Related domains:

Air quality and respiratory health; health; health (disabilities); health (health conditions); physical protection policy; safety (free of violence, abuse, neglect).

Recommended measures:

- Rate of elevated blood lead levels[21]
- Number of reported cases of children under age 5 with blood lead levels exceeding 10ug/dl per 100,000 children[23]
- Percentage of children aged 12-36 months: a) screened for elevated blood lead levels and b) found to have elevated blood lead levels[33]
- Number of hospitalisations of children aged 0-14 for respiratory disease[47]
- Existence of legislation and regulations that limit the use of lead in building and decorating materials, and establish bio-monitoring of babies and children at high risk[48]
- Lead exposure detected in children screened[51]

EXPOSURE TO ENVIRONMENTAL HAZARDS, NOISE POLLUTION

Related domains:

Physical protection policy

Recommended measures:

- Existence of policies aimed at assessing and reducing the exposure of babies and young children to potentially harmful noise in ICU units, day-care centres, schools and kindergartens[48]

FAMILY STRUCTURE AND LIVING ARRANGEMENTS

Related domains:

Child well-being relating to the family; children in strong, stable families; demographic; demographic and socio-economic determinants of child health; demographic characteristics; demographic indicators; demographics (family structure and living arrangements); family; family and community (family); family and community context; family and household; family environment (household structure); home (demographics and family composition); parenting and cultural resources; population and family characteristics; population, family and neighbourhood (family structure); risk and enabling factors; social determinants of health (development); stable and economically independent families.

Recommended measures:

- Percentage of children living in households headed by a single parent[1]
- Percentage of children living in two-working or single parent homes: lack of parental supervision[1]
- Percentage of children living in single parent families[3]
- Percentage of all families with 'own children' under age 18 living in the household, who are headed by a person (male or female) without a spouse present in the home. 'Own children'

are never-married children under 18 who are related to the householder (head of household) by birth, marriage or adoption[4]

- Family type[7]
- Level of contact with non-resident father[7]
- Percentage of families headed by lone-parent, by region[8]
- Living arrangements of children under 18, i.e. the percentage living with: a) two parents present; b) mother only present; c) father only present; and d) living with no parent present[10]
- Family structure[14]
- Relationships between separated parents[14]
- Percentage of children under age 18 by presence of parents in household: a) two parents; b) mother only; c) father only; d) no parent[18]
- Percentage of lone-parent families[19]
- Percentage of children under age 18 in the USA who are living with two parents[20]
- Percentage distribution of living arrangements of children under age 18 in the USA in two-parent, one-parent or no parent families[20]
- Percentage distribution of living arrangements of children under age 18 in the USA (two parents, mother only, father only, no parent)[20]
- Percentage of children in each of the following living conditions: married couple, step-parent, co-habiting parents, single female parent, single male parent, no parent[21]
- Percentage of all families with 'own children' under age 18 living in the household, who are headed by a person, male or female, without a spouse present in the home. 'Own children' are never-married children under 18 who are related to the householder by birth, marriage or adoption[24]
- Asylum-seeking children: the total number of asylum-seeking children in direct provision accommodation[27]
- Asylum-seeking children: the total number of asylum-seeking children in private rented accommodation[27]
- Percentage of dependent children under 18 living with one parent[29]
- Percentage of families with children headed by a single parent[31]
- Percentage of children living in: a) households with their own parents (married couple, single parent, single mother, single father); and b) other households with children[32]
- Proportion of census families in private households with children living at home by family structure (husband/wife families with children at home, common-law couples with children at home, male lone-parent families with children at home, female lone-parent families with children at home)[38]
- Number of families with children headed by a single parent[42]
- Percentage of children who live in family household units with only one parent or primary care-giver resident, by male, female and in total, in age groups 0-4, 5-9 10-14, 15-17[48]
- Number and percentage of own children under 18 years in married couple and single parent families, by race/ethnicity of family householder[50]
- Number and percentage of families with own children under 18 years, by family type (married couple families, single parent families) and race/ethnicity of family householder[50]
- Number of children under age 18 living in single parent families[51]
- Percentage of population living in urban areas as defined according to the national definition used in most recent population census[56]

FOOD SECURITY

Related domains:

Child health and development (nutrition); economic security; economic security (consumption); economic security (housing/other); economic security (income security); family environment (housing and food security); risk and enabling factors; social determinants of health (development).

Recommended measures:

- Percentage on school dinners[7]
- Cost and quality of food by geographic location, families living in lower income[8]
- Percentage of children ages 2 to 9 by age and diet quality (poor diet, needs improvement, good diet), as measured by the Healthy Eating Index[18]
- Percentage of children under age 18 in households experiencing food insecurity reporting child hunger[18]
- Percentage of children under age 18 in the USA in households experiencing food insecurity, measured using the food security scale[20]
- Percentage of families that sometimes do not have enough to eat[21]
- Proportion of households with children aged 5-14 for which an adult in the household responded 'always' to the statement, 'we can afford to eat properly' in the 2002 National Children's Nutrition Survey[29]
- Percentage of children under 18 served by food banks[36]
- Number of children served by school breakfast programmes[36]
- Food insecurity – asked respondents how often this statement is true: 'I worried whether my food would run out before I got money to buy more'[45]
- Average weekly cost of a Nutritious Food Basket for a family of four[47]

GESTATIONAL AGE

Related domains:

Entry (pregnancy, birth); health; healthcare services; health conditions and health care (health conditions); healthy children; maternal and neo-natal conditions; neo-natal health; physical health; pre-natal period (healthy babies).

Recommended measures:

- Gestational age at birth[1]
- Overall pre-term (<37 weeks) birth rate (%)[8]
- Percentage post-term (>42 weeks), percentage term (>37 <41 weeks), percentage premature (<37 weeks), percentage very premature (<32 weeks), percentage extremely premature (<28 weeks)[9]
- Percentage of children born before 37 weeks of gestation[19]
- Percentage of pre-term births[20]
- Percentage of all births that are premature (per 1,000 live births)[22]
- Percentage of live births with a gestational age at birth of less than 37 completed weeks (less than 259 days)[28]
- Pregnancy lasts 37-42 weeks, ends with labour[36]
- Babies born before 37 weeks[36]
- Number of live births and foetal deaths at each completed week of gestation (starting from 22 weeks), expressed as a proportion of all live and stillbirths. This distribution is presented as follows: a) 22-36 weeks of gestation (pre-term births); b) 37-41 weeks (term births); and c) 41+ weeks (post-term). Pre-term births can be subdivided into: a) 22-27 weeks (extremely pre-term); b) 28-32 weeks (very pre-term); and c) 32-36 weeks (moderate pre-term)[58]
- Percentage of pre-term live and stillbirths less than 32 weeks of gestation that are born in a maternity unit without an on-site neo-natal intensive care unit. The percentage of very pre-term births should be presented by level of maternity unit using local official definitions or unofficial definitions[58]

GOALS, VALUES AND IDENTITY

Related domains:

Citizenship and values; civic life skills; pro-social behaviour; social and emotional development (emotional and personal development); social development, behavioural health and teen fertility (social development).

Recommended measures:

- Percentage who report an interest in current events and in social problems[5]
- Percentage of children who report having political, religious or social discussions with family and friends[5]
- Percentage of high school seniors in the USA who rate selected personal life goals as being 'extremely important': a) being successful in my line of work; b) having a good marriage and family life; c) having lots of money[20]
- Percentage of high school seniors in the USA who rate selected social life goals as being 'extremely important': a) making a contribution to society; b) working to correct social and economic inequalities; and c) being a leader in my community[20]
- Percentage of high school seniors who believe that the following life goals are 'extremely important': being successful at work; having strong friendships; having a good family life; having lots of money; making a contribution to society; working to correct social inequalities; and being a leader in the community[21]
- Percentage of youth who perceive socio-economic opportunities and believe they can attain them[21]
- Percentage of high school seniors who often worry about the following national problems: crime and violence, drugs, hunger and poverty, race relations, nuclear war, economic problems, pollution[21]
- Percentage of students (Grades 6, 8 and 11) who report that 'I think things through carefully before I make a decision; I can say 'no' when someone wants me to do things I know are wrong or dangerous'. Data collected as part of the indicator: social competencies (I think things through carefully before I make a decision; I can say 'no' when someone wants me to do things I know are wrong or dangerous; I am accepting of those different than me (racially, culturally, socio-economically); It is wrong to discriminate against someone because of his/her race, appearance, culture, religion, etc; and I am good at making friends)[42]
- Positive identity (Grades 6, 8 and 11) – I feel I do not have much to be proud of; I accept responsibility for my actions when I make a mistake or get into trouble; When I have problems, I am good at finding a way to fix them; and I believe that working hard now will make my life successful in the future[42]
- Percentage of high school seniors who felt that certain life values (work success, providing better opportunities for children, having lots of money, strong friendships) were 'very important', by sex[50]
- Percentage of high school seniors indicating that they agree with their parents on selected topics (what to do with your life, how to dress, how to spend money, what is permitted on a date, value of an education, roles for women, environmental issues, racial issues, religion, politics)[50]

HEALTH INSURANCE COVERAGE

Related domains:

Children's economic well-being; economic security (access to health care); health; health (healthcare); health (inadequate health care); health and safety (youth health: youth access to services); health conditions and health care (health care); health services utilisation (healthcare financing); healthy children; income, assets and work (poverty, wealth, income); infant, child and teen health indicators.

Recommended measures:

- Percentage of potentially Medicaid-eligible children who have received a service paid by the Medicaid programme[1]
- Percentage of children without health insurance[1]
- Percentage of children with Special Health Care Needs in the State CSHCN programme with a source of insurance for primary and speciality care[1]
- Percentage of children with access to medical care: Medicaid, Denalik, KidCare, Indian Health Service[1]

- Percentage of children under age 18 living in low-income working families who were not covered by health insurance at any point during the year. Children are considered living in low-income working families if the family income was less than 150% of the federal poverty level and if at least one parent worked 50 or more weeks during the year[4]
- Percentage of children under age 18 who were not covered by health insurance at any point during the year. Health insurance includes private sector insurance generally provided through work, as well as insurance provided through the public sector, such as Medicare and Medicaid[4]
- Percentage of children under 18 who are covered by health insurance[10]
- Percentage of children under age 18 with no usual source of health care[18]
- Percentage of children under age 18 covered by health insurance[18]
- Percentage of children under age 18 in the USA who are covered by health insurance[20]
- Percentage of children under age 18 in the USA who are covered by Medicaid[20]
- Percentage of children covered by health insurance (public, private, none)[21]
- Percentage of persons eligible for but not enrolled in Medi-cal. Medi-cal can provide access to healthcare services for people whose assets and income are insufficient to pay medical bills and/or to meet basic monthly needs. Those enrolled receive free or reduced cost healthcare. The following are eligibility thresholds for pregnant women and families wishing to enrol in Medi-cal: pregnant women with incomes <=200% FPL, children ages 1-5 with family incomes <=133% FPL and children ages 6-19 and parents in families with incomes =100% FPL[23]
- Number of eligible children and pregnant women enrolled in Healthy Families, Medi-Cal, AIM, and/or programmes available for health coverage[23]
- Number of children aged 0 through 5 and pregnant women enrolled in Medi-cal. Medi-cal can provide access to healthcare services for people whose assets and income are insufficient to pay medical bills and/or to meet basic monthly needs. Those enrolled receive free or reduced cost healthcare. The following are eligibility thresholds for pregnant women and families wishing to enrol in Medi-cal: pregnant women with incomes <=200% FPL, children ages 1-5 with family incomes <=133% FPL and children ages 6-19 and parents in families with incomes =100% FPL[23]
- Health insurance coverage (no coverage, public coverage, private coverage) for children under 18 years of age[25]
- Children enrolled in Medicaid, ages 0-18[32]
- Percentage of Medicaid-enrolled children (ages 0-18) receiving preventative care[33]
- Health choice enrolment (ages 0-18)[33]
- Medicaid enrolment (ages 0-18)[33]
- Percentage of all children (ages 0-18) uninsured[33]
- Percentage of all children (ages 0-18) in target group uninsured[33]
- Number of Medicaid/HealthChoices treatments (day treatment, in-home, in-patient, out-patient, other)[34]
- Number of Medicaid/HealthChoices primary diagnoses[34]
- Number of children enrolled in a) Medicaid and b) CHIP[34]
- Births to women with primary financial coverage of Medicaid or self-pay[39]
- Title XIX participation rate (Medicaid B1)[42]
- Health insurance coverage[42]
- Number of youth who have access to quality healthcare through Illinois KidCare and Medicaid[43]
- Percentage of 18-years-olds and older who have health insurance[45]
- Percentage of children under age 18 with health insurance[45]
- Percentage of population with health insurance, by age, poverty status (in poverty, not in poverty), race/ethnicity and type of coverage (private health insurance, Medicaid, Medicare)[50]
- Rate of uninsured children and youth under age 18 in families with incomes under/above 200% of poverty[51]
- Number of children, birth through to 18, enrolled in Medicaid[51]

- Total TennCare population (per cent)[53]
- TennCare enrolees younger than 21 (per cent)[53]

HELMET USE

Related domains:
Health (health-related behaviour); health and safety (youth health: good health and health habits among youth); healthy children.

Recommended measures:
- Helmet use: bicycle, skating, skiing[1]
- Rate of bicycle helmet use[21]
- Percentage of youth who report to have worn a helmet when riding a bicycle in the past 12 months[43]

HIGHER EDUCATION, ATTAINMENT

Related domains:
Education; education and achievement (enrolment and attendance); school (outcomes).

Recommended measures:
- Percentage of high school graduates ages 25 to 29 who have completed a bachelor's degree or higher[18]
- Percentage of 25- through 29-year-old high school graduates in the USA who have attended some college or who have received a bachelor's degree or higher[20]
- Percentage of 25- through 29-year-old high school graduates in the USA who received a bachelor's degree[20]
- Percentage of bachelor's, masters, first-professional and doctor's degrees awarded to women[50]

HIGHER EDUCATION, COSTS

Related domains:
Education and childcare (enrolment); school (description).

Recommended measures:
- Average net cost of college tuition for low, middle and high income students (net of grants)[21]
- Long-term pay-off to post-secondary education of various sorts[21]
- Average charges for full-time undergraduate students, by type and control of college[50]

HIGHER EDUCATION, ENROLMENT

Related domains:
Citizenship and values; education; education and achievement (enrolment and attendance); education aspirations; education outcome; education and childcare (behavioural characteristic); education and childcare (enrolment); pro-social behaviour; youth successfully transition to adulthood.

Recommended measures:
- Percentage post-compulsory enrolment[7]
- Percentage of 25- through 29-year-old high school graduates in the USA who have attended some college[20]
- Percentage of 25- through 29-year-old high school graduates in the USA who have attended some college or who have received a bachelor's degree or higher[20]
- Percentage of youth who have high aspirations for post-secondary education[21]
- Percentage of youth involved in post-secondary education[21]
- Percentage of post-secondary students enrolled in 2-year, 4-year and vocational schools[21]
- Percentage of high school seniors who intend to go to college[21]

- Number of 18-24-year-olds who graduated or completed a qualification at a tertiary education institute, as a proportion of all 18-24-year-olds[29]
- Percentage of high school seniors with plans for education, vocational training or employment[31]
- Percentage of graduating high school seniors who continue their education within 6 months[31]
- Percentage of graduating seniors planning to continue education[34]
- Percentage of seniors who plan to go to college after graduation (right after high school, a year or more after graduation, no or don't know) and educational aspirations (high school diploma or less, two years or less of college or vocational school, college graduate, post-graduate degree), by selected characteristics[50]
- Higher education enrolment (gross rates, per cent of 19-24 population)[55]

HIV/AIDS

[*SEE ALSO* INFECTIOUS DISEASES AND SEXUALLY TRANSMITTED DISEASES]

Related domains:

Development indicators; health; health (communicable diseases); health (health conditions); health (health status and disability); health (illness); health conditions and health care (health conditions); health status (adolescents); health status (children); HIV/AIDS.

Recommended measures:

- Number of newly diagnosed AIDS cases among children and adolescents[10]
- Reported peri-natally acquired AIDS cases among children under age 13 in the USA[20]
- Reported AIDS rate (per 100,000) among children under 13 in the USA[20]
- AIDS cases in adolescents ages 13 through 19 in the USA[20]
- Incidence of AIDS in children and youth (0-13, 14-19, 20-24 years)[20]
- Young adult AIDS cases by gender and exposure category (risk not reported/identified, receipt of blood/blood components, injecting drug use (IDU), heterosexual contact, men having sex with men) for ages 20-24[25]
- Paediatric AIDS by race/ethnicity and exposure category (peri-natal transmission, receipt of blood/blood components, risk not reported/identified)[20]
- Adolescent AIDS cases by gender and exposure category (risk not reported/identified, receipt of blood/blood components, injecting drug use (IDU), heterosexual contact, men having sex with men) for ages 13-19[25]
- Adolescent HIV infection cases by gender and race/ethnicity for ages 13-19 at diagnosis[25]
- Number of newly reported cases of peri-natal HIV/AIDS[33]
- HIV prevalence in 15-24-year-old pregnant women[35]
- Total number of reported cases of selected youth-related diseases (polio, measles, tuberculosis, gonorrhoea, syphilis, AIDS) for all age groups[50]
- Self-reported knowledge of persons 18-years-old and over about AIDS (a lot or some, a little or nothing), by level of education (less than 12 years of education, 12 years of education, more than 12 years of education)[50]
- Child HIV: number of new cases/year per 1,000 children 0-14 years[52]
- Newly registered cases of HIV[55]
- Estimated number of adults and children living with HIV/AIDS as of end-2003[56]
- Percentage of blood samples taken from pregnant women (15-49 years) that test positive to HIV during 'unlinked anonymous' sentinel surveillance at selected ante-natal clinics[56]
- Percentage of young women and men (15-24 years) who report through prompted questions that condom use can prevent HIV transmission[56]
- Percentage of young men and women (15-24 years) who know that a healthy-looking person can have the AIDS virus[56]
- Estimated number of children (0-17 years) as of end-2003 who have lost one or both parents to AIDS[56]
- Percentage of young women (15-24 years) who correctly identify the two major ways of preventing the sexual transmission of HIV (using condoms and limiting sex to one faithful,

uninfected partner), who reject the two most common misconceptions about HIV transmission and who know that a healthy-looking person can have the AIDS virus[56]
- Percentage of adults (15-49 years) living with HIV/AIDS as of end-2003[56]

HOSPITALISATION, AGE AND/OR CAUSE-SPECIFIC

Related domains:

Child health and development (health); childhood morbidity and mortality; disability; health; health (health conditions); health (health service utilisation); health (healthcare); health (quality of care); health services utilisation; health status (children); health systems policy; healthcare; leading causes of child mortality and hospitalisation; morbidity.

Recommended measures:

- Tonsillectomy and adenoidecomy rates per 1,000 for children (0-19), by region[8]
- Percentage of children hospitalised by age group (<1, 1-4, 5-9, 10-14, 15-19), by income and by region hospitalised per 1,000[8]
- Hospitalisation rates per 1,000 for children aged 0-19 for immunisable and preventable infections, by region, income quintile[8]
- Hospital re-admission rates of live newborns within their first 6 weeks post-discharge and reasons given for re-admission (respiratory, jaundice, etc)[8]
- Ten most common diagnoses for healthcare visits for children 0-19[8]
- Hospital separation rate per 1,000 (0-4, 5-9, 10-14, 15-19 and 20-24 years)[9]
- Ten most frequent conditions resulting in hospital separation among children (<1, 2-9, 10-19, 20-24 years)[9]
- Morbidity (refers to all cause of illness for which children and young people may enter hospital) rates for children aged 0-18 (by male, female and in total, where appropriate, by age categories <1 year, 1-3 years, 4-6 years, 7-9 years, 10-12 years, 13-15 years and 16-18 years and in total, where appropriate, and by geographic location and in total, where appropriate)[13]
- Hospitalisations for ambulatory sensitive conditions (i.e. preventable or treatable through good primary care)[21]
- Proportion of infants admitted to neo-natal intensive care unit[21]
- Major causes of hospitalisation by age (1-4, 5-9, 10-14, 15-19, 20-21)[25]
- Hospital utilisation (number of nights in hospital), by income (under $20,000, $20,000 or more) and race[25]
- Discharge rate of patients 1-14 years for selected diagnoses (diseases of the respiratory system, injury, diseases of the digestive system)[25]
- Hospital admission rate of 0-14-year-olds[27]
- Surgery for undescended testes (orchidopexy): the proportion of surgery for undescended testes (orchidopexy) among children before their fifth birthday[27]
- Day surgery: the proportion of surgery in children 0-15 years as day cases for: a) grommet surgery; b) hernia repair; and c) squint correction[27]
- Leading causes of hospitalisation in children aged under 1, 1-4 and 5-9[36]
- Number, proportion and crude hospitalisation rate per 100,000 by leading cause for children aged 10-19 by sex (complications of pregnancy, injury and poisoning, digestive system diseases, respiratory system, mental disorders, musculo-skeletal system and connective tissue, genito-urinary system, disorders of blood and blood-forming organs, infectious and parasitic diseases, nervous system and sense organ disorders, endocrine, nutritional and metabolic diseases and immunity disorders, all other causes)[38]
- Number, proportion and crude hospitalisation rate per 100,000 by leading cause for children aged 1-9 by sex (respiratory system, injury and poisoning, digestive system diseases, infectious and parasitic diseases, endocrine, nutritional and metabolic diseases and immunity disorders, disorders of blood and blood-forming organs, congenital anomalies, nervous system and sense organ disorders, diseases of the skin and subcutaneous tissue, musculo-skeletal system and connective tissue, all other causes)[38]

- Percentage of in-patient bed days of children under 16 occurring in hospitals where accompanying by 'parent' day and night is offered, as a percentage of all bed days for this age group[48]
- Number of admissions to hospital 0-14 years per 1,000 population 0-14[52]
- Number of admissions to hospital 15-19 years per 1,000 population 15-19[52]
- Number of admissions to hospital outside area of residence of people aged 0-19 years per 1,000 population aged 0-19 years[52]

HOSPITALISATION, INJURY-RELATED
[INTENTIONAL AND UNINTENTIONAL]

Related domains:
Child health and development (health); disability; health; health (healthcare); health (injuries); health and safety (youth engaging in risky behaviour: youth accidents and injuries); healthy children; illness and injury; injuries and violence; injuries and violence (intentional injuries); injuries and violence (unintentional injuries); injuries to children; pregnant women and young children thrive; safety (safe environment); safety and physical status; safety and security; youth choose healthy behaviour.

Recommended measures:
- Hospitalisation rate for children aged 0-14 years for injuries from assault[2]
- Hospitalisation rate for children aged 0-14 years for accidental injuries (poisoning, burns and scalds, pedestrian accidents, pedal cycling)[2]
- Rate of hospitalisation due to trauma[5]
- Child road fatal and severe accident rates per 1,000[6]
- Hospitalisation for injury[7]
- Hospitalisation rates for self-harm[7]
- Percentage injury hospitalisation by cause of injury in children aged 0-19 (motor vehicle, violence by others, suffocation/choking, drowning, fire, violence by self, falls, natural environment, poisoning, other vehicle, sports, other, undetermined and late effects), by income quintile and region[8]
- Hospitalisation rates per 10,000 by age (<1, 1-4, 5-9, 10-14, 15-19), gender, location of injury sustained (farm, traffic, home, workplace, hospital and other), by region and cause[8]
- Injury-related hospital separation rates[9]
- Admission rate to hospital as a result of unintentional injury resulting in a hospital stay of longer than 3 days for children aged under 16[15]
- Hospitalisations resulting from injuries (falls, motor vehicle traffic crashes, other unintentional, assault, self-inflicted, other) to children from birth to 5 years of age, by category[19]
- Rate of teens seen in the emergency room with an intentional or unintentional injury[21]
- Percentage of children with accidental injuries requiring medical attention[21]
- Rate of injuries per 1,000 children that require in-patient hospitalisation in three broad injury categories: accidents (motor vehicle or other), attempted homicide or attempted suicide[24]
- Proportion of children aged 0-5 years who are hospitalised for treatment of injuries[28]
- Rate (per 1,000) of injuries among children aged 0-9 resulting in hospitalisations[31]
- Rate (per 1,000) of injuries among children aged 10-17 resulting in hospitalisations[31]
- Percentage of leading causes of hospitalisation due to injury in children aged under 1, 1-4 and 5-9[36]
- Leading causes of hospitalisation per 100,000 for unintentional injury by age group (under 1, 1-4, 5-9, 10-14, 15-19)[38]
- Hospitalisation per 100,000 for unintentional injury by age group (under 1, 1-4, 5-9, 10-14, 15-19) and sex[38]

- Hospitalisation per 100,000 for intentional injury by age group (under 1, 1-4, 5-9, 10-14, 15-19) and sex[38]
- Hospitalisation per 100,000 due to assault by age group (under 1, 1-4, 5-9, 10-14, 15-19)[38]
- Hospitalisations resulting from unintentional injuries (motor vehicle crashes, drowning, fires and falls) among children aged 0-19[39]
- Hospitalisations resulting from assault among children aged 0-19 (rate per 100,000)[39]
- Percentage of hospitalisation due to injury[43]
- Number of hospitalisations of children aged 0-14 for all types of injuries[47]
- Annual rate of overnight hospital in-patient admissions of children suffering burns, per 100,000 population, by male, female and in total, in age groups 0-4, 5-9, 10-14 and 15-17, and by socio-economic group when available[48]
- Annual rate of overnight hospital in-patient admissions of children suffering from poisoning, per 100,000 population, by male, female and in total, in age groups 0-4, 5-9, 10-14 and 15-17, and by socio-economic group when available[48]
- Annual incidence per 100,000 population of fracture of long-bones defined by specific ICD-10 code, by male, female and in total, in age groups 0-4, 5-9, 10-14 and 15-17, and by socio-economic group when available[48]
- Number of times children went to the emergency room because of injuries[51]

HOSPITALISATION, MENTAL HEALTH-RELATED

Related domains:
Child health and development (health); disability; health; health (healthcare); health (injuries); health and safety (youth engaging in risky behaviour: youth accidents and injuries); healthy children; illness and injury; Injuries and violence; injuries and violence (intentional injuries); injuries and violence (unintentional injuries); injuries to children; pregnant women and young children thrive; safety (safe environment); safety and physical status; safety and security; youth choose healthy behaviour.

Recommended measures:
- Psychiatric hospitalisation: percentage of children hospitalised for a psychiatric diagnosis[1]
- Mental health-related hospital separations[9]
- Number of incidences requiring hospitalisation for mental health issues (by male, female and in total, where appropriate, by age categories <1 years, 1-3 years, 4-6 years, 7-9 years, 10-12 years, 13-15 years and 16-18 years and in total, where appropriate, and by geographic location and in total, where appropriate)[13]
- Hospitalisation for selected mental disorders (organic psychotic conditions, other psychoses and neurotic disorders, personality disorders and other non-psychotic mental disorders), by age group (age 10-14, 15-19) and sex[38]

HOUSING, CROWDED CONDITIONS

Related domains:
Deprivation (other); economic security (housing and other); environment; social determinants of health (development)

Recommended measures:
- Household crowding index (number of persons per room) by housing type (owned and rental housing) and region[8]
- Separate-sex bedrooms for older children (10+)[12]
- Percentage of children living in crowded conditions (<1 room per person)[21]
- Proportion of children under 18 years and young people aged 18-24 living in crowded households. A crowded household is defined as a household that requires one or more additional bedrooms, as defined by the Canadian National Occupancy Standard[29]

HOUSING, HOMELESSNESS

Related domains:
Children in strong, stable families; economic security (stable, affordable housing); family environment (housing and food security); homelessness; social determinants of child health; stable and economically independent families.

Recommended measures:
- Number of homeless children[1]
- Rate of children aged 0-15 accompanying a parent or guardian seeking assistance from Supported Accommodation Assistance Program[2]
- Rate per 100,000 Maryland residents of homeless adults and children served by all shelter programmes in Maryland[24]
- Number of persons presented as homeless who had child dependents with them[27]
- Percentage of youth aged 0-17 living in homeless or emergency shelters in a one-month period[45]
- Percentage of households staying in an emergency shelter that were families with children[47]

HOUSING, HOUSING COSTS AND AFFORDABLE HOUSING

Related domains:
Economic security (consumption); economic security (housing and other); economic security (stable, affordable housing); family environment (housing and food security).

Recommended measures:
- Percentage of households containing children under age 18 and paying over 30% of their income on housing[20]
- Percentage of children in families where housing costs exceed 50% of family income[21]
- Percentage living in affordable housing (paying less than 30% of gross income for housing costs including rent or mortgage, taxes and utilities)[31]
- Number of occupied housing units owner-occupied[34]
- Percentage of people who pay more than 30% of income on housing[45]
- Number of families with children paying more than 30% of their income on rent[47]

HOUSING, HOUSING NEED

Related domains:
Access to housing; community and school environment strengths (community economic and geographic stability); economic security (government support programmes); economic security (stable, affordable housing); material well-being.

Recommended measures:
- Families in need of housing[12]
- Number of children enrolled on the Supported Accommodation Assistance Program (SAAP) database, by male, female and in total, where appropriate, by age categories <1 year, 1-3 years, 4-6 years, 7-9 years, 10-12 years, 13-15 years and 16-18 years and in total, where appropriate, and by geographic location and in total, where appropriate[13]
- Percentage of children in families in subsidised or public housing[21]
- Housing vacancy rate[42]
- Number of families with children on the active waiting list for subsidised housing[47]

HOUSING, HOUSING PROBLEM INDEX

Related domains:
Children in strong, stable families; economic security; economic security (consumption).

Recommended measures:
- Percentage of children in households reporting housing that is physically inadequate, too costly or overcrowded[1]

- Percentage of households with children under age 18 that report housing problems (cost burden, inadequate housing, crowded housing)[18]
- Percentage of households with children under age 18 in the USA having selected housing problems. Housing problems include physical problems, excessive cost burden and overcrowding. 'Crowded' is defined as having more than one person per room. Physical problems include plumbing, heating, electricity, upkeep and/or condition of apartment hallways. Cost burden is the ratio of housing costs to reported housing income[20]

HOUSING, PHYSICAL PROBLEMS

Related domains:

Economic security (consumption); economic security (housing and other); economic security (poverty and income); family environment (housing and food security); family well-being; home (demographics and family composition); living conditions.

Recommended measures:

- Proportion of dependent children (aged 0-15 or 16-18 in full-time education) who live in a home that does not meet the set standard of decency. The definition of a decent home is one that meets all of the following criteria: a) it is above the current statutory minimum standard for housing; b) it is in a reasonable state of repair; c) it has reasonably modern facilities and services; and d) it provides a reasonable degree of thermal comfort[15]
- Percentage of households with access to sanitary excreta disposal[17]
- Percentage of households with children under age 18 in the USA living in housing with moderate to severe physical problems[20]
- Percentage of children's households containing selected durables[21]
- Percentage of children living in inadequate housing (severe or moderate physical problems)[21]
- Percentage of children living in houses without complete plumbing or kitchen facilities[21]
- Percentage of families who have inadequate housing during the time a service case is open[30]
- Percentage of respondents who reported housing problems, by income (e.g. lacking complete plumbing for exclusive use, and multiple upkeep problems such as water leakage, open cracks or holes, broken plaster or signs of rats)[45]
- Number of households, by housing status and condition, and presence of children under 18[50]

IMMUNISATION

Related domains:

Child health; child health and development (health); childhood morbidity and mortality; children are ready for school; communicable disease; health; health (children stay healthy); health (health care); health (quality of care); health and safety (youth health: youth access to services); health conditions and health care (health care); health services utilisation; health system quality; healthy children; immunisation; participation.

Recommended measures:

- Percentage of children through age 2 who have completed immunisations for measles, mumps, rubella, polio, diphtheria, tetanus, pertussis, Haemophilus influenza, Hepatitis B1
- Immunisation rate[1]
- Proportion of children who are fully vaccinated at 1, 2 and 6 years of age[2]
- Percentage of 2-year-olds who have been immunised. This is derived from the National Immunisation Survey, which provides State estimates of vaccination coverage levels among children aged 19 months to 35 months. The figures given reflect the percentage of children who have 4:3:1 coverage[4]
- MMR uptake[6]
- Percentage of children with complete immunisation schedules at ages 1, 2 and 7 years, by region[8]
- Percentage 1st milestone when children are 6 months old (includes: 3 doses of DTPa/DTPw, OPV (Sabin vaccine) and Hib vaccine (HbOC or 2 doses of PRP-OMP); and

percentage 3rd milestone when children are 18 months old (includes: all 1st milestone vaccinations, in addition to MMR (mumps, measles, rubella) and Hib at 12 months and DTPa/DTPw and Hib at 18 months)[9]

- Percentage of children aged 19-35 months receiving the combined series vaccination (4:3:1:3). This includes 4 or more doses of diphtheria and tetanus toxoids and the pertussis vaccine, 3 or more doses of an oral polio vaccine, 1 or more doses of a measles-containing vaccine, and 3 doses of Haemophilus influenza type b vaccine[10]
- Percentage of children aged 12-15 months assessed as fully immunised by jurisdiction (by male, female and in total, where appropriate, by age categories <1 year, 1-3 years, 4-6 years, 7-9 years, 10-12 years, 13-15 years and 16-18 years and in total, where appropriate, and by geographic location and in total, where appropriate)[13]
- Percentage of mothers of children under one who received at least 2 doses of TT within 3 years of the child's birth[17]
- Percentage of children aged 12-23 months who received: a) triple polio; b) measles; c) Hb3; d) DPT3; and e) BCG vaccination according to card or history[17]
- Percentage of children aged 19-35 months with the 4:3:1:3 combined series of vaccinations[18]
- Percentage of children aged 19-35 months in the USA who have received routinely recommended vaccinations[20]
- Rate of full immunisation (ages infant, 2, 5, teens)[21]
- Number of children who have obtained the recommended immunisations by 2 years of age. Children who are completely immunised by 24 months of age (2 years) have completed the following immunisations: 4 doses of diphtheria, tetanus and pertussis (DPT); 3 doses of polio; and one dose of measles, mumps and rubella (MMR)[23]
- Percentage of children aged 19-35 months who have received the full schedule of appropriate immunisations against diphtheria, tetanus, pertussis, measles, mumps, rubella and polio. Haemophilus influenza type B (HIB), Hepatitis B and chicken pox vaccines are also part of the immunisation series, but coverage with these vaccines is measured separately by the National Immunisation Survey[24]
- Estimated vaccination coverage among children aged 19-35 months by type and doses of vaccine (>=4 DTP, >=3 polio, >= 1 MMR, >=3 Hib, >=3 Hep B, >=1 varicella)[25]
- Percentage of uptake of MMR (mumps, measles and rubella) vaccine[27]
- Percentage of uptake, at 24 months, of diphtheria and tetanus (D3, T3 - 3 doses) and Haemophilus influenza b (Hib) and oral polio vaccine[27]
- Immunisation coverage at aged 2 years[29]
- Percentage of kindergartners fully immunised[31]
- Percentage of children with appropriate immunisations at: a) age 2 and b) at school entry[33]
- Percentage of children immunised between ages 4-9 against diphtheria, pertussis, tetanus, measles, mumps, rubella and polio[36]
- Proportion of children in licensed day care centres immunised against Haemophilus influenza type b, by birth year and child age[38]
- Proportion of children in Grade 7 immunised against hepatitis by school year[38]
- Proportion of children fully immunised against DPT-Polio and MMR, by birth year and child age[38]
- Percentage of youth who receive age-appropriate immunisations[43]
- Percentage of young children, aged 19-35 months, who are age-appropriately immunised (i.e. have 4:3:1 coverage)[45]
- Percentage of children fully immunised by age 2[46]
- Immunisation coverage rate[47]
- Immunisation rates for childhood immunisation, expressed as children aged 24-35 months inclusive having completed primary courses of immunisation as a percentage of all children in that age group, separately for the following antigens: diphtheria, pertussis, tetanus, poliomyelitis, Haemophilus influenza type B, measles, mumps, rubella, hepatitis B, meningococcus C[48]

- Percentage of children under 2 years seen in public health clinics not fully immunised against such preventable diseases as polio, measles, diphtheria, tetanus, haemophilus influenza B and whooping cough[51]
- Number of 24-month-old children immunised against measles per 1,000 24-month-old children[52]
- Percentage of children under 2 immunised against: a) tuberculosis; b) polio; c) measles; and d) diphtheria, pertussis and tetanus[55]
- Percentage of infants that received 3 doses of diphtheria, pertussis (whooping cough) and tetanus vaccine[56]
- Expanded Programme on Immunisation: the immunisations in this programme include those against TB, DPT, polio and measles, as well as protecting babies against neo-natal tetanus by vaccination of pregnant women. Other vaccines (e.g. against hepatitis B or yellow fever) may be included in the programme in some countries[56]
- Percentage of vaccines routinely administered in a country to protect children that are financed by the national government (including loans)[56]
- Percentage of infants that received 3 doses of hepatitis B vaccine[56]

INDICES

Related domains:
Adolescent risk behaviours; children in strong, stable families; family and household; family environment (household structure); health; health (health conditions); health and safety (youth engaging in risky behaviour); health conditions and health care (health conditions); neighbourhood; social development, behavioural health and teen fertility (social development); youth health (access to services).

Recommended measures:
- Stable new family index: percentage of stable new families with the first birth to a mother who has completed high school and who is age 20 or older; and with the father's name recorded on the child's birth certificate[1]
- Family risk index: percentage of children living in 'high risk' families. The family risk index is a composite of four risk factors: 1) child lives in a family with income below the poverty line; b) child lives in a single parent family; c) child lives in a family where no parent has full-time, year-round employment; and d) child lives with a household head who is a high school drop-out[3]
- 'At risk' births index: percentage of live babies deemed 'at risk' (low birth weight <2,500g; high birth weight >4,000g)[8]
- Healthy births index: percentage of all births in the USA defined as healthy (gestational age 37 weeks+, birth weight 2,500 grams+, APGAR score 7 or above, pre-natal care 1st trimester)[20]
- Low risk teen cumulative risk index: percentage of youth by their 12th through 18th birthdays in the USA with no risks on cumulative risk measure. The behaviours examined for this cumulative index are suspension or expulsion from school, engaging in sexual intercourse, use of illegal drugs, unsupervised consumption of alcohol and regular smoking of cigarettes. A status of 'no risk' indicates that a youth reported involvement in none of the five tracked behaviours[20]
- Low risk teen cumulative risk index: percentage of youth by their 12th through 18th birthdays in the USA who have engaged in selected risk behaviours. The behaviours examined for this cumulative index are suspension or expulsion from school, engaging in sexual intercourse, use of illegal drugs, unsupervised consumption of alcohol and regular smoking of cigarettes. A status of 'no risk' indicates that a youth reported involvement in none of the five tracked behaviours[20]
- Child health index: percentage of children born with 0, 1, 2, 3+ of the following risk factors: late or no pre-natal care; low maternal weight gain (<21 lbs); having 3 or more siblings; mother smoked while pregnant; mother drank alcohol while pregnant; birth <18 months from previous birth[21]

- Severely distressed neighbourhood index: percentage of children living in severely distressed neighbourhoods defined as census tracts 1+ standard deviation beyond the mean level in 4 or 5 characteristics: poverty, female-headed families, high school drop-outs, males unattached to the labour force and families receiving public assistance[21]
- Child health index: percentage of births rated positively on all four of the following indicators: APGAR score 9+; birth weight of 2,500+ grams; gestational age of 37+ weeks; mother received pre-natal care in 1st trimester of pregnancy[21]
- New family index: percentage of first births to women with <12 years schooling, unmarried and under age 20[21]
- New families at risk index: percentage of first births that are to unmarried women younger than 20, with less than 12 years of education[31]
- New family stability index: percentage of all births that occur to high school graduates, first birth mothers over age 19 and that have a father recorded on the child's birth certificate, 1996-2000[45]
- New family index: percentage of stable new families (the percentage of all births that occur to high school graduates, first birth mothers over age 20 and that have a father recorded on the child's birth certificate)[46]
- Healthy start index: percentage of infants born to mothers who did not drink alcohol or smoke during pregnancy; born weighing 2,500 grams or more, and born to mothers who received pre-natal care in the 1st trimester[46]
- Risk behaviour: percentage of high school students who would 'not likely' or 'very unlikely' tell an adult if a) they heard a student threaten to harm another; b) saw a student with a handgun at school; c) saw a student with a knife at school; d) saw a student with drugs at school[51]
- Risk behaviour: percentage of high school students who participated in the following risk behaviours in the past 12 months: a) carried a handgun or knife for self-defence; b) carried a handgun or knife as a weapon; c) been in a fight with someone; d) hit boyfriend or girlfriend; e) been hit by boyfriend or girlfriend; f) received detention or in-school suspension; g) been suspended from school; h) stolen anything more than $5; i) had an accident while driving; j) been arrested and booked; k) felt hopeless or sad for two weeks; l) seriously considered attempting suicide[51]

INFANT MORTALITY, FOETAL DEATHS

Related domains:
Health (mortality); neo-natal health.

Recommended measures:
- Foetal mortality rate (per 1,000 live births and foetal deaths)[21]
- Number of foetal deaths per 1,000 births[52]
- Number of intrauterine deaths (22-27 weeks of gestational age) per 1,000 births[52]
- Number of antenatal deaths (>27 weeks of gestational age) per 1,000 births[52]
- Number of foetal deaths during delivery per 1,000 births[52]
- Number of foetal deaths at or after 22 completed weeks of gestation in a given year per 1,000 live and stillbirths in the same year[58]

INFANT MORTALITY, NEO-NATAL DEATHS

Related domains:
Health; health (mortality); health conditions and health care (mortality); health status (infant); maternal and neo-natal conditions; neo-natal health.

Recommended measures:
- Number of infant deaths under one-year-old per 1,000 live births per year, further separated into neo-natal (<28 days) and post-neonatal (28 days to one year), and by income quintile[8]

- Causes of death in neo-nates (congenital anomalies, short gestation, respiratory system, complications of labour)[8]
- Percentage neo-natal deaths (<28 days)[9]
- Neo-natal mortality rates (deaths per 1,000 live births) in the USA[20]
- Neo-natal mortality rates (per 1,000 live births)[21]
- Preliminary neo-natal (younger than 28 days) mortality rates by race of mother[25]
- Neo-natal mortality rate: number of deaths under 28 days of age per 1,000 live births[52]
- Birth weight-specific neo-natal mortality rate: a) number of deaths under 28 days of age in infants <1,500g per 1,000 live births <1,500g; b) number of deaths under 28 days of age in infants weighing 1,500-2,499g per 1,000 live births in infants weighing 1,500-2,499g; c) number of deaths under 28 days of age in infants >= 2,500g per 1,000 live births >= 2,500g[52]
- Number of deaths in the neo-natal period (up to 28 completed days after birth) after live birth at or after 22 complete weeks of gestation in a given year, expressed per 1,000 live births in the same year. This rate is subdivided by timing of death into early neo-natal deaths (at 0-6 days after live birth) and late neo-natal deaths (at 7-27 days after live births)[58]

INFANT MORTALITY, PERI-NATAL DEATHS

Related domains:
Child health and development (health); infant health – the first year of life; maternal and neo-natal conditions; neo-natal health.

Recommended measures:

- Percentage stillborn (<20 weeks gestation/<400 grams who did not breathe after delivery or show any evidence of life such as a heart beat)[9]
- Peri-natal mortality, number per 1,000 total births[38]
- Causes of peri-natal death[58]

INFANT MORTALITY, POST-NEONATAL DEATHS

Related domains:
Health; health (mortality); health conditions and health care (mortality); health status (infant).

Recommended measures:

- Number of infant deaths under one-year-old per 1,000 live births per year, further separated into neo-natal (<28 days) and post-neonatal (28 days to one year), and by income quintile[8]
- Causes of death in post-neonates (congenital anomalies, respiratory system, nervous system, infectious/parasitic diseases)[8]
- Post neo-natal mortality rates (deaths per 1,000 live births) in the USA[20]
- Post neo-natal mortality rates (per 1,000 live births)[21]
- Preliminary post neo-natal mortality rates (between 28 days and 1 year) by race of mother[25]
- Rate per 1,000 total births of death from 28 weeks to 1st week of life[36]

INFANT MORTALITY, SUDDEN INFANT DEATH SYNDROME-RELATED DEATHS

Related domains:
Childhood morbidity and mortality; mortality; physical health.

Recommended measures:

- Sudden infant death syndrome (SIDS) rate[2]
- Infant mortality (<1 year) related to SIDS, rate per 1,000 live births[9]
- Number of deaths occurring from SIDS per 1,000 live births[27]
- Sudden infant death rate, when an infant less than one-year-old dies suddenly and the cause of death is unknown[28]
- Number of deaths under 1 year of age due to SIDS per 1,000 live births[52]

INFANT MORTALITY

Related domains:

Babies born healthy; basic indicators; child and maternal mortality; child health and development (health); childhood morbidity and mortality; children's health and well-being; deaths; demographics (death); development indicators; exit (deaths); health; health (violence); health and safety (youth engaging in risky behaviour: youth death); health conditions and health care (mortality); health status (infant); healthy children; infant health – the first year of life; infant, child and teen health indicators; mortality; neo-natal health; physical health; pregnant women and young children thrive.

Recommended measures:

- Infant mortality[1]
- Infant mortality rate[2]
- Number of deaths occurring to infants under 1 year of age per 1,000 live births[4]
- Infant mortality rates[6]
- Infant mortality[7]
- Rate of infant mortality in babies weighing 500g or more, or of 20 weeks or more gestational age[8]
- Infant mortality (<1 year): rate per 1,000 live births[9]
- Death rate (per 100,000) for infants (less than 1 year); for children (ages 1-14 years); and youth (ages 15-19 years)[10]
- Homicide rate (per 100,000) for infants under 1 year. Infant homicides are classified as deaths purposefully inflicted by other persons on children less than 1 year[10]
- Infant mortality rate per 1,000 live births[15]
- Infant mortality rates (per 1,000 live births [18]
- Infant mortality rate, per 1,000 live births[19]
- Infant mortality rates (deaths per 1,000 live births) in the USA[20]
- Infant mortality rates (per 1,000 live births)[22]
- Rate (per 1,000 live births) of all births, births in various racial/ethnic groups and births to mothers who do not survive beyond year one[24]
- US infant mortality rates by race of mother[25]
- Comparison of national mortality rates[25]
- Number of deaths occurring in the first year of life per 1,000 total births occurring over the same time period in the same population[27]
- Number of infants who die in the first year of life per 1,000 live births[28]
- Annual number of deaths of infants aged less than one year, per 1,000 live births in that year[29]
- Infant mortality (children under 1 year age)[31]
- Infant mortality[32]
- Number of infant deaths per 1,000 live births[33]
- Number of deaths per 1,000 infants[34]
- Number of children who have died between birth and their first birthday, expressed per 1,000 live births[35]
- Percentage of leading cause of death in children under the age of one[36]
- Selected causes of death in infants (peri-natal conditions, congenital anomalies, ill-defined conditions, injuries and poisonings, nervous system and sense organ disorders, respiratory diseases, infectious diseases, all others)[38]
- Infant mortality: number per 1,000 total births[38]
- Number of deaths to infants under one year of age[39]
- Number of deaths of infants under one year of age per 1,000 infants under one year of age[41]
- Total infant mortality rate (IMR) between birth and exactly one year of age expressed per 1,000 live births, by male, female and in total, and by socio-economic group when available[48]
- Infant mortality rate per 1,000 live births[51]
- Number of deaths under 1 year of age per 1,000 live births[52]

- Number of deaths under 1 year of age due to accidents per 1,000 live births[52]
- Infant mortality (per 1,000 live births)[53]
- Infant mortality rate (per 1,000 live births)[55]
- Probability of dying between birth and exactly one year of age, expressed per 1,000 live births[56]
- Number of deaths (day 0-364) after live birth at or after 22 completed weeks gestation in a given year, expressed per 1,000 live births in the same year[58]

INFECTIOUS DISEASE

[*SEE ALSO* HIV/AIDS; IMMUNISATION; SEXUALLY TRANSMITTED DISEASES]

Related domains:

Child health and development (health); child health status and well-being (child morbidity); childhood morbidity and mortality; communicable disease; health (health conditions); health (illness); health (quality of care); health (vaccine preventable communicable diseases; health status (children: vaccine preventable diseases); health; health (communicable diseases); immunisation; physical health.

Recommended measures:

- Distribution of hospitalisation due to immunisable-preventable infections by age (0-4, 5-9, 10-14, 15-19) and cause (pertussis, tuberculosis and other)[8]
- New cases of vaccine preventable diseases: Hepatitis B, mumps, measles, rubella and pertussis[9]
- Number of cases of meningococcal Group C disease (vaccine preventable disease) in children aged 0-5 years[19]
- Number of cases of measles (vaccine preventable disease) in children aged 0-5 years[19]
- Number of cases of Haemophilus influenza-B (vaccine preventable disease) in children aged 0-4 years[19]
- Rates of communicable diseases[21]
- Incidence of vaccine-preventable diseases during infancy[21]
- Incidence of measles in children under age 18[21]
- Number of cases of reportable vaccine-preventable diseases among children under 5 (diphtheria, tetanus, rubella, measles, hepatitis B, mumps, haemophilus influenzae-B, hepatitis A, pertussis)[25]
- Bacterial meningitis: the crude rate of invasive meningococcal disease (IMD) among children aged 0-18[27]
- Tuberculosis: the crude incidence of TB among children aged 0-18[27]
- Meningococcal disease is the rate of new cases reported by year in children 5 years of age and younger[28]
- Measles is the rate of new cases reported by year in children 5 years of age and younger[28]
- Haemophilus influenza B disease in children is the rate of new cases reported by year in children 4 years of age or younger[28]
- Number of newly reported cases of tuberculosis (age 0-19)[33]
- Number of reported cases (age 0-18): measles, mumps, rubella, diphtheria, pertussis, tetanus and polio[33]
- Rates of most common childhood disease reported in children aged 0-9[36]
- Incidence of: a) salmonellosis; b) rubella; c) pertussis; d) mumps; e) meningococcal meningitis; f) measles; g) influenza; h) Haemophilus influenza type B; i) hepatitis B; j) giardiasis; and k) campylopacteriosis, in children aged 0-19 years[38]
- Annual incidence per 100,000 population of: a) measles; b) bacterial meningitis; and c) tuberculosis, in age groups 0-4, 5-9, 10-14, 15-17, by socio-economic group[48]
- Total number of reported cases of selected youth-related diseases (polio, measles, tuberculosis, gonorrhoea, syphilis and AIDS) for all age groups[50]
- New cases of: a) tuberculosis; b) tetanus; c) rubella; d) pertussis; e) measles; f) hepatitis; and g) diphtheria, per 100,000 population[55]

LITERACY, GENERAL

Related domains:
Basic indicators; development indicators; education; education and personal development; family; women.

Recommended measures:
- Child literacy[12]
- Proportion of the population aged 15-24 that is literate. A person is said to be literate when he/she can both read and write with understanding of a short and simple statement on his/her everyday life[35]
- Female adult literacy rate (15-24) as a percentage of the male adult literacy rate in a given age group[35]
- Percentage of persons aged 15 or over who can read and write[56]
- Male literacy rate[57]
- Female literacy rate[57]

LITERACY ACTIVITIES, LIBRARY REGISTRATION

Related domains:
Access to developmental opportunities (recreation and skill development opportunities); children succeeding in school; education and achievement (related behaviours and characteristics: family-child engagement in literacy activities); education and childcare (behavioural characteristic).

Recommended measures:
- Number of children who have public library cards[1]
- Percentage of 3- through 5-year-olds (not yet in kindergarten) in the USA who have participated in literacy activities with a family member, a) read to everyday, b) told a story at least three times a week, c) visited a library at least once in the past month[20]
- Percentage of pre- kindergarten children ages 3-5 who were taken to the library 1+ times in the last month[21]
- Number of children aged 0-12 currently registered with the Toronto Public Library[47]

LITERACY ACTIVITIES, LIMITED ENGLISH PROFICIENCY

Related domains:
Children ready for school and vice versa; education and achievement (related behaviours and characteristics); education and childcare (childcare); education and childcare (school characteristics); population; population and family characteristics.

Recommended measures:
- Percentage of children with difficulty speaking English[1]
- Percentage of children ages 5-17 who have difficulty speaking English[3]
- Percentage of children ages 5 to 17 who speak a language other than English at home and who have difficulty speaking English[18]
- Percentage of children ages 5 through 17 in the USA who speak a language other than English at home and who are reported to have difficulty speaking English. Parents were asked if their child spoke a language other than English at home and how well the child could speak English. Categories used for reporting were 'very well', 'well', 'not well' and 'not at all'. All children who were reported to speak below the level of 'very well' were considered to have difficulty speaking English[20]
- Where English is not the primary language, the proportion of children who are instructed in their native language[21]
- Proportion of children from non-English speaking homes who have access to providers that speak the home language[21]

- Percentage of children who are linguistically isolated, defined as living in a household where no-one age 14 or older speaks English exclusively or very well[21]
- Percentage of public school students with limited English proficiency[34]

LITERACY ACTIVITIES, READING HABITS OF CHILDREN

Related domains:
Education and achievement (related behaviours and characteristics); education and childcare (behavioural characteristics).

Recommended measures:
- Percentage of students aged 9, 13 and 17 in the USA who read for fun on a daily basis[20]
- Percentage of children reading 10+ pages per day (4th, 8th, 12th Grades)[21]

LITERACY ACTIVITIES, READING TO CHILDREN

Related domains:
Daily interactions; early learning and school readiness; education; education and achievement (related behaviours and characteristics: family-child engagement in literacy activities); education and childcare (behavioural characteristic); education and skills (behaviour affecting learning); family and community (parental educational attainment); family-related indicators; parent-child interaction; risk and enabling factors; social and emotional development (social community relationships: positive parent-child relationships: closeness to mother and father: parental involvement in activities with youth).

Recommended measures:
- Proportion of children aged <1 year and 4 years of age who are read to by an adult on a regular basis[2]
- Level of involvement by resident father (reading)[7]
- Percentage of children aged 3-5 who were read aloud to every day in the past week by a family member[10]
- Percentage of children aged 3 to 5 who were read to every day in the last week by a family member[18]
- Frequency that young Canadian children are read to: a few times a week or less, daily, many times a day[19]
- Percentage of 3- through 5-year-olds (not yet in kindergarten) in the USA who have participated in literacy activities with a family member, a) read to everyday, b) told a story at least three times a week, c) visited a library at least once in the past month[20]
- Percentage of pre-kindergarten children ages 3-5 who are told stories 3+ times per week by a parent or household member[21]
- Percentage of children ages 3-5 who are read to (every day, frequently) by a parent or household member[21]
- Distribution of children aged 2-5 by how often an adult reads to the child or listens to the child read[28]
- Reading to children – asked adults with children under 19 at home: 'have you or anyone in your family read to your child in the past week?' Of those who say they did, how often did they do that (once or twice a week, three or more times per week, every day)?[45]
- Times per week 3-5 year olds are read to by race/ethnic group of parent and poverty status[49]
- Percentage distribution of number of times per week family members read to children under 12 years old: a) not read to at all; b) read to 1-6 times per week; and c) read to 7 or more times per week[54]

MATERNAL AGE

Related domains:
Natality; parenting and cultural resources; population characteristics; population characteristics or risk factors; risk and enabling factors.

Recommended measures:
- Age of parent when child born[7]
- Percentage distribution of births by race and maternal age (less than 15, 15-17, 18-19, 20-29, 30-39, 40-54)[25]
- Average age at mother's first birth (years)[55]
- Distribution of age in years at delivery for women delivering a live or stillbirth. Recommended presentation as follows: 10-14, 15-19, 20-24, 25-29, 30-34, 35-39, 40-44, 45+[58]

MATERNAL LEAVE

Related domains:
Children in strong, stable families; economic security (employment).

Recommended measures:
- Length of maternal leave taken[1, 21]

MATERNAL MORBIDITY

Related domains:
Maternal health

Recommended measures:
- Number of women experiencing any combination of the following conditions or procedures as a proportion of all women delivering live or stillborn babies: 1) eclamptic seizures; 2) surgery (other than tubal ligation or caesarean section) or embolisation; 3) blood transfusion; and 4) ICU >24 hours[58]
- Number of women who had an episiotomy or a first-, second-, third- or fourth-degree tear of the perineum expressed as a proportion of all women who had a vaginal delivery. Tears (definitions from ICD-10 and Perinatal Health Indicators for Canada, 2000, p. 35): a) 1st degree tear (ICD O70.0) involves the fourchette, perineal skin and vaginal membrane; b) 2nd degree tear (ICD O70.1) includes the skin and mucous membrane, and the fascia and muscles of the perineal body; c) 3rd degree tear (ICD O70.2) extends through skin, mucous membrane and perineal body and involves the muscle of the anal sphincter; and d) 4th degree tear (ICD O70.3) extends through the rectal mucosa to expose the lumen of the rectum[58]
- Prevalence of faecal incontinence[58]

MATERNAL MORTALITY

Related domains:
Child and maternal mortality; development indicators; health status (infant); maternal health; women.

Recommended measures:
- Maternal mortality rates by race of mother (per 100,000 live births)[25]
- Annual number of maternal deaths, per 100,000 live births. A maternal death is the death of a woman while pregnant or within 42 days of termination of pregnancy, irrespective of the duration and site of pregnancy, from any cause related to, or aggravated by, the pregnancy or its management, but not from accidental or incidental causes (as cited in ICD-10)[35]
- Maternal mortality rate (per 100,000 live births). Annual number of deaths of women due to pregnancy or childbirth-related causes[55]
- Annual number of deaths of women from pregnancy-related causes per 100,000 live births. This 'reported' column shows country reported figures that are not adjusted for underreporting and misclassification[56]
- Lifetime risk of maternal death takes into account both the probability of becoming pregnant and the probability of dying as a result of that pregnancy accumulated across a woman's reproductive years[56]

- Number of maternal deaths (the death of a woman while pregnant or within one year of the termination of pregnancy, irrespective of the duration and site of the pregnancy, from any cause related to, or aggravated by, the pregnancy or its management, but not from accidental or incidental causes), per 100,000 live and stillbirths[58]
- Number of maternal deaths (during pregnancy or within one year following the end of pregnancy) per 100,000 live births subdivided into the following causes: a) thromboembolism; b) hypertension; c) haemorrhage; d) amniotic fluid embolism; e) sepsis; f) early pregnancy deaths; g) anaesthesia; h) genital tract trauma and other direct causes; I) indirect causes (as defined in ICD-10, WHO); and j) coincidental (fortuitous) and late deaths (between 43-365 days following the end of pregnancy)[58]

MEDICATION

Related domains:
Health (health service utilisation)

Recommended measures:

- Top ten categories of prescription drugs in children (0-19): systematic anti-bacterials, anti-asthmatics, analgesics, topical steroids, anti-depressants/stimulants, oral contraceptives, ophthalmic preparations, anti-acne products, anxiolytics/anti-psychotics, NSAIDS (non-steroidal anti-inflammatory drugs)[8]
- Rate per 1,000 children with one or more prescriptions for psycho-stimulants and anti-depressants, by age (0-4, 5-9, 10-14, 15-19), region and income quintile[8]
- Rate per 1,000 children with one or more prescriptions for non-steroidal anti-inflammatory drugs, by age (0-4, 5-9, 10-14, 15-19), region and income quintile[8]
- Rate per 1,000 children with one or more prescriptions for narcotic analgesics, by age (0-4, 5-9, 10-14, 15-19), region and income quintile[8]
- Rate per 1,000 children with one or more prescriptions for iron supplements, by age (0-4, 5-9, 10-14, 15-19), region and income quintile[8]
- Rate per 1,000 children with one or more prescriptions for anti-psychotics and anxiolytics, by age (0-4, 5-9, 10-14, 15-19), region and income quintile[8]
- Rate per 1,000 children with one or more antibiotic prescriptions, by age (0-4, 5-9, 10-14, 15-19), number of prescriptions, region and income quintile[8]
- Rate of children per 1,000 with at least one prescription, by age (0-4, 5-9, 10-14, 15-19) and region[8]
- Medication: levels of medication, over-prescribing, prescribing medication not suited to children[48]

MENTAL HEALTH REFERRALS

Related domains:
Childhood morbidity and mortality; children succeeding in school; family and social functioning; health; health (mental and behavioural disorders); health and safety (youth health: youth access to services); healthy children; mental health.

Recommended measures:

- Percentage of children hospitalised for a psychiatric diagnosis[1]
- Number of children receiving mental health services[1]
- Referrals to mental health services[7]
- Mental health-related hospital separations[9]
- Number of referrals to mental health services among children[9]
- Number of incidences requiring hospitalisation for mental health issues (by male, female and in total, where appropriate, by age categories <1 year, 1-3 years, 4-6 years, 7-9 years, 10-12 years, 13-15 years and 16-18 years and in total, where appropriate, and by geographic location and in total, where appropriate)[13]

- Total number of referrals to child and adolescent psychiatry services among children aged 0-18[27]
- Hospitalisation for selected mental disorders (organic psychotic conditions, other psychoses and neurotic disorders, personality disorders and other non-psychotic mental disorders), by age group (10-14, 15-19) and sex[38]
- Number of youth receiving treatment for mental health problems[43]
- Percentage of 9-17-year-olds who meet diagnostic criteria for some form of mental disorder[51]

MOVING, HOUSE

Related domains:

Population; population, family and neighbourhood (neighbourhoods); residential stability; risk and enabling factors; transience.

Recommended measures:

- Risk of moving house/school in any given year[7]
- Percentage of children in the USA under age 18 who have moved within the last year[20]
- Percentage of children who have moved within the last year by type of move (intra-county, inter-county, inter-State)[21]

MOVING, SCHOOL

Related domains:

Academic achievement; children succeeding in school; children's academic experiences; neighbourhood stability; risk and enabling factors; social determinants of health (educational); transience.

Recommended measures:

- Number of school transfers, except in the case of migratory students[1]
- Risk of moving house/school in any given year[7]
- Percentage of enrolled students who transferred from a school in each of the areas to some other school[8]
- Children changing schools[11]
- Children who have ever changed schools by family poverty status and home ownership[49]
- Percentage of children aged 6-11 and 12-17 who have changed schools at some time during their educational career, as reported by parents[54]

NUTRITION

Related domains:

Condition manifested in childhood; deprivation (other); diet and nutrition; health; health (health-related behaviour); health (healthy lifestyles); health and safety (youth health: good health and health habits among youth); healthy children; nutrition, physical activity and obesity; safety and physical status.

Recommended measures:

- Percentage of people who eat 5 or more daily servings of vegetables and fruits[1]
- Percentage of children receiving adequate nutrition: food stamps, WIC[1]
- Eating habits and diet[5]
- Diet and nutrition: rank order of poor diets[6]
- Percentage having breakfast 5 or more days/week[9]
- Percentage who eat 4 or more servings of vegetables/day[9]
- Percentage who consume: a) whole milk; b) skim milk; and c) low/reduced fat milk[9]
- A nutritious breakfast with cereal, a hot dinner, a third meal, fruit or vegetables 4 times a day[12]
- Percentage of 9th to 12th Graders with a healthy diet[21]
- Trends in daily fruit and vegetable consumption among Grade 6 children by sex (the proportion of children who ate fruit and raw vegetables daily)[38]

- Percentage of youth who eat 5 or more servings of fruit and vegetables per day during the past 7 days[43]
- Nutrition and food consumption[48]
- Percentage of high school students who reported eating fruit, eating salad and eating vegetables weekly[51]
- Percentage of high school students who reported eating 5 or more servings of fruit or vegetable per day[51]
- Percentage of children aged 6-59 months who have received at least one high dose of vitamin A capsules in 2002[56]
- Malnourished children under 5[57]

OUT-OF-HOME PLACEMENTS

Related domains:

Care and protection; child and teen well-being indicators; child health and development (developmental); child protection; children in non-parental care; children in strong, stable families; children live in stable, supported families; daily interactions; demographics (family structure and living arrangements); educational development; family; family and household; health and safety (youth engaging in risky behaviour); other determinant factors of child health, risk and protective factors; participation, quality of life and social inclusion; permanency for children; population, family and neighbourhood (family structure); safety (free of violence, abuse, neglect); social determinants of child health; social well-being; stable and economically independent families.

Recommended measures:

- Rate of out-of-home placements[1]
- Out-of-home placement: what percentage of children are placed outside of their home into public custody because of abuse or neglect for the first time in a particular year[1]
- Rate of children aged 0-14 years in out-of-home care[2]
- Percentage of those looked after in foster placements[6]
- Children looked after per 1,000[6]
- Number and rate (per 1,000 children) of foster children aged 17 and under. Foster arrangements include non-relative foster homes, relative foster homes (also known as 'kinship care'), group homes, institutions and pre-adoptive homes[10]
- Children in out-of-home placements/rate per 1,000[11]
- Children out of home[12]
- Children in care[12]
- Number and rate (per 1,000) of children in the USA living in foster care[20]
- Percentage of children who went to live with someone other than their parents for 1+ months in previous year[21]
- Percentage of children living in institutions or group quarters[21]
- Non-custodial parent: legal custody arrangements, proximity, time spent with child[21]
- Percentage of children who ever lived in foster care[21]
- Percentage of children who are living in foster care[21]
- Percentage of children living in related and unrelated sub-families[21]
- Rate per 1,000 children placed in foster care, juvenile justice, mental health, substance abuse treatment and education, out-of-home placements[24]
- Percentage of children who leave out-of-home care for a more permanent living arrangement. Permanent care status as defined by (1) adoption/adoptive placement, (2) custody or guardianship (where relatives or others have custody or guardianship in place of the State). Permanent foster care is when the court has sanctioned by name a kin or non-kin foster parent. When a child returns home, legal responsibility usually is returned to parents 3-6 months after a child returns to the home[24]

- Number of children in care by category: foster care general, foster care special, foster care - relative, pre-adoptive foster care, residential general, residential special, at home under supervision, other, and in total[27]
- Percentage of children in care as a percentage of the total child population[27]
- Number of children in care, by age category, <1 year, 1-5 years, 6-12 years, 13-18 years and in total[27]
- Number of children in care by length of stay, <1 year, 1-5 years, >5 years[27]
- Number of admissions to care[27]
- Number of children in care by family type, married/cohabiting couple, lone parent/other[27]
- Percentage of children who are adopted within 12 months of filing an adoption petition[30]
- Percentage of children not placed with kin who remain in their home school during placement[30]
- Percentage of children for whom adoption petitions are filed within 12 months of pre-adoptive placements[30]
- Number of transfers of legal and physical custody of a child to a relative[30]
- Median length of time from the date of parental rights' termination to placing a child in a permanent living arrangement[30]
- Median length of time between termination of parental rights and placement of a child in a pre-adoptive home[30]
- Percentage of children whose parents' rights have been terminated and who have not declined adoption, 'aged out' of the system, and are not adopted[30]
- Percentage of children whose parents' rights have been terminated and who are adopted within 12 months of termination of parents' rights[30]
- Percentage of children residing in a permanent living arrangement within 12 months of initial out-of-home placement[30]
- Percentage of children in placement more than 12 months during the last 60 months[30]
- Number of petitions filed to terminate parental rights and the percentage of those petitions granted[30]
- Number of children in out-of-home placement in a given year[30]
- Median number of placements per out-of-home placement episode[30]
- Median number of out-of-home placement episodes per child during the past 24 months[30]
- Rate (per 1,000) of out-of-home placements in children aged 0-17. This includes persons not living with biological or adoptive parents and not living independently[31]
- Average number of moves within the child substitute care system. For cases closed within the year, not counting the initial removal from and return to home or planned short-term visits[31]
- Children in foster care[32]
- Percentage of children in 1,000 placed out of home (per 1,000)[34]
- Number of children in care[36]
- Number of children <16 years using the YWCA Peterborough Crossroads Shelter Programme[36]
- Number of children, ages 0-17, in foster care[39]
- Duplicated average daily rate of children, ages 0-17, in State-supervised, family-based foster care, regardless of parental rights' termination or length of care per 1,000 children per year[41]
- Foster care of youth, the percentage of youth attaining permanency[43]
- Number of children, ages 0-17, in State custody/care on January 1 each year[45]
- Number of children entering care, re-entering care and discharged from care[47]
- Percentage of children who are under the care or formal supervision of statutory Social Welfare or Social Services Agencies, by male, female and in total, and in age groups 0-4, 5-9, 10-14, 15-17[48]
- Percentage of children who do not live with their natural parents[51]
- Percentage of children in foster care under a plan for: placement in adoptive homes, return to a parent or guardian, placement with a relative, independent living, permanent foster care, other[51]

- Number of children under 18 in foster care (0-2, 3-5, 6-10, 11-13, 14 and above)[51]
- Median age at first placement in foster care[51]
- Number of children aged 0-14 years admitted full-time to special care institutions per 1,000 children aged 0-14 years[52]
- Children remaining in State custody (per 1,000 children younger than age 20)[53]
- Children committed to State custody (per 1,000 children younger than age 20)[53]
- Percentage of children under age 18 who have never lived apart from their designated parent for more than one month[54]
- Rate of children in the care of foster parents or guardians (per 100,000 population, aged 0-17)[55]
- Rate of children in residential care (per 100,000 population, aged 0-17)[55]
- Rate of children in infant homes (per 100,000 population, aged 0-3)[55]
- Gross adoption rate (per 100,000 population, aged 0-3)[55]
- Children in the care of foster parents or guardians (thousands)[55]
- Children in residential care (thousands)[55]
- Children in infant homes (thousands)[55]

PARA-SUICIDE

Related domains:
Exit (deaths); health (emotional and behavioural disorders); health (mental health); health (mortality); health and safety (youth mental health); health conditions and health care (health conditions); mental health; mental health of children.

Recommended measures:

- Hospitalisation rates for self-harm[7]
- Percentage of students in Grades 9-12 who in the past 12 months: a) thought seriously about attempting suicide; b) attempted suicide; and c) whose suicide attempts required medical attention[10]
- Percentage of teens in the USA in Grades 9 through 12 who report having attempted suicide in the previous 12 months[20]
- Percentage of 9th-12th Graders who have attempted suicide in the past 12 months[21]
- Self-reported suicidal thoughts and behaviour (thought seriously about attempting suicide, attempted suicide, made a suicide plan, suicide attempt required medical attention), by sex[22]
- Self-inflicted injuries (ages 1-19). Data collected as part of the indicator: injuries (unintentional, assaults and self-inflicted injuries)[24]
- Hospitalisation for attempted suicide, by age (10-14, 15-19) and sex[38]
- Suicide attempts. 'Have you ever tried to kill yourself?' and 'In the past 12 months, did you make a plan about how you would attempt suicide?'[42]
- Percentage of students in Grades 9-12 reporting each of the following in the last year: seriously considered suicide, made a suicide plan, attempted suicide, were treated for a suicide attempt[45]
- Annual incidence of attempted suicide, defined by in-patient hospital stays with a discharge diagnosis of attempted suicide, per 100,000 population, by male, female and in total, in age groups 10-14, 15-17, and by socio-economic group when available[48]
- Percentage of high school students who reported to have attempted suicide in the past year and whose suicide attempt required medical attention[51]

PARENTAL EDUCATION

Related domains:
Children in strong, stable families; demographic and socio-economic determinants of child health; family; family and community (family); family environment (household structure); family-related indicators; income, assets and work (parental educational attainment); parenting and cultural resources; population characteristics or risk factors; risk and enabling factors.

Recommended measures:

- Educational level of parents or mother[1]
- Percentage of children living with a household head who is a high school drop-out[3]
- Parental level of education[7]
- Parent's own family background as a child (family type, unemployment, social class)[7]
- Highest level of educational attainment among parents of children aged 6-18 (less than high school, high school diploma or equivalent, some college including vocational/ technical, bachelor's degree or higher)[10]
- Highest level of education attained by parents of young children (less than secondary, secondary school graduation, beyond high school, college or university degree (including trade), by mother, father and in total[19]
- Adult literacy rates for parents of newborn children. The number of years completed in school by parents of newborn is being used to measure adult literacy: none, 1-3 years, 4-6 years, 7-9 years, 10-11 years, 12 years, 13-15 years, 16 years and over, unknown[23]
- Highest level of education attained by the mother of children aged 0-5 years[28]
- Highest level of education attained by the father of children aged 0-5 years[28]
- Percentage of babies born to mothers with less than a high school education (per 100 live births)[34]
- Rate of live births to mothers who have not completed high school per 1,000 women[41]
- Percentage of children whose current 'mother' has attained elementary/lower secondary/ upper secondary/tertiary education, as a percentage of all children, in the age group 0-4, 5-9, 10-14, 15-17[48]
- Number of babies born to mothers who had not completed the 12th Grade[51]
- Distribution of education level of women delivering live or stillborn babies, expressed as highest completed level of education, or number of completed years of education[58]

PARENTAL EMPLOYMENT

Related domains:

Child well-being relating to the family; childcare; children in strong, stable families; demographic characteristics; economic security; economic security (employment); economic security (parental employment); family; family and community context; home (family income); income, assets and work (employment); material well-being; population characteristics; risk and enabling factors; social inclusion.

Recommended measures:

- Secure parental employment: one parent working full-time, at least 35 hours per week, 50-52 weeks a year[1]
- Proportion of children aged 0-14 years living in families where no parent is employed[2]
- Percentage of children living in families where no parent has full-time, year-round employment[3]
- Share of children under age 18 living in families where no parent has regular, full time employment. For children living in single-parent families, this means the resident parent did not work at least 35 hours per week, at least 50 weeks in the previous calendar year. For children living in married-couple families, this means neither parent worked at least 35 hours per week, at least 50 weeks in the previous calendar year. Children living with neither parent also were listed as not having secure parental employment[4]
- No working adults in household[7]
- Percentage of children under 18 living with at least one parent employed full-time all year[10]
- Unemployment among families[12]
- Availability of flexi-time, job-sharing and part-time work options[14]
- Percentage of children aged under 16 in a working-age household where no adults work. A working-age household is a household that includes at least one person of working age (a woman aged between 16 and 59 or a man aged between 16 and 64). Workless individuals are those who are either International Labour Organisation unemployed or economically inactive (that is not in employment)[15]

- Percentage of children under age 18 living with at least one parent employed full-time all year[18]
- Percentage of mothers in the USA with children under age 18 who were employed, full-time and part-time[20]
- Percentage of children under age 18 in the USA with no resident parent in the labour force[20]
- Percentage of children under age 18 in the USA with both or only resident parent in the labour force[20]
- Number of job changes in the previous year[21]
- Percentage of mothers who are in the labour force; unemployed; employed[21]
- Percentage of fathers who are in the labour force; unemployed; employed[21]
- Percentage of children with no parents in the labour force[21]
- Occupational complexity of parents' jobs[21]
- Level of maternal job satisfaction[21]
- Percentage of children with 1+ parents working long hours (50+ hours per week)[21]
- Percentage of children where no parent is fully employed (full time, full year)[21]
- Percentage of children less than age (1, 3, 6, 18) whose mothers are in the labour force[21]
- Percentage of children less than age (1, 3, 6, 18) where both parents or only parent are working[21]
- Parental unemployment rate by season for and length of unemployment[21]
- Average hours worked per week by parents (both mother and father)[21]
- Mothers with pre-school children (less than 6 years old) and mothers with children ages 6-17 in the workforce[25]
- Households with children (aged 0-14) with no working adult (percentage)[26]
- Percentage of dependent children under 18 in two-parent and one-parent families by parental employment status[29]
- Percentage of all children with all available parents in the labour force and percentage of school-age children with all available parents in the labour force[34]
- Percentage of households with no-one at work[37]
- Unemployment rates of parents with children at home (children under age 6 and children age 6 and older)[38]
- Employment status of parents with own children under 18 years old, by type of family (married couple families, female-headed families, male headed-families)[50]
- Employment status of married, separated and divorced women with children under 18 years old, by age of children[50]
- Number of mothers with children under 6 and with children 6-17 in the labour force[51]
- Number of children under 6 in families where the single parent or both parents work[51]

PARENTAL INVOLVEMENT IN SCHOOLING

Related domains:
Child well-being within education; children ready for school and vice versa; education and achievement (related behaviours and characteristics); education and childcare (behavioural characteristic); education outcome; families, youth and individuals are engaged in their community's decisions and activities; family and community (family); family and community (school and community); social and emotional development (social community relationships: positive parent-child relationships: closeness to mother and father).

Recommended measures:

- Percentage of classrooms with parent involvement components[1]
- Degree of school/home contact[7]
- Percentage of students whose parents reported involvement in their child's school. Involvement is defined as parent participation during the school year in any of the following activities at least once: a) attending a general school meeting: b) attending scheduled meetings with their child's teacher; c) attending a school event; or d) volunteering in the school or serving on a school committee[10]

- Parental involvement in school[14]
- Percentage of children in the USA whose parents are involved in their schools, by level of involvement. Low involvement = involvement in 0 or 1 activity. Moderate involvement = involvement in 2 activities. High involvement = involvement in 3 or more activities. Possible activities include: 1) attending general school meetings, 2) going to a regularly scheduled parent-teacher conference, 3) attending a school or class event, and 4) volunteering at the school or serving on a school committee[20]
- Parental involvement in school and school-related activities[21]
- Percentage of youths in Grades 8 and 12 who report parental involvement in schooling - youth who report that their parents are actively involved in helping them succeed in school[31]
- Parental involvement in schooling (Grades 6, 8 and 11): 'Someone in my home helps me with my school work and at least one of my parents/guardians goes to school activities that I am involved in'[42]
- Percentage of parents with children in public schools who attended 1-5, 6-10, 11-20 or 20+ meetings/events at their children's school; also asked adults with children under 19 at home how much they agreed/disagreed with the following: 'I am pleased with how much our local school reached out to involve me in my child(ren)'s education'[45]

PARENTAL MENTAL HEALTH

Related domains:

Family and community (family); family-related indicators (parental health); health (mental health); maternal health; parental mental health; parenting and cultural resources; risk and enabling factors.

Recommended measures:

- Proportion of parents with a mental health problem[2]
- Depression/work orientation of mother[7]
- Percentage of parents reporting two or more depressive symptoms during the past 30 days. Depressive symptoms include the following: felt sad, hopeless, worthless, restless, or that everything was an effort all of the time or most of the time[10]
- Proportion of children aged 0-5 years whose primary care-giver exhibits high symptoms of depression[28]
- Indicator of post-partum depression[58]

PARTICIPATION IN DECISION-MAKING

Related domains:

Child well-being within education; civic life skills; families, youth, and individuals are engaged in their community's decisions and activities; participation, quality of life and social inclusion; social and emotional development (social community relationships: civic engagement); social and emotional development (social community relationships: leadership).

Recommended measures:

- Degree of child participation in decision-making about their lives[5]
- Adult/government reaction to children's participation[5]
- Percentage of children who are attending schools with student governments[5]
- Ability to influence decisions[12]
- Pupil participation in the running of the school[14]
- Percentage of youth in Grades 8 and 12 who report that they are given useful roles in their school[31]
- Percentage of youth in Grades 8 and 12 who report that they help decide what goes on in their school – the percentage of youth agreeing with the statement, 'students help decide what goes on in my school'[31]
- Opportunities to develop class rules, the percentage of students in Grades 6, 8, 10 and 12 who answered 'yes' to the statement 'in my school, students have lots of chances to help decide things like class activities and rules'[41]

PARTICIPATION IN OUT-OF-SCHOOL AND/OR COMMUNITY-BASED ACTIVITIES

Related domains:
Civic life skills; families, youth, and individuals are engaged in their community's decisions and activities; participation in extra-curricular activities; participation, pro-social behaviour, quality of life and social inclusion; risk and enabling factors; school (out-of-school experiences); school-age enrichment activities; social and emotional development (social community relationships: civic engagement); youth choose healthy behaviour.

Recommended measures:

- Percentage of children who belong and are active in a civic organisation (political, community service, religious or in general)[5]
- Perceived importance of contributing to the community and society[5]
- Membership of church, PTA, trade union, social clubs[7]
- Involvement in non-school activities (club, etc)[12]
- Percentage of high school seniors who see friends, read, do sports, work around the house, play music, do art or write on a daily basis[21]
- Percentage of community and consumer representation in regional partnerships[31]
- Percentage of youth in Grades 8 and 12 who report that they are given useful roles in their community[31]
- Percentage of youth in Grades 8 and 12 participating in youth programmes – students who report spending 1+ hours per week in an average week in clubs or organisations outside of school (not including sports)[31]
- Youth involvement (Grades 6, 8, 10 and 12) in activities outside of school[40]
- Percentage of students in Grades 6, 8, 10 and 12 who answered 'yes' when asked, 'which of the following activities for people your age are available in your community?' Service clubs, scouting groups, 4-H clubs, boys and girls clubs, and community sports programmes'[41]
- Youth programmes (Grades 6, 8 and 11)[42]
- Number of youth participating in 4-H[43]
- Number of active members in Girls Scouts of America[43]
- Asked youth aged 13-19 how much they agree/disagree with the following: 'I'm given lots of chances to help make my town or city a better place in which to live'. Data collected as part of the indicator: youth opportunity for community involvement (I'm given lots of chances to help make my town or city a better place in which to live; In my family I feel useful and important; and Students help to decide what goes on in my school)[45]
- Children aged 6-17 participating in activities, by parents' assessment of the neighbourhood[49]
- Children aged 6-17 participating in activities, by family poverty status[49]
- Percentage of seniors who say they engage in various activities (driving around at least once per week, 5 or more hours of television on a school night, use of a personal computer at least once a week, do things with friends at least once a week, do things with parent at least once a week, read more than one hour per week not related to school work)[50]
- Percentage of children aged 6-17 participating in: a) sports; b) clubs; and c) lessons, as reported by parents[54]

PARTICIPATION IN SCHOOL ACTIVITIES

Related domains:
Family and community (school and community); school (description); school (out-of-school experiences); school-age enrichment activities; social and emotional development (pro-social activities and attitude); social and emotional development (social community relationships: civic engagement).

Recommended measures:

- Percentage of students in Grades 8, 10 and 12 who reported to participate in school music or other performing arts programmes[10]

- Percentage of students in Grades 6, 8, 10 and 12 who answered 'yes' to the question 'there are lots of chances for students in my school to get involved in sports, clubs and other school activities outside of class?'[41]
- Children aged 6-17 participating in activities, by parents' assessment of the neighbourhood[49]
- Children aged 6-17 participating in activities, by family poverty status[49]
- Percent of high school seniors who reported being in various high school programmes (general, college preparatory/academic, vocational)[50]
- Percentage of high school seniors who participate in selected school-sponsored extra-curricular activities (academic clubs, honorary societies, student government, newspaper or yearbook)[50]

PHYSICAL ACTIVITY AND SPORT

Related domains:
Child lifestyle determinants of child health, risk and protective factors; condition manifested in childhood; family and community (school and community); health; health (children stay healthy); health (health-related behaviour); health and safety (youth health: good health and health habits among youth); health status (adolescents); healthy children; nutrition, physical activity and obesity; pro-social behaviour; safety and physical status; school (out-of-school experiences); social and emotional development (pro-social activities and attitude); social connectedness; social determinants of health (development); social development, behavioural health and teen fertility (physical health and safety).

Recommended measures:

- Percentage of children with physical fitness in curriculum[1]
- Level and incidence of physical activity[5]
- Percentage of 11-16-year-olds exercising at least 4 hours per week outside school[6]
- Regular exercise[7]
- Percentage of children who participate in sports activities by income quintile[8]
- Percentage engaging in games/sports at least 20 minutes 4+ days/week[9]
- Percentage of students in Grades 9-12 who participated in vigorous physical activity in the past week. Activities that caused sweating and hard breathing for at least 20 minutes on at least 3 of the past 7 days[10]
- Percentage of students in Grades 8, 10 and 12 who participate in school athletics[10]
- Percentage of children by age (11, 13, 15) and gender who report exercising twice a week or more[16]
- Percentage of students in Grades 9 through 12 in the USA who report having exercised vigorously 3 or more times in the past 7 days. Vigorous exercise is defined as activities that cause sweating and hard breathing for at least 20 minutes[20]
- Percentage of 8th, 10th and 12th Grade students in the USA who report that they actively participate in sports or exercise 'almost every day'[20]
- Rate of participation in organised sports among teens[21]
- Percentage of high school students who participate in vigorous (activities that caused sweating and hard breathing for at least 20 minutes on >=3 of the 7 days preceding the survey), moderate (activities that did not cause sweating and hard breathing for at least 30 minutes on >=5 of the 7 days preceding the survey) or strengthening physical activity (such as push-ups, sit-ups or weight-lifting on >=3 of the 7 days preceding the survey), by race[25]
- Percentage of high school students who reported to play on one or more sports team[25]
- Percentage of high school students enrolled in a physical education class[25]
- Proportion of children and young people aged 5-17 years and 18-24 years who participated in sport and active leisure, as measured by the Sport and Physical Activity Surveys. For the 5-17 age group, the reference period for participation was the previous 2 weeks; for the 18-24 age group, it was the previous 12 months[29]
- Percentage (Grades 9-12) who exercised at least 20 minutes a day, at least 3 days in the past week[33]

- Trends in Grades 6, 8 and 10 children who exercise 2 or more times per week outside school hours, by sex[38]
- Percentage of children aged 12-19 who reported they participated in regular exercise. Regular exercise referred to physical activity lasting more than 15 minutes, at least 12 times in the past 12 months[38]
- Percentage of children aged 12-19 considered inactive using the Physical Activity Index (PAI)[38]
- Percentage of youth who participate in strengthening exercises[43]
- Percentage of youth who attend physical education classes daily[43]
- Percentage of high school youth (Grades 9-12) involved in vigorous physical activity (at least 20 minutes of exercise that made them sweat and breathe hard on 3 or more of the last 7 days) or moderate physical exercise (at least 30 minutes of exercise that did not cause sweating or hard breathing on at least 5 of the last 7 days)[45]
- Average number of hours children aged 1-4 spend in: a) physically active play; and b) sedentary activities per week[47]
- Percentage of children aged 5-12 who are on average physically active enough (i.e. an average daily expenditure of at least 8 kilocalories/kilogram of body weight/day)[47]
- Percentage of children reporting that they undertake vigorous activity outside of school hours for at least 2 hours a week, by male, female and in total, at ages 11, 13 and 15, and by socio-economic group when available[48]
- Percentage of population 7-years-old and over participating in sports activities (basketball, bicycle riding, exercising with equipment, running or jogging, swimming, camping) in the past year[50]
- Percentage of high school seniors who participate in sports, athletics or exercise every day or almost every day, by sex[50]
- Percentage of high school students who reported to exercise 3 or more times per week for 20 minutes in sports that made them sweat or breathe hard[51]
- Percentage of high school students who reported doing stretching or muscle strengthening exercise weekly[51]
- Percentage of high school students who do not engage in vigorous or moderate activity at all during a week[51]

PHYSICAL FIGHTING

Related domains:
Conditions (juvenile delinquency); health (violence); health and safety (youth engaging in risky behaviour: youth use of violence and weapons); problem behaviour; social and emotional development (delinquency and crime); social development, behavioural health and teen fertility (physical health and safety).

Recommended measures:

- Percentage of students in Grades 9-12 who reported physical fighting at least once in the past year[10]
- Percentage of students in Grades 9 through 12 in the USA reporting that they have been in a physical fight within the past year[20]
- Percentage of teens who were in a fight in the last 30 days[21]
- High school students' report of physical fighting in Mississippi (fight on school property, require medical attention)[22]
- Percentage of students in Grades 9-12 who were in a physical fight on school property during the past 12 months[31]
- Percentage of students in Grades 6, 8, 10 and 12 who answered 'not wrong at all' to the question 'how wrong do your parents feel it would be for you to pick a fight with someone?'[41]
- How wrong would your parents/guardian feel it would be for you to start a physical fight with someone? (Grades 6, 8 and 11)[42]
- Attitudes of friends toward violent behaviour (Grades 6, 8 and 11)[42]

POVERTY AND INCOME, CHILDREN IN POVERTY

Related domains:

Children in strong, stable families; children live in stable, supported families; children's economic well-being; demographic and socio-economic determinants of child health; economic resources and contribution; economic security; economic security (income security); economic security (poverty and income); economic status; family environment (family socio-economic status); family environment (household structure); family-related indicators; family well-being; general economic well-being; home (family income); income, assets and work (employment); income, assets and work (poverty, wealth, income); material well-being; population characteristics; poverty; risk and enabling factors (transience); social determinants of child health; social determinants of health (development); social inclusion; stable and economically independent families.

Recommended measures:

- Percentage of households with employment and above poverty level[1]
- Percentage of children living at 50% of Federal Poverty Level, 100% FPL, 150% FPL[1]
- Percentage of children living in low-income working families[3]
- Percentage of children living in poverty[3]
- Share of children under age 18 who live in families with incomes below the US poverty threshold, as defined by the US Office of Management and Budget[4]
- Number and percentage of children under age 18 living in families where they were related to the head of the household and the family income was less than 150% of the Federal Poverty Level and at least one parent worked 50 or more weeks a year[4]
- Relative poverty rates before and after taxation and transfers[5]
- Child poverty rates (income <50% average before housing costs)[6]
- Child poverty rates (income <50% average after housing costs)[6]
- Risk of experiencing poverty/family break-up in any given year[7]
- Proportion of households with children, that have incomes below 50% of average (median) household income[7]
- Duration or repeated experience of poverty/unemployment/family type[7]
- Percentage of children (age 0-19) in families from low-income households (lowest income quintile), by region[8]
- Percentage of children under 18 living in poverty for: a) at least 6 years; and b) at least 9 years. Families are considered to be in poverty if their pre-tax money income (not including in-kind benefits such as food stamps and not including the earned income tax credit) is less than a money income threshold that varies by family size and composition[10]
- Percentage of children under 18 living below selected poverty thresholds. Families are considered to be in poverty if their pre-tax money income (not including in-kind benefits such as food stamps and not including the earned income tax credit) is less than a money income threshold that varies by family size and composition[10]
- Among poor children, the percentage in working poor families. Working poor families are defined as families whose income is below the official Federal Poverty Level and in which either two-parent family members work for a total of at least 35 hours per week or a single parent works at least 20 hours per week[10]
- Children in poverty[11]
- Child poverty (income and deprivation)[12]
- Percentage of children living in low-income households. Low-income households are 50%, 60% and 70% of median household income (before and after housing costs): a) relative low income - median income moving each year; b) absolute low-income – median income fixed at 1996/1997 levels in real terms; and c) persistent low-income – low incomes (before housing costs only) in 3 out of last 4 years (60% and 70% of median only)[15]
- Percentage of related children under age 18 in poverty[18]
- Percentage of related children under age 18 by family income relative to the poverty line[18]

- Percentage of families with young children living below the low-income cut-off, by two-parent families, lone parent families and in total[19]
- Percentage of children in the USA under age 18 living below the poverty level[20]
- Percentage of children in the USA under age 18 living below selected poverty thresholds: under 50% of poverty, under 100% of poverty, under 150% of poverty and under 200% of poverty[20]
- Rates of transitions into and out of poverty[21]
- Percentage of children in poverty[21]
- Percentage of children in extreme poverty (<50% of poverty line)[21]
- Percentage of children at or near poverty (<150% or <200% of poverty line)[21]
- Multi-year rates of poverty for children[21]
- Average monthly poverty rate for children[21]
- Percentage of people under 18 (SAIPE statistics) or related children under 18 (CPS statistic) whose families have incomes below the US poverty threshold, as defined by the US Office of Management and Budget. 'Related children' include the householder's children by birth, marriage or adoption under age 18, as well as other persons under 18, such as nieces or nephews, who are related to the family head[24]
- Related children under 18 years of age living in families below 100% of poverty level by race/ethnicity and household status (male head of household, female head of household, married head of household)[25]
- Children (aged 0-15) in poor households (percentage). The poverty line is 50% of the national median of equivalised income[26]
- SARHU deprivation index[27]
- HASE index[27]
- Proportion of the population aged 0-14 in each socio-economic group (SEG)[27]
- Pre-tax low-income cut-off (LICO) rate is the proportion of children aged 0-5 years living below the pre-tax LICO[28]
- Post-tax low-income cut-off (LICO) rate is the proportion of children aged 0-5 years living below the post-tax LICO[28]
- Percentage of families with incomes under federal poverty guidelines during the time a service case is open[30]
- Percentage children in poverty: 1999[31]
- Children in poverty[32]
- Families earning less than LIS[32]
- Percentage of children living in low-income families[34]
- Percentage of children under age 5 living below 185% poverty[34]
- Percentage of children ages 5-17 living below 185% poverty[34]
- Percentage of the population whose income/consumption falls below the line ($1 per person per day)[35]
- Percentage of children living below half average income[37]
- Prevalence of low income by type of families (married or common-law couple with children less than 18 years, lone parent families with children less than 18 years, male lone parent families with children less than 18 years, female lone parent families with children less than 18 years) with children (families with children 0-9 years, families with children 10-17 years) [38]
- Child poverty, youth poverty and family poverty[39, 42, 45, 46]
- Percentage of female-headed families with children living in poverty[46]
- Proportion of children under the age of 15 living in families with incomes below LICO[47]
- Percentage of children living in households with a household income below the national 60% median, equivalised using the modified OECD equivalence scale in at least 2 of the previous 3 years, in age groups 0-4, 5-9, 10-14, 15-17[48]
- Percentage of children living in households in each of the six socio-economic categories of upper manual, lower non-manual skilled, manual, unskilled manual, self-employed and farmer, derived from the International Standards Classification of Occupations (ISCO)

classification, and determined by resident parental occupation (highest of father or mother, or single parent) as a percentage of all children, in age groups 0-4, 5-9, 10-14, 15-17[48]

- Number and percentage of related children under 18 living in poverty, by family status and race/ethnicity of family householder[50]
- Number of children and youth under the age of 18 living in families with income below poverty[51]
- Number of children and youth under the age of 18 living in families with income below selected poverty thresholds (under 50%, under 100%, under 125%, under 150%, under 175%, under 185%, under 200%)[51]

POVERTY AND INCOME, CHILDREN LIVING IN POOR NEIGHBOURHOODS

Related domains:
Neighbourhood; population, family and neighbourhood (neighbourhoods); quality of care.

Recommended measures:

- Low-income neighbourhoods, defined as those where the residents are among the lowest 20% of the population in terms of household income[8]
- Percentage of related children under age 18 in the USA below the poverty level by the poverty level of their neighbourhood[20]
- Percentage of children under age 18 below the poverty level in the USA who live in very poor (40%+ poverty) neighbourhoods[20]
- Percentage who live in high poverty neighbourhoods (40%+ poor)[21]
- Percentage of children living in high-poverty neighbourhoods[34]

POVERTY AND INCOME, FAMILY INCOME

Related domains:
Basic indicators; child well-being relating to the family; children in strong, stable families; development indicators; economic indicators; economic resources and contribution; economic security (housing/other); economic security (poverty and income); economic status; family and community context; family environment (family socio-economic status); general economic well-being; health; home (family income).

Recommended measures:

- Median annual income for families with related children under age 18 living in the household. Related children include the householder's children by birth, marriage or adoption, as well as other persons under age 18 (such as nieces or nephews) who are related to the householder and living in the household[4]
- Share of equalised income quintiles represented by each age group[5]
- Income status of family[14]
- Median income of families in the USA with related children under age 18[20]
- Median income of families with children[21]
- Annual average consumption of children's families, for each income quintile[21]
- Percentage of children in high-income households[21]
- Proportion of dependent children aged under 18 who were living in economic family units receiving an equivalent income, net of housing costs, below the low-income threshold. The measure takes account of income, housing costs and family size, and is adjusted for inflation and taxes. The low-income threshold used in this measure is 60% of the 1998 median equivalent disposable family income net of housing costs[29]
- Proportion of dependent children aged under 18 and young people aged 18-24 living in economic family units with a low standard of living. A family unit with a low standard of living is one with a 'somewhat restricted', 'restricted' or 'very restricted' standard of living as measured by the Economic Living Standards Index (ELSI)[29]

- Average annual wage. Includes private-sector jobs covered by unemployment compensation[31]
- Median family income[31, 32, 44]
- Family income for necessities[32]
- Median family income for families with children under age 18 by family type (married couple families, single mother families, single father families)[34]
- Poverty Gap Ratio is the combined measurement of incidence of poverty and depth of poverty. Depth of poverty is the difference between the poverty line and the average income of the population living under the poverty line, expressed as a fraction of the poverty line. By multiplying the incidence of poverty by the depth of poverty, we get a measure of the magnitude of poverty[35]
- Inequality is defined as the income/expenditure of the poorest 20% of the population divided by total income/expenditure of the whole population[35]
- Distribution of report census family income (under $10,000, $10,000-$39,999, $40,000-$79,999, $80,000 and over)[38]
- Median family income, by race/ethnicity of head of household[50]
- Median income of full-time, year-round workers, by sex and age[50]
- Presence of related children under 18 years by money income of families (less than $15,000, $15,000-$24,999, $25,000-$34,999, $35,000-$49,999, $50,000-$74,999, $75,000 and over)[50]
- Mean income of families with children[51]
- Percentage of income received by the 20% of households with the highest income and by the 40% of households with the lowest income[56]
- Percentage of population living on less than $1.08 a day at 1993 international prices (equivalent to $1 a day in 1985 prices, adjusted for purchasing power parity). As a result of revisions in purchasing power parity exchange rates, poverty rates for individual countries cannot be compared with poverty rates reported in previous editions[56]

POVERTY AND INCOME, MEASURES OF DEPRIVATION

Related domains:
Demographic characteristics, deprivation (other).

Recommended measures:

- Percentage of children living in households without a vehicle[3]
- Percentage of children living in households without a telephone[3]
- Warm winter clothes and adequate wet weather clothing[12]
- Some toys and books appropriate to his/her stage of development[12]
- Shoes that fit[12]
- School trips[12]
- School-related items (books, clothing, footwear, lunches, outings)[12]
- Special needs equipment e.g. for a child with a disability[12]
- Regular pocket money[12]
- Participation in after-school classes (drama, swimming, music)[12]
- New toys on birthdays, Christmas or other special occasions[12]
- Involvement in organised sports or a club (scouts, etc)[12]
- Having friends home to play[12]
- Having a regular home (not B&B/hostel), which is warm and dry with indoor toilet and a bath or shower[12]
- An occasional family outing to the zoo, cinema or similar special event[12]
- A quiet place to do homework[12]
- A birthday party with friends and relations[12]
- Percentage of children under 18 living in households with access to a motor vehicle[29]

PRE-NATAL CARE

Related domains:

Children's health well-being; communities which support family life; demographics (birth and related outcomes); health; health (health care); health and safety (youth health: youth access to services); healthcare services; health conditions and health care (health care); health services utilisation; healthy children; infant, child and teen health indicators; maternal and neo-natal conditions; pregnancy and early childhood services; pregnant women and young children thrive.

Recommended measures:

- Adequate pre-natal care[1]
- Percentage of women who reported not receiving pre-natal care[8]
- Percentage with no care at week 8 and percentage with no care at week 12[9]
- Percentage of births to women receiving late pre-natal care (in 3rd trimester) or no pre-natal care[10]
- Percentage of women in the USA receiving pre-natal care in the 1st trimester[20]
- Percentage of women in the USA receiving late or no pre-natal care[20]
- Percentage of live births to mothers receiving pre-natal care in 1st trimester[21]
- Percentage of live births to mothers receiving late or no pre-natal care[21]
- Measures of adequacy of pre-natal care (Kessner and Kotelchuck indexes)[21]
- Number of pregnant women who received pre-natal care during the 1st trimester of pregnancy. Early pre-natal care is defined as at least one pre-natal care visit during the 1st trimester (3 months) of pregnancy. Adequate pre-natal care is usually defined as starting care in the first 3 months of pregnancy and at least 9 visits for women giving birth to full-term infants after 40 weeks[23]
- Number of pregnant women who began pre-natal care after the 1st trimester of pregnancy or receive no pre-natal care during pregnancy. Late pre-natal care is defined as pre-natal care that begins after the 1st trimester (3 months) of pregnancy. No pre-natal care is defined as no visitations to a hospital, clinic or any other pregnancy-related agency prior to the delivery of the child[23]
- Percentage of live births for which pre-natal care was initiated in the 1st trimester[24]
- Percentage of mothers receiving late (in the 3rd trimester) or no pre-natal care, by age (<18, 18-19, 20-24, 25-29, 30-34, 35-39, 40+) and race[25]
- Percentage of mothers beginning pre-natal care in the 1st trimester, by age (<18, 18-19, 20-24, 25-29, 30-34, 35-39, 40+) and race[25]
- Percentage of pregnant women availing of early pre-natal care (1st trimester)[31]
- Births to mothers who had inadequate pre-natal care[32]
- Percentage of children born to mothers without early pre-natal care (per 100 births)[34]
- Births to women receiving early (1st trimester) pre-natal care[39]
- Rate of women receiving pre-natal care in the first 3 months of pregnancy per 1,000 pregnancies[41]
- Percentage of women receiving pre-natal care during the 1st trimester[45]
- Number of pregnant women receiving no pre-natal care in the first three months of pregnancy[51]
- Number of pregnant women receiving no pre-natal care at all[51]
- Adequate pre-natal care (per cent)[53]
- Distribution of timing of first ante-natal visit by trimester of pregnancy for all women delivering live or stillborn babies. Trimesters are defined as: a) 1st trimester = <15 weeks; b) 2nd trimester = 15–27 weeks; and c) 3rd trimester = 28 weeks or more[58]

PUBLIC EXPENDITURE

Related domains:

Conditions (education); economic indicators; economic resources and contribution; education; education and childcare (school characteristics); educational well-being; health.

Recommended measures:

- Percentage of public expenditures by age group[5]
- Average expenditures per student[21]
- Per pupil expenditures in Mississippi[22]
- Public school per pupil expenditure[32]
- Education expenditure per pupil[34]
- Instructional expenditures per pupil[34]
- Public expenditure on health as a percentage of GDP[55]
- Public expenditure on education as a percentage of GDP[55]
- General government expenditure (per cent of GDP)[55]

RELATIONSHIPS WITH OTHER ADULTS IN THE COMMUNITY

Related domains:

Child well-being relating to the family; communities provide safety and support for families and individuals; personal life skills; social and emotional development (emotional and personal development: positive relationship with an (other) adult); social and emotional development (social community relationships: positive relationship with an (other) adult); social support networks.

Recommended measures:

- Proportion of households with children under 15 years of age where respondent was able to get support in time of crisis from persons living outside the household[2]
- Support from family, friends and others[5]
- Presence of role model for child of single parent family[14]
- Percentage of youths in Grades 8 and 12 who report that they are valued by their community – 'in my community I feel like I matter to people'[31]
- Percentage of youths in Grades 8 and 12 who report positive relationships with adults – youth who report they receive support from 3+ non-parent adults[31]
- Adults in my community care about people my age (Grades 6, 8 and 11). Data collected as part of the indicator: youth perception of neighbourhood safety: my neighbourhood is a safe place to live; in my neighbourhood there are lots of fights, crime, or illegal drugs; adults in my community care about people my age; and adults in my community let me know they are proud of me when I do something well)[42]
- Caring neighbourhood[42]
- Community values youth (Grades 6, 8 and 11)[42]
- Percentage of youths in Grades 8, 10 and 12 who report neighbours are involved positively in their lives[43]
- Youth (ages 13-19) who feel cared for in their community – asked youth ages 13-19 how much they agree/disagree with the following: 'adults in my town or city care about people my age'[45]
- Perceptions of youth as community assets – asked adults with children under 19 at home how much they agree/ disagree with the following: 'young people in my community are more of an asset to the community rather than a burden'[45]
- Youth (ages 13-19) with caring neighbours – asked youth ages 13-19 how much they agree/disagree with the following: 'in my neighbourhood or town, there are a lot of people who care about me'[45]
- Youth (ages 13-19) feeling important – asked youth ages 13-19 how much they agree/ disagree with the following: 'adults in my town or city make me feel important', 'adults in my town or city listen to what I have to say' and 'in my town or city, I feel like I matter to people'[45]
- Youth (ages 13-19) with positive adults in their lives – asked youth ages 13-19 'tell me how many adults (excluding parents or relatives) who you have known for at least 2 years a) give you encouragement whenever you see them; b) you look forward to spending time with; c) spend a lot of time helping other people; and d) talk with you at least once a month'[45]

RELATIONSHIPS WITH PARENTS, PARENTAL ATTACHMENT AND EMOTIONAL SUPPORT

Related domains:

Care and support; children live in stable, supported families; family and community (family); family-related indicators; mental health; personal life skills; parental determinants of child health, risk and enabling factors; risk and protective factors (parental support for children); pro-social behaviour; social and emotional development (early development); social and emotional development (social community relationships: positive parent-child relationships); social development, behavioural health and teen fertility (social development).

Recommended measures:

- Child/young person assessment of quality of parent/child relationship[7]
- Levels of family conflict[7]
- Support from family, friends and others[5]
- Percentage of parents with children under 13 who reported to provide various forms of warmth and affection every day during the past month – a) hugged or showed physical affection to their children; b) told their child that they loved him/her; and c) told their child that they appreciated something he/she did[10]
- Percentage of youth ages 12 through 17 in the USA who report feeling very close to their parents[20]
- Percentage of 0-3 year-olds with trusting relationship with primary care-giver[21]
- Proportion of children aged 0-5 years in families with high levels of dysfunction[28]
- Proportion of secondary school students aged 12-18 years who reported that their mum and/or dad (or someone who acts as mum and/or dad) care a lot about them, that they feel close to mum and/or dad most of the time and that they are able to spend enough time with mum and/or dad[29]
- Percentage of youths in Grades 8 and 12 who report their families provide high levels of love and support[31]
- Percentage of youths in Grades 8 and 12 who report that they are given useful roles in their family[31]
- Percentage of students in Grades 6, 8, 10 and 12 who answered 'yes' to the question 'do you feel very close to your mother?'[41]
- Percentage of students in Grades 6, 8, 10 and 12 who answered 'yes' to the question 'do you feel very close to your father?'[41]
- I feel very close to at least one of my parents/guardians (Grades 6, 8, and 11)[42]
- I have a happy home; I can talk about the things that bother me or I don't understand with someone in my house; I can get help and support when I need it from someone in my home; a parent/guardian knows where I am and who I am with, especially in the evening and on weekends; and people in my home shout at each other (Grades 6, 8 and 11)[42]
- Youth (ages 13-19) feeling supported in their family – asked youth ages 13-19 how much they agree/disagree with the following: 'my parents give me help and support when I need it', 'my parents often tell me they love me', 'in my family I feel useful and important', 'in my family there are clear rules on what I can and cannot do'[45]
- Percentage of children who report that they find it easy or very easy to talk with their parents when something is really bothering them, expressed as a percentage of all children, by male, female and in total, at ages 11, 13 and 15, and by socio-economic group when available[48]

RELATIONSHIPS WITH PARENTS, PARENTAL ENCOURAGEMENT

Related domains:

Daily interactions; social and emotional development (social community relationships: positive parent-child relationships).

Recommended measures:

- A parent/guardian checks to make sure I have done the things that I am supposed to do (school homework, household chores, get home on time, etc); when I am doing a good job, someone in my home lets me know about it; and a parent/guardian generally finds out if I have done something wrong and then punishes me (Grades 8, 10 and 12)[42]
- Percentage of youths in Grades 8, 10 and 12 who report that their parents notice them when they are doing a good job and let them know about it[43]
- Percentage of parents who reported to praise their children ages 0-6 and 6-17 three or more times per day[54]

RELATIONSHIPS WITH PARENTS, PARENTAL FEELINGS TOWARDS THEIR CHILD

Related domains:
Educational expectations; family-related indicators; parents' feelings towards their children.

Recommended measures:

- Proportion of children aged 0-5 years whose parents did not exhibit low positive interaction with the child[28]
- Percentage of parents who reported they a) often or very often; b) sometimes; and c) never, felt angry with their children[54]
- Percentage of parents who reported that they a) often or very often; b) sometimes; and c) never, felt that their child was much harder to care for than most children[54]
- Percentage of parents who reported that their children's needs a) often or very often; b) sometimes; and c) never, took more of their life than expected[54]
- Percentage of parents who reported that their child a) often or very often; b) sometimes; and c) never, does things that bother them[54]
- Percentage of parents who wanted the following education level for their children: a) less than college graduate; b) college graduate; and c) more education and training after college, and the percentage of parents who think their children will achieve the following education level: a) less than college graduate; b) college graduate; and c) more education and training after college[54]

RELATIONSHIPS WITH PARENTS, PARENTAL INVOLVEMENT IN ACTIVITIES WITH YOUTH

(*SEE ALSO* LITERACY, READING TO CHILDREN AND PARENTAL TIME)

Related domains:
Daily interactions; education and childcare (behavioural characteristic); social and emotional development (social community relationship: positive parent-child relationships); social development, behavioural health and teen fertility (social development).

Recommended measures:

- Percentage of parents in the USA who engage in selected activities with their children ages 5 through 17[20]
- Percentage of pre-kindergarten children who engaged in songs, music or art with parent or other household member in last month[21]
- Learning opportunities: percentage of pre-kindergarten children ages 3-5 whose parents regularly engage them in the following activities: play, concert, art gallery, museum, zoo, errands, household chores, discussion of family history or ethnic heritage, events sponsored by community or religious groups[21]
- Family learning and cultural activities – asked adults with children under 19 at home: 'in the past month, has anyone in your family done the following with your child(ren): visited a library; gone to a play/concert/other live show; visited a zoo/aquarium; talked about family history/ethnic heritage; attended an event sponsored by a community/ religious group?'[45]
- Percentage of children under 12-years-old having one or more outing, and average number of outings in the last month[54]

RELATIONSHIPS WITH PARENTS, PARENTAL RULES

Related domains:

Children live in stable, supported families; daily interactions; parent-child interaction; social and emotional development (social community relationships: positive parent-child relationships: communication between parents and children).

Recommended measures:

- Percentage of youth in Grades 8 and 12 whose parents set clear rules and consequences – the percentage of youth who report their families have clear rules and consequences and that parents monitor their whereabouts[31]
- In my home there are clear rules about what I can and cannot do; and I often get disciplined for not doing the same thing at another time (Grades 6, 8 and 11)[42]
- Percentage of youth in Grades 8, 10 and 12 who report that family rules are clear[43]
- TV rules by age group of child and race/ethnic group of parents[49]
- Percentage of children aged 3-5, 6-11 and 12-17 living in households with at least one type of family TV rule: type of programme watched, time of day, number of hours[54]

RELATIONSHIPS WITH PARENTS, PARENTAL STYLE

Related domains:

Risk and enabling factors (parenting and cultural resources)

Recommended measures:

- Parenting style (ignoring/open/authoritarian)[7]
- Self-assessed coping level of main care-giving parent[7]
- Percentage of parents of young children displaying positive parenting styles[14]
- Percentage of adult care-givers who have the capacity to raise their children without outside assistance during the time a service case is open[30]
- Number of parents/care-givers/families accessing parent support programmes[36]
- Percentage of children under 1 year of age whose parents have access to a programme of education, psychological and social support in parenting during the first year of life[48]

RELATIONSHIPS WITH PARENTS, PARENTAL TIME

Related domains:

Child well being relating to the family; daily interactions; economic security (employment); education and childcare (childcare); social and emotional development (social community relationships: positive parent-child relationships).

Recommended measures:

- Length of active time spent between child and parent[14]
- Time spent with children from birth to 5 years of age, minutes per day, by an employed, married parent[19]
- Average hours per week of parental time available to children[21]
- Amount of time parent spends with child on a typical day[21]
- Family time for leisure and recreation – asked adults with children under 19 at home how much they agree/disagree with the following: 'I believe that our family has adequate time for leisure and recreation'[45]
- Percentage of children under age 6 and 6 to 17 who have mealtimes (breakfast, dinner) each day with their father/step-father (if male parent is present in household)[54]
- Percentage of children under age 6 and 6 to 17 who have mealtimes (breakfast, dinner) each day with their designated parent[54]

RELATIONSHIPS WITH PEERS

Related domains:

Child well-being within community; participation, quality of life and social inclusion; personal life skills; social and emotional development (emotional and personal development: sense of personal identity and mattering).

Recommended measures:

- Support from family, friends and others[5]
- Friends in local neighbourhood[12]
- Level of contact with peers[14]
- Percentage of students (Grades 6, 8 and 11) who report 'I am good at making friends'. Data collected as part of the indicator: social competencies (I think things through carefully before I make a decision; I can say 'no' when someone wants me to do things I know are wrong or dangerous; I am accepting of those different than me (racially, culturally, socio-economically); it is wrong to discriminate against someone because of his/her race, appearance, culture, religion, etc; and I am good at making friends)[42]

RELATIONSHIPS WITH TEACHERS

Related domains:

Social and emotional development (emotional and personal development: positive relationship with an (other) adult).

Recommended measures:

- Teachers care (Grades 9-12). Data collected as part of the indicator: youth perception of schools (teachers care, safety, students are respectful)[40]
- Positive interaction with teachers, percentage of students in Grades 6, 8, 10 and 12 who answered 'yes' to the statement 'my teacher notices when I am doing a good job and lets me know about it'[41]
- Teachers care about me (Graces 6, 8 and 11). Data collected as part of the indicator: school climate (my teachers care about me; students in my school treat each other with respect; and I feel safe at school)[42]
- Percentage of youths in Grades 8, 10 and 12 who report that their school lets parents know when students have done something well[43]
- Percentage of youths in Grades 8, 10 and 12 who report teachers affirm good work[43]
- Percentage of youths in Grades 8, 10 and 12 who report that there are many opportunities for students to talk with a teacher one-on-one[43]

RELIGIOSITY

Related domains:

Citizenship and values; family and community (school and community); pro-social behaviour; social and emotional development (pro-social activities and attitude); social development, behavioural health and teen fertility (social development).

Recommended measures:

- Percentage of students in Grades 8, 10 and 12 who reported that religion plays a very important role in their lives[10]
- Percentage of 8th, 10th and 12th Grade students in the USA reporting that religion plays a very important role in their lives[20]
- Percentage of high school seniors for whom religion plays an important role in their lives[21]
- Religious involvement of high school seniors: importance of religion in my life (very important, pretty important, a little, not important)[50]

RELIGIOUS SERVICE ATTENDANCE

Related domains:
Citizenship and values; family and community (school and community); pro-social behaviour; social and emotional development (emotional and personal development); social and emotional development (pro-social activities and attitude); social development, behavioural health and teen fertility (social development).

Recommended measures:
- Percentage of students in Grades 8, 10 and 12 who reported to attend religious service at least once a week[10]
- Percentage of 8th, 10th and 12th Grade students in the USA reporting weekly religious attendance[20]
- Frequency of church attendances among high school seniors[21]
- Religious community – Grades 6, 8 and 11 – on the average during the school year, how many hours per week do you spend at church or synagogue worship services, programmes or activities?[42]
- Religious involvement of high school seniors: attending religious services (weekly, 1 to 2 times per month, rarely, never)[50]

RESPECT:

Related domains:
Civic life skills; neighbourhood; social and emotional development (emotional and personal development: character); social and emotional development (social community relationships: cultural sensitivity).

Recommended measures:
- Degree of support for tolerance and expression of minority views and other forms of civil rights[5]
- Percentage of high school seniors who would not want to live in an area where most of the neighbours were of other races[21]
- Students (Grades 9-12) are respectful. Data collected as part of the indicator: youth perception of schools (students are respectful, safety and teachers care)[40]
- Percentage of students (Grades 6, 8 and 11) who report that 'students in my school treat each other with respect'. Data collected as part of the indicator: school climate (my teachers care about me; students in my school treat each other with respect; and I feel safe at school)[42]
- Percentage of students (Grades 6, 8 and 11) who report that 'I think things through carefully before I make a decision; I can say 'no' when someone wants me to do things I know are wrong or dangerous'. Data collected as part of the indicator: social competencies (I think things through carefully before I make a decision; I can say 'no' when someone wants me to do things I know are wrong or dangerous; I am accepting of those different than me (racially, culturally, socio-economically); it is wrong to discriminate against someone because of his/her race, appearance, culture, religion, etc; and I am good at making friends)[42]
- Youth (ages 13-19) respecting others – asked youth ages 13-19 if people who know them would say they 'respect values and beliefs of people who are a different race or culture than I am', 'respect values and beliefs of people who are of a different sexual orientation than I am', 'know a lot about people of other races' and 'enjoy being with people who are of a different race than I am'[45]

RUNAWAY YOUTH

Related domains:
Conditions (juvenile delinquency); social and emotional development (social community relationships: behaviour problems).

Recommended measures:

- Reported rates of running away[6]
- Runaway youth rates per 100,000 population (ages 0-19) in Mississippi[22]
- Runaway reports[42]

SAFETY AT SCHOOL:

Related domains:

Family and community (school and community); health (violence); health status (adolescents: violence); safety; school violence; social and emotional development (emotional and personal development: youth perceptions of safety in/at school).

Recommended measures:

- Percentage of students who reported fearing attack at school or on the way to and from school during the last 6 months[10]
- Percentage of high school students who were threatened or injured with a weapon on school property, by race[25]
- Percentage of high school students who reported to miss one or more days from school because they felt unsafe at school or on their way to school[25]
- Percentage of secondary school students aged 12-18 years reporting that they had been bullied or felt unsafe at school in the Youth 2000: A National Secondary School Youth Health Survey[29]
- Percentage of students in Grades 9-12 who did not go to school during the past 30 days because they felt unsafe[31]
- Number of weapon-related incidents reported in school, per 1,000 students[34]
- Number of assaults per 1,000 students[34]
- Number of assaults on staff and students[34]
- Safety (Grades 9-12) – data collected as part of the indicator: youth perception of schools (safety, teachers care, students are respectful)[40]
- Percentage of students in Grades 6, 8, 10 and 12 who answered 'yes' to the statement 'I feel safe at my school'[41]
- Percentage of students (Grades 6, 8 and 11) who report feeling safe in their school. Data collected as part of the indicator: school climate (my teachers care about me; students in my school treat each other with respect; and I feel safe at school)[42]
- Caring school climate (Grades 6, 8 and 11)[42]
- Percentage of students in Grades 9-12 who did not go to school on at least 1 of the past 30 days because they felt unsafe at school or on their way to or from school[45]

SAFETY IN THE COMMUNITY

Related domains:

Community and school environment strengths; neighbourhood safety; safety; safety and physical status; social and emotional development (emotional and personal development).

Recommended measures:

- Proportion of households with children aged 0-14 years where neighbourhood is perceived to be unsafe[2]
- Perception of safety among children from different age groups[5]
- Proportion of young people aged 15-24 who reported that they felt unsafe in their neighbourhood at night or, if they did not walk alone at night, reported that they would feel unsafe doing so[29]
- My neighbourhood is a safe place to live; and in my neighbourhood there are lots of fights, crime or illegal drugs (Grades 6, 8 and 11). Data collected as part of the indicator: youth perception of neighbourhood safety: my neighbourhood is a safe place to live; in my neighbourhood there are lots of fights, crime or illegal drugs; adults in my community care

about people my age; and adults in my community let me know they are proud of me when I do something well[42]
- Percentage of students (Grades 8, 10 and 12) who report feeling safe in their neighbourhood[43]
- Community safety: asked respondents, 'overall, how safe do you feel in your community?'[45]

SCHOOL, ABSENTEEISM

Related domains:
Children successful in school; education; education and achievement (enrolment and attendance); education and childcare (behavioural characteristic); education and personal development; education outcome.

Recommended measures:
- Truancy rates[7]
- Non-attendance at school (including children excluded from school)[12]
- Percentage of truancies and students excluded from school. (Truancies: proportion of half days missed a year through unauthorised absence. Exclusion: proportion of students excluded)[15]
- Percentage of 8th and 12th Grade students in the USA who were absent from school 3 or more days in the preceding month[20]
- Percentage of students absent 3+ days in previous month (4th, 8th and 12th Grades)[21]
- Percentage of students in all Grades missing more than 20 days of the school year. School attendance data is calculated as the percentage of students present in school for at least half the average school day throughout the year[24]
- Average (mean) daily number of unjustified absences and intermittent unjustified absences from school per 100 students enrolled, as measured in the Survey on Attendance, Absences and Truancy 2002. Unjustified absences are defined as those that are not explained or not explained to the satisfaction of the school. Intermittent unjustified absences occur when a student is absent for part of a morning (or afternoon) or part of a period, without justification[29]

SCHOOL, ATTENDANCE

Related domains:
Basic indicators; children succeed in school; children succeeding in school; education; HIV/AIDS.

Recommended measures:
- School attendance rate[1]
- Percentage of boys aged 6-14 who never attended school[17]
- Percentage of girls aged 6-14 who never attended school[17]
- School attendance rate[31]
- Attendance rates for a) elementary and b) secondary students[34]
- Percentage of children in the age group that officially corresponds to primary schooling who attend primary school. These data come from national household surveys[56]
- Net primary school attendance, derived from national household survey reports of attendance at primary school[56]
- Percentage of children entering the first Grade of primary school who eventually reach Grade 5[56]
- Percentage of children (10-14 years) who lost both biological parents and who are currently attending school as a percentage of non-orphaned children of the same age who live with at least one parent and who are attending school[56]

SCHOOL, CHARACTERISTICS

Related domains:

Child well-being within education; children ready for school and vice versa; education/childcare (school characteristics); school (description); school (outcomes); social policy indicators.

Recommended measures:

- Percentage of schools with on-site family advocate/school nurse/counsellor[1]
- Number of schools with on-site before or after school care programmes[1]
- Number of schools ranked in the 'distinguished' and 'successful' categories by the Quality Schools designations[1]
- Number of schools with formal transition plan for entry from pre-school into kindergarten[1]
- Adoption by the school of a holistic approach regarding education[14]
- Percentage of children in troubled schools, defined as schools with significant student behavioural, conduct or staff morale problems[21]
- Proportion of children exposed to bilingual education[21]
- Percentage of elementary school classes with fewer than 20 students[34]
- Percentage of children attending schools with a written anti-bullying policy in operation, as a percentage of all school children[48]
- Pupil/teacher ratios and expenditures per student in public elementary and secondary schools[50]
- Characteristics of educational systems (average days of instruction in the school year, age for starting school, average minutes of instruction in the school day, average number of hours of instruction per school year, per cent of students who spend 2 or more hours on homework daily) in selected countries[50]

SCHOOL, COMPLETION

Related domains:

Children completing school; education; education and achievement (enrolment and attendance); education and childcare (enrolment); educational well-being; school (description).

Recommended measures:

- Percentage of young adults ages 18 to 24 who have completed high school[18]
- High school completion rates (percentage) for 18 through 24 years in the USA[20]
- Proportion of 21-22 year-olds who have completed high school[21]
- On-time graduation (the percentage of 9th Graders who graduate from high school 4 years later)[21]
- Percentage of children with ED who exit special education by graduating or completing school. The denominator does not include those students with ED who exited the programme to return to general education or to transfer to another programme. The denominator does include those students who reached maximum age, dropped out, were expelled, or exited with a diploma or certificate[24]
- Four-year public high school completion rate[32]
- Percentage of 25- to 29-year-olds completing high school and college, by age and race/ethnicity[50]

SCHOOL, DROP-OUTS

Related domains:

Achievement; children completing school; children succeed in school; conditions (education); education and achievement (enrolment and attendance); education and childcare (enrolment); education and skills (attendance and attainment); education indicators; education outcome; educational well-being; other determinant factors of child health, risk and protective factors; population characteristics; school (description); social determinants of child health.

Recommended measures:

- Percentage of teens ages 16-19 who are high school drop-outs[3]
- Percentage of teens between ages 16 and 19 who are not enrolled in school and are not high school graduates. Those who have a GED or equivalent are included as high school graduates in this measure[4]
- Percentage leaving school with no qualifications[7]
- Percentage of young adults aged 16-24 in the civilian non-institutionalised population who are not enrolled in a high school programme and have not received a high school diploma or obtained an equivalency certificate[10]
- Event drop-out rate (percentage) for youth in the USA in Grades 10 through 12 (ages 15 through 24). The event drop-out rate is the proportion of students enrolled in Grades 10 through 12 one year earlier who were not enrolled and not graduated in the year for which the data are presented[20]
- Proportion of 10th to 12th Graders who dropped out of high school during the past year[21]
- Percentage of 19-20 year-olds who lack a high school credential[21]
- Percentage of 18-24 year-olds who are high school drop-outs[21]
- Percentage not graduating from high school in Mississippi[22]
- Percentage of public school students in 9th through 12th Grade who withdrew from school before graduation or before completing a Maryland approved educational programme during the July-to-June academic year[24]
- Status school drop-out rates for ages 16-24 by race/ethnicity[25]
- Percentage high school drop-outs[31]
- Junior cycle year 3, percentage of students from the initial cohort who were retained in the system and entered year 3 of the junior cycle[27]
- Public school annual drop-out rate[32]
- Percentage of students in Grades 9 through 12 who drop out[34]
- Percentage gaining no GCSE Grade C or above[37]
- Percentage of children who leave school (voluntarily or by exclusion) before the statutory school-leaving age, by male, female and in total[48]
- Percentage of high school drop-outs among persons 16 to 24 years old, by sex and race/ethnicity[50]
- Percentage of 8th Graders failing to graduate from State schools 5 years later[51]
- Event drop-outs (percentage)[53]
- Cohort drop-outs (percentage)[53]

SCHOOL, ENROLMENT (PRIMARY AND SECONDARY)

Related domains:

Basic indicators; children in learning; development indicators; education; education and childcare (enrolment); education and development; education and personal development; school (description); women.

Recommended measures:

- Participation in education at age 15 years[12]
- Percentage of 16-18 year-olds in learning – defined as being in education or training[15]
- Net enrolment ratio among children aged 6-10 years[17]
- Percentage of 14-17 year-olds enrolled in school[21]
- Enrolment of 16-year-olds in education (percentage)[26]
- Minority share of public school enrolment[34]
- Combined primary and secondary gross enrolment ratio for girls as a percentage of the combined primary and secondary gross enrolment for boys[35]
- Survival to 5th Grade of primary education measures the proportion of school children enrolled in Grade 1 of primary education who have enrolled in Grade 4 and as a percentage of the initial number of school children in Grade 1[35]

- Net enrolment in primary school is defined as the percentage of children of primary school age who are enrolled in primary education[35]
- Percentage of population 14 to 29 years enrolled in school, by age (14-17, 18-19, 20-21, 22-24, 25-29)[50]
- Vocational/technical secondary enrolment rate (gross rates, per cent of 15-18 population)[55]
- General secondary enrolment rate (gross rates, per cent of 15-18 population)[55]
- Basic education enrolment rate (gross rates, per cent of relevant population)[55]
- Girls' gross enrolment ratio divided by that of boys, as a percentage. The gross enrolment ratio is the number of children enrolled in a schooling level (primary or secondary), regardless of age, divided by the population of the age group that officially corresponds to that level[56]
- Number of children enrolled in a primary level, regardless of age, divided by the population of the age group that officially corresponds to the same level[56]
- Number of children enrolled in a secondary level, regardless of age, divided by the population of the age group that officially corresponds to the same level[56]
- Number of children enrolled in primary school who belong to the age group that officially corresponds to primary schooling, divided by the total population of the same age group[56]

SCHOOL, FORMAL QUALIFICATIONS

Related domains:
Achievement; children completing school; development and behaviour measures; education; education and skills (attendance and attainment); education outcome; educational development; social determinants of child health.

Recommended measures:
- Percentage achieving 5 or more A*-C[6]
- Percentage achieving 2 or more A levels[6]
- Percentage achieving standard high school (age 16) qualification[7]
- Level of education completed by adults aged 25-29 (less than high school, high school diploma or equivalent, some college including vocational/technical, bachelor's degree or higher)[10]
- Percentage of 19-year-olds with a Level 2 qualification or above. Examples of a Level 2 qualification are: one A level, NVQ level 2, GNVQ intermediate, 5 or more GCSEs at Grade A*-C or any equivalent qualifications[15]
- Percentage of 15-year-olds (at the start of the academic year) with one or more GCSEs at Grade A*-G or GNVQ equivalents in all schools[15]
- Percentage of young people leaving care with one or more GCSEs (Grade A*-G) or a vocational qualification – examinations sat during the care period are included even if results were announced after leaving care[15]
- Percentage of all persons over 25 years residing in Maryland who have a high school diploma or equivalent[24]
- Percentage of high school graduates who complete minimum course requirements needed for career and technology programmes, or requirements needed to enter the University of Maryland, or who completes both[24]
- Senior cycle retention, percentage of students who have completed the leaving certificate[27]
- Junior certificate exam 'sits', percentage of students who were graded in at least one junior certificate subject[27]
- Number of secondary school students who left school with no formal educational qualifications, as a proportion of all secondary school-leavers[29]
- Percentage of children ages 16 to 19 who are no longer in high school but receive their high school diploma or equivalent by the time of case closing[30]
- Educational outcome at 15[48]
- Percentage of 10th Grade students not passing all parts of high school exit exam[51]

SCHOOL, READINESS

Related domains:
Access to developmental opportunities (childhood learning and care); children are ready for school; children enter school ready to learn; children ready for school and vice versa; community and school environment strengths (effective services: schools); education and childcare (achievement and proficiency); education and skills (learning assessments); education outcome; educational development; readiness and early school performance; social and emotional development (early development).

Recommended measures:
- Percentage of children ready for kindergarten/appropriate early childhood experiences[1]
- 'School readiness' at age 4 or 5[7]
- Percentage of children aged 3-5 reported to have three or four cognitive/literacy school readiness skills. The school readiness indicator taps four skills related to early literacy and cognitive development: the ability to 1) recognise letters; 2) count to 20 or higher; 3) write own name; and 4) read or pretend to read[10]
- Proportion of kindergarteners who are 'unready' for kindergarten[21]
- Percentage of kindergarten students who have reached one of the three levels on the Work Sampling System Kindergarten Assessment: full readiness, approaching readiness or developing readiness. The three levels of readiness are based upon teacher ratings in the following seven domains: social and personal, language and literacy, mathematical thinking, scientific thinking, social studies, the arts and physical development. Full readiness is defined as consistently demonstrating skills, behaviours and abilities, that are needed to meet kindergarten expectations successfully. Approaching readiness indicates that a student is inconsistently meeting those goals and requires targeted instructional support. Students who are developing readiness do not successfully meet kindergarten readiness goals and require considerable support[24]
- Percentage of children ages 3 to 5 who pass pre-school screening by the time of case closing[30]
- Percentage of children ready for kindergarten (children were rated by kindergarten teachers 4-6 weeks into the school year on four dimensions of readiness for school)[31]
- Percentage of children who are ready to enter school[43]
- Percentage of TDSB elementary schools reporting to have at least one quarter of their young students at very low readiness scores in two or more domains[47]
- Percentage of children assessed not ready for the 1st Grade[51]

SCHOOL, RETENTION

Related domains:
Academic achievement; children succeeding in school; children's academic experiences; education and childcare (enrolment).

Recommended measures:
- Number of student retentions and social promotions[1]
- Percentage needing to repeat a year[7]
- Proportion of children enrolled in one year of those enrolled in the previous year[9]
- Percentage of 2nd Graders in the USA who were retained in kindergarten and/or 1st Grade[20]
- Percentage of children ages 6-7 who have repeated 1st or 2nd Grade[21]
- Children ages 12-17 who have repeated grades by residential characteristics[49]
- Percentage of children ages 6-11 and 12-17 who have repeated a grade, as reported by parents[54]

SCHOOL, SUSPENSION AND EXPULSION

Related domains:

Academic achievement; child well-being within education; education and childcare; education indicators; education outcome; social and emotional development (social community relationships: behaviour problems).

Recommended measures:

- School exclusions[7]
- Rate of disciplinary action (student absences from a State school as a result of suspensions, exclusions or cancellations of enrolment) per 1,000 students per school day (by male, female and in total, where appropriate, by age categories <1 year, 1-3 years, 4-6 years, 7-9 years, 10-12 years, 13-15 years and 16-18 years and in total, where appropriate, and by geographic location and in total, where appropriate)[13]
- Ability of the school to deal with disruptive pupils without excluding them[14]
- Percentage of truancies and students excluded from school. (Truancies: proportion of half days missed a year through unauthorised absence. Exclusion: proportion of students excluded)[15]
- Number permanently excluded from school[37]
- Percentage of students in Grades 6, 8, 10 and 12 who reported having been suspended from school at least once in the past 12 months[41]
- Average age students in Grades 6, 8, 10 and 12 who were first suspended from school, as reported by students[41]
- Number of incidents/number of incidents per 100 students resulting in student removal from school (includes personal offence violations, alcohol/ tobacco/other drug-related incidents, weapon-related incidents, other acts/criminal and other acts/policy violations)[45]
- School expulsions (per 1,000 students)[53]
- School suspensions (percentage)[53]
- Percentage of children aged 12-17 ever expelled or suspended from school, as reported by parents[54]

SCREENING

Related domains:

Access to developmental opportunities (inclusive services for children); children are ready for school; condition manifested in childhood; developmental measures; health (healthcare); healthy children; pregnant women and young children thrive; youth health (access to services: pregnancy and early childhood services).

Recommended measures:

- Percentage of newborns who have been screened for hearing impairment before hospital discharge[1]
- Percentage of newborns in the State with at least one screening for each of PKU, hypothyroidism, galactosemia, hemoglobinopathies[1]
- Percentage of teens who have a preventative visit during which they were screened for sexual behaviour, use of tobacco products and use of alcohol and other drugs[21]
- Percentage of births where families receive 'new baby' visits[31]
- Percentage of children screened by 1st Grade for vision and hearing problems[31]
- Number of babies who have had their hearing screened and the number of whom were found to be deaf or hard of hearing[47]
- Number of children assessed for speech and language problems[47]

SEAT BELT/RESTRAINT USE

Related domains:

Health (health-related behaviour); health and safety (youth health: good health and health habits among youth); healthy children; physical protection policy (child transportation safety); social development, behavioural health and teen fertility (physical health and safety).

Recommended measures:

- Seat-belt use[1]
- Infant car seat use[1]
- Percentage of children and youth who wear seat belts or restraints[10]
- Percentage of children and youth in the USA who are observed to have worn a seat belt or been placed in a child safety seat[20]
- Percentage of children who regularly use seat belts[21]
- Percentage of youth who report to wear a seat belt when riding in a car driven by someone else[43]
- Existence and actual enforcement of legislation and regulations establishing mandatory requirements for safe mobility and transport of children[48]

SELF-ESTEEM

Related domains:
Mental health; pro-social behaviour.

Recommended measures:

- Self-esteem measures[7]
- Percentage of children with strong, positive self-image (competent, efficacious)[21]

SELF-REPORTED HAPPINESS AND PSYCHOLOGICAL WELL-BEING

Related domains:
Health (health conditions); mental health; personal life skills; survival and health, material well-being, education and development, social inclusion.

Recommended measures:

- Perceived well-being[5]
- Psychological well-being scores at different ages[7]
- Percentage of high school seniors who report being very happy[21]
- Life satisfaction, 15-19 year-olds (percentage)[26]
- Perceived well-being, quality of life and positive mental health[48]

SELF-REPORTED HEALTH STATUS

Related domains:
Health (health conditions); health conditions and health care (health conditions); healthy children.

Recommended measures:

- Parent/caretaker rating of child's health: good, fair, poor[1]
- Percentage of related children under age 18 in very good or excellent health[18]
- Percentage of children under age 18 in the USA who are reported by their parents to be in very good or excellent health[20]
- Global assessment of child's health (excellent, good, etc)[21]

SELF-REPORTED MENTAL HEALTH

Related domains:
Health; health (mental health); personal life skills; pro-social behaviour.

Recommended measures:

- Anxiety, depression and general well-being[5]
- Percentage of 15-year-olds who report feeling low at least once a week in the last 6 months, by male, female and in total[6]
- Percentage of students in Grades 9-12 who, in the past 12 months, reported feeling sad or hopeless almost every day for 2 or more weeks in a row[10]

- Capacity to cope with stress and to engage in personally meaningful activities[21]
- Prevalence of significant symptoms of depression[29]
- Percentage of high school students who reported that during the past year they felt so sad and hopeless almost every day for 2 weeks or more that they stopped doing some usual activity[51]

SEXUAL PARTNERS

Related domains:
Adolescent risk behaviours; entry (pregnancy, birth); health status (adolescents); problem behaviour; sexual activity and condom use; sexual activity and pregnancy; sexual behaviour; sexual health; social development, behavioural health and teen fertility (sexual activity and fertility); teenage fertility.

Recommended measures:
- Number of sexual partners by age 20[7]
- Percentage of students in Grades 9 through 12 in the USA who reported having 4 or more sex partners during lifetime[20]
- Percentage of sexually active 20-year-olds in the USA with 6 or more lifetime sex partners[20]
- Percentage distribution of number of sexual partners in a year among sexually active teens aged 15 through 19 in the USA[20]
- Percentage distribution of number of lifetime sexual partners among sexually active 20-year-olds in the United States by age at first intercourse (first intercourse at a) age 14 or younger; b) age 15 or 16; and c) age 17 or older)[20]
- Number of sexual partners[21]
- Sexual behaviour (4 or more sexual partners during lifetime) of Mississippi youth, by sex[22]
- Percentage of high school students who have had 4 or more sexual partners in their lifetime, by Grade (9th, 10th, 11th, 12th) and gender[25]
- Proportion of teens aged 15-19 years who reported having multiple sexual partners in the past 12 months[38]
- Percentage of high school students in Grade 12 who reported having 4 or more sexual partners in their lifetime[51]

SEXUALLY ACTIVE TEENS

Related domains:
Adolescent risk behaviours (sexual activity and pregnancy); health (health-related behaviour); health status (adolescents: sexual activity and condom use); problem behaviour; social and emotional development (sexual activity and teen child-bearing); social development, behavioural health and teen fertility (sexual activity and fertility); teenage fertility.

Recommended measures:
- Percentage sexually active in last 3 months[7]
- Percentage of students in Grades 9-12 who reported to be sexually active. Sexually active is defined as having had sexual intercourse in the past 3 months[10]
- Percentage of students in Grades 9 through 12 in the USA who reported having sexual intercourse in the previous 3 months[20]
- Percentage of teens who are sexually active[21]
- Percentage of 9th to 12th Graders who are sexually active[21]
- Sexual activity (sexual intercourse in last 3 months preceding survey) by high school students by Grade (9th, 10th, 11th, 12th)[25]
- Percentage of high school students in Grade 11 and 12 who reported having sexual intercourse in the past 3 months[51]

SEXUALLY EXPERIENCED TEENS

Related domains:

Adolescent risk behaviours (sexual activity and pregnancy); adolescents (reproductive health: onset of sexual activity); entry (pregnancy, birth); health status (adolescents: sexual activity); sexual health; social and emotional development (sexual activity and teen child-bearing); social development, behavioural health and teen fertility (sexual activity and fertility); teenage fertility.

Recommended measures:

- Percentage of those aged 14-18 who are sexually experienced[7]
- Proportion of 15-19 adolescents who have had sexual intercourse ever and within the past year by age, gender, parental status, income and geographical location[8]
- Percentage rates of age at first intercourse of adolescents aged 17-19 years by geographical location[8]
- Percentage of students in Grades 9-12 who reported to be sexually experienced. Sexually experienced is defined as having had sexual intercourse in one's lifetime[10]
- Percentage of youth in the USA who have ever had intercourse[20]
- Percentage of students in Grades 9 through 12 in the USA who reported ever having sexual intercourse[20]
- Sexual behaviour (ever had sexual intercourse) of Mississippi youth, by sex[22]
- Percentage of high school students who have ever had sexual intercourse, by Grade (9th, 10th, 11th, 12th) and gender[25]
- Proportion of population aged 15-19 years that reported having had sexual intercourse, by sex[38]
- Percentage of high school students who reported having sexual intercourse by the age of 13, 15[51]

SEXUALLY TRANSMITTED DISEASES [STDs]
[*SEE ALSO* INFECTIOUS DISEASES AND HIV/AIDS]

Related domains:

Adolescents (reproductive health); health; health (health conditions); health and safety (youth engaging in risky behaviour: youth sexual activities); health conditions and health care (health conditions); health status (adolescents); infant, child and teen health indicators; sexual health; teenage fertility; youth choose healthy behaviour.

Recommended measures:

- STD rate for those aged 15-19[7]
- Rates per 1,000 of *Chlamydia* for males and females, by age group (15-19) and gender[8]
- Reported rates of youth primary and secondary syphilis in the USA (per 100,000 population), ages 10-14, 15-19[20]
- Reported rates of youth gonorrhoea in the USA (per 100,000 population), ages 10-14, 15-19[20]
- Reported rates of primary and secondary syphilis for youth aged 15 through 19 in the USA (per 100,000 population), aged 15 through 19[20]
- Reported rates of gonorrhoea for youth aged 15 through 19 in the USA (per 100,000 population), aged 15 through 19[20]
- Rate of syphilis, gonorrhoea in 15-19 years-olds[21]
- Rates of sexually transmitted diseases (*Chlamydia*, gonorrhoea, syphilis) per 100,000 adolescents by age (15-19, 20-24) and race[25]
- Reported incidence of *Chlamydia*, gonorrhoea and syphilis among teens aged 10-19[31]
- Number of newly reported cases of congenital syphilis[33]
- Incidence of Hepatitis B by sex, youth aged 15-19 years (cases per 1,000)[38]
- Incidence of gonorrhoea by sex, youth aged 15-19 years (cases per 1,000)[38]
- Incidence of *Chlamydia* by sex, youth aged 15-19 years (cases per 1,000)[38]
- Sexually transmitted diseases (ages 15-19) (includes syphilis and gonorrhoea)[39]

- Rate of 10-17 year-olds who were diagnosed with gonorrhoea, *Chlamydia* or syphilis per 1,000[41]
- Percentage of youth contracting a sexually transmitted disease[43]
- Total number of reported cases of selected youth-related diseases (polio, measles, tuberculosis, gonorrhoea, syphilis, AIDS) for all age groups[50]
- Number of children and youth infected with STDs[51]
- Teens with STD (per cent for ages 15-17)[53]
- Newly registered cases of syphilis and gonorrhoea per 100,000 population between ages 15-19[55]
- Newly registered cases of syphilis and gonorrhoea per100,000 population[55]

SLEEP

Related domains:
Health (health-related behaviour); healthy children; social development, behavioural health and teen fertility (physical health and safety).

Recommended measures:
- Percentage of mothers putting infant down to sleep in the supine position (on their back)[1]
- Percentage of adolescents aged 12 through 17 in the USA who report that they get enough sleep[20]
- Percentage of teens getting adequate sleep[21]

SOCIAL WELFARE DEPENDENCE, RECEIPT OF AID FOR FAMILIES WITH DEPENDENT CHILDREN (AFDC)/TEMPORARY ASSISTANCE FOR NEEDY FAMILIES (TANF)

Related domains:
Children's economic well-being; community and school environment strengths (community economic and geographic stability: receipt of public transfer); conditions (poverty); economic security (financial support: means-tested assistance); economic security (government support programmes); economic security indicators; economic status; home (family income: federal aid to families); income, assets and work (social support benefits); youth self-sufficiency (family).

Recommended measures:
- Number of child recipients of AFDC/TANF (in thousands)[10]
- Among children in families ever receiving AFDC/TANF, percentage of children under 18 receiving them for: a) at least 6 years; and b) at least 9 years[10]
- Percentage and number (in thousands) of children in the USA under age 18 in families receiving AFDC or General Assistance[20]
- Percentage of children under age 6 in the USA receiving any AFDC benefit[20]
- Average monthly rate of AFDC recipiency for children[21]
- Percentage children on AFDC in Mississippi[22]
- Children who are Work First/TANF recipients[32]
- Percentage of children receiving TANF/AFDC under age 18 (per 100)[34]
- Rate of persons (all ages) participating in Temporary Assistance for Needy Families Programme per 1,000 population[41]
- Percentage of children under 18 years receiving Aid to Families with Dependent Children (AFDC) payments[50]
- Number of children and youth under the age of 18 living in families receiving Temporary Aid to Needy Families[51]
- Children younger than age 18 on Families First/TANF (per cent)[53]

SOCIAL WELFARE DEPENDENCE, RECEIPT OF ENERGY ASSISTANCE

Related domains:

Economic security (government support programmes).

Recommended measures:

- Percentage of children receiving energy assistance in past year[21]

SOCIAL WELFARE DEPENDENCE, RECEIPT OF FOOD STAMPS

Related domains:

Children live in stable, supported families; children's economic well-being; economic security (financial support: means-tested assistance); economic security (government support programmes); economic security indicators; income, assets and work (social support benefits); youth self-sufficiency (family: responsible management of finances: receipt of public transfers).

Recommended measures:

- Percentage of children under age 18 living in low-income working families where someone in the household participated in the federal Food Stamp Program. Children are considered living in low-income working families if the family income was less than 150% of the federal poverty level and if at least one parent worked 50 or more weeks during the year[4]
- Number of child recipients of food stamps (in thousands)[10]
- Children receiving food stamps (<130% poverty)[11]
- Percentage of children in the USA under age 18 in households receiving AFDC and food stamps[20]
- Percentage of children in the USA under age 18 in families receiving AFDC or General Assistance, and in households receiving food stamps[20]
- Percentage and number (in thousands) of children in the USA under age 18 in households receiving food stamps[20]
- Percentage of children in families receiving food stamps in past year[21]
- Percentage of children in families receiving AFDC or food stamps in past year[21]
- Percentage of children in families receiving food stamps (proxy for children in poverty)[31]
- Children on food stamps[32]
- Children, youth and families receiving food stamps[39, 41, 42]
- Total recipients of food stamps (percentage)[53]
- Children younger than age 18 receiving food stamps (percentage)[53]

SOCIAL WELFARE DEPENDENCE, RECEIPT OF FREE OR REDUCED PRICE LUNCHES

Related domains:

Children ready for school and vice versa; children's economic well-being; economic security (government support programmes); education indicators; youth self-sufficiency (family: responsible management of finances: receipt of public transfers).

Recommended measures:

- Number of children enrolled in free or reduced lunch program[1]
- Children receiving free/reduced price school lunches (<185% poverty)[11]
- Percentage of children receiving free or reduced price lunches[21]
- Children enrolled in free/reduced price school meals[32]
- Percentage of public school students eligible for free or reduced price lunch[34]
- Free and reduced lunch programme[41, 42]
- Free or reduced lunch participation (percentage)[53]

SOCIAL WELFARE DEPENDENCE, RECEIPT OF GENERAL MEANS TESTED ASSISTANCE

Related domains:
Children in strong, stable families; community and school environment strengths (community economic and geographic stability: receipt of public transfer); economic resources and contribution; economic security (government support programmes); economic security (income security: children on social assistance); infant, child and teen health indicators; material well-being; pregnant women and young children thrive; youth self-sufficiency (family: responsible management of finances: receipt of public transfers).

Recommended measures:
- Percentage of children in a particular region or city dependent on government for shelter, nutrition, parenting or special needs at a particular point in time, not including regular education[1]
- Benefits/transfers paid directly to children or to families on behalf of children[5]
- Children in families in receipt of social welfare, in particular SWA[12]
- Percentage of children in families receiving any means-tested federal support[21]
- Rate of intergenerational welfare dependence[21]
- Percentage of children (ages 0-4 and 5-17) in families receiving welfare[31]
- Percentage of children and youth (ages 0-19) receiving Supplemental Security Income (SSI). This programme provides monthly cash benefits to aged, blind and disabled persons with income and resources below certain limits[39]
- Percentage of children and youth (ages 0-17) receiving public assistance. Public assistance programmes provide cash and in-kind aid to meet the basic support needs of individuals and families[39]
- Percentage of low-income youth participating in available nutritional programmes, such as Women, Infants and Children[43]
- Number of recipients of public welfare, 1993 - 2000[45]
- Number of children under the age of 15 living in families in receipt of social assistance[47]
- Children younger than age 6 on WIC (per cent)[53]

STILLBIRTHS

Related domains:
Child health and development (health); infant health – the first year of life.

Recommended measures:
- Stillbirths rate per thousand by age of mother (15-19, 20-24, 25-29, 30-34, 35-39 and 40-44)[36]
- Number of stillbirths per 1,000 total births[38]

STUNTING

Related domains:
Healthy children; nutrition.

Recommended measures:
- Child's height/weight for age is below the 5th percentile[1]
- Percentage of under-5 girls with moderate stunting[17]
- Percentage of under-5 boys with moderate stunting[17]
- Moderate and severe – below two standard deviations from median height for age of reference population[56]

SUICIDE IDEATION

Related domains:
Exit (deaths); health (health conditions); health (mental health); health conditions and health care (health conditions); mental health.

Recommended measures:

- Self-reported suicidal feelings among young people[7]
- Percentage of students in Grades 9-12 who in the past 12 months: a) thought seriously about attempting suicide; b) attempted suicide; and c) whose suicide attempts required medical attention[10]
- Percentage of teens in the USA in Grades 9 through 12 who report having seriously considered suicide in the previous 12 months[20]
- Percentage of 9th to 12th Graders who have seriously considered suicide in past 12 months[21]
- Self-reported suicidal thoughts and behaviour (thought seriously about attempting suicide; attempted suicide; made a suicide plan; suicide attempt required medical attention), by sex[22]

SUICIDE

[*SEE ALSO* MORTALITY, INJURY-RELATED, INTENTIONAL AND UNINTENTIONAL]

Related domains:

Adolescent risk behaviours; child and maternal mortality; childhood morbidity and mortality; community and school environment deficits (negative adult behaviour: adult suicide); deaths; exit (deaths); health; health and safety (youth mental health); health and survival; health conditions and health care (mortality); mental health; social inclusion.

Recommended measures:

- Suicide death rate for children aged 10-14 years[2]
- Suicides 15-24 per 100,000, by male, female and in total[6]
- Suicide rate (by gender, age, race)[7]
- Child suicide[12]
- Suicide rate for children aged 18 years and younger (by male, female and in total, where appropriate, by age categories <1 year, 1-3 years, 4-6 years, 7-9 years, 10-12 years, 13-15 years and 16-18 years and in total, where appropriate, and by geographic location and in total, where appropriate)[13]
- Youth suicides (rate per 100,000) in the USA by age 10-14 and 15-19[20]
- Child/youth suicide rate per 100,000 population (ages 0-19)[22]
- Suicide among children aged 19 and under, can be grouped by age: 0, 1-4, 5-9, 10-14, 15-19 and all). Data collected as part of the indicator: deaths due to injury (accidents, homicides and suicides)[24]
- Male suicides (15-24 year-olds) per 100,000[26]
- Suicide frequency among children aged 0-18, by male, female and in total[27]
- Number of suicide deaths of persons aged 15-24 years as a proportion (per 100,000) of the population in that age group[29]
- Suicide (ages 18+). Deaths reported as suicides. Rate per 100,000[31]
- Suicide deaths among youth aged 15-19, by sex[38]
- Hospitalisations resulting from self-inflicted injuries (ages 10-14 and 15-19)[39]
- Number of successful suicides by juveniles ages 10-17 per 1,000 juveniles[41]
- Number of successful suicides by adults age 18 and older per 1,000 adults age 18 and older[41]
- Suicide death rates by age (ages 0-65+)[42]
- Suicide and suicide rate[42]
- Percentage of suicides by youth[43]
- Number of suicides among children aged 15-19[51]
- Age 15-19 suicide rate (per 100,000 population), by male, female and in total[55]

TEEN ABORTIONS

Related domains:

Demographics (birth and related outcomes); home (demographics and family composition); natality; problem behaviour; sexual health; social and emotional development (sexual activity and teen child-bearing); social development, behavioural health and teen fertility (sexual activity and fertility).

Recommended measures:

- Abortion rate (per 1,000) for females ages 15-19[10]
- Pregnancy, birth and abortion rates for teenagers: a) 15-17 years; and b) 18-19 years[20]
- Teen abortion rate[21]
- Abortions per 1,000 women aged 15-19 years[38]
- Number of estimated pregnancies, abortions, and births per 1,000 teenage women, by age (10-14, 15-19)[50]
- Number of voluntary abortions/year in women aged <19 years per 1,000 women aged <19 years[52]
- Abortion rate among women under 20 (per population)[55]
- Abortion rate among women under 20 (per births)[55]

TEEN BIRTHS AND REPEAT BIRTHS

Related domains:

Babies born healthy; child health and lifestyle behaviours; children as carers; children in strong, stable families; children's health and well-being; demographics (birth and related outcomes); education and development; entry (pregnancy, birth); family; family/household; health; health and safety (youth engaging in risky behaviour: youth sexual activities); health and survival; health status (adolescents: adolescent child-bearing); home (demographics and family composition); infant, child and teen health indicators; material well-being; maternal and neo-natal conditions; natality; population and family characteristics; population, family and neighbourhood (child population characteristics); reproductive health; sexual health; social and emotional development (sexual activity and teen child-bearing); social development, behavioural health and teen fertility (sexual activity and fertility); social inclusion.

Recommended measures:

- Percentage of live births to teen parents 19 years of age or younger[1]
- Number of births to teenagers between 15 and 17, per 1,000 females in this age group[4]
- Under age 20 specific fertility rate per 1,000[6]
- Percentage of births to women under 20 years of age[9]
- Birth rate (per 1,000) for females ages 15-19[10]
- Children born to teenage mothers (under 18-years-old)[11]
- Birth rate for teenagers[12]
- Birth rates for unmarried women (per 1,000) ages 15-17, 18-19, 20-24, 25-29, 30-34, 35-39, 40-44[18]
- Birth rates (per 1,000) among females ages 15 to 17[18]
- Percentage of all births to unmarried women ages 15 through 19 in the United States[20]
- Pregnancy, birth and abortion rates for teenagers: a) 15-17 years; and b) 18-19 years[20]
- Teen birth rates in the USA (births per 1,000 females in each age group: 10-14, 15-17, 18-19 and 15-19) [20]
- Rate of second births to teenagers who have had a first birth[20]
- Percentage of all births to women under age 20 in the USA that are second or higher order[20]
- Teen birth rate (ages 15-17, 18-19) [21]
- Percentage of teen births to unmarried teen females[21]
- Second births to teen females, rate per 1,000[21]
- Percentage of all registered births to single teen mothers[22]
- Rate of births (per 1,000) for adolescents less than 15 years (10-14 year-olds) and for adolescents between the ages of 15 and 17, as well as those between the ages of 15 and 19, in various racial/ethnic groups, and adolescents in various age groups[24]
- Adolescent birth rates by age (10-14, 15-17, 18-19) and race of mother[25]
- Births to 15-19 year-olds per 1,000[26]
- Births to females less than 18 years old, rate per 1,000[27]

- Number of live births to females under 18 years of age, per 1,000 females aged 15-17[29]
- Percentage of youth under age 18 who become parents during the time a service case is open[30]
- Teen birth rate (15-19) [31]
- Births to teens, ages 15-19[32]
- Percentage of children born to mothers under age 20 (per 100 live births)[34]
- Number of births to girls under 16[37]
- Live births per 1,000 women aged 15-19 years[38]
- Rate of out-of-wedlock live births per 1,000 live births to women ages 10-17[41]
- Rate of live births per 1,000 live births to women ages 10-19[41]
- Percentage of births to mothers under age 20[42]
- Teen birth rate[42]
- Percentage of teenage mothers who give birth to another child[46]
- Number of births per 1,000 unmarried women 15 to 44 years old, by age (15-19, 20-24, 25-29, 30-34, 35-39, 40-44) and race[50]
- Number of estimated pregnancies, abortions and births per 1,000 teenage women, by age (10-14, 15-19)[50]
- Number of babies born to mothers younger than 20[51]
- Number of babies born to mothers younger than 18[51]
- Births to teens (per 1,000 females ages 15-17)[53]
- Share of non-marital births to mothers under age 20 (percentage of live births to mothers under age 20)[55]
- Live births, per 1,000 women aged 15-19[55]
- Share of births to mothers under 20 (percentage of total live births)[55]

TEEN PREGNANCY AND REPEAT PREGNANCY

Related domains:
Adolescent risk behaviours (sexual activity and pregnancy); adolescents (reproductive health); demographics (birth and related outcomes); health; health (health conditions); health and safety (youth engaging in risky behaviour: youth sexual activities); home (demographics and family composition); infant, child and teen health indicators; pre-natal period (demographics); sexual health; social and emotional development (sexual activity and teen child-bearing); social development, behavioural health and teen fertility (sexual activity and fertility); youth choose healthy behaviour.

Recommended measures:

- Teen pregnancy rates ages 15-19, (includes all live births, stillbirths and abortions per 1,000 females aged 15-19 years-old)[8]
- Pregnancy rate (per 1,000) for females ages 15-19[10]
- Teenage pregnancy: a) under-18 conception rates per 1,000 females aged 15-17; b) percentage of teenage mothers who are not in education, employment or training. The under-18 conception rate is the number of conceptions (resulting in one or more live births and legal abortions) to females under 18, per thousand females aged 15 to 17. The figures on teenage mothers not in education, employment or training are for the 16-19 year-old range[15]
- Pregnancy, birth and abortion rates for teenagers: a) 15-17 years; and b) 18-19 years[20]
- Percentage of teens who have had a pregnancy[21]
- Young teen (ages 15-17) pregnancy rate (includes resident births, abortions and foetal deaths. Does not include abortions outside the State)[31]
- Number of pregnancies per 1,000 girls (ages 15-17)[33]
- Pregnancy rate (per 1,000) for females aged 15-19[36]
- Total number of live births, stillbirths and abortions per 1,000 women aged 15-19 years[38]
- Adolescent pregnancy rate is the number of pregnancies per 1,000 females aged 10-14, 15-17 and 15-19. Pregnancies are the sum of the number of live births, reported induced terminations of pregnancies and reported foetal deaths of all gestations[39]

- Rate of pregnancies (live births, abortions and miscarriages) per 1,000 females aged 10-17[41]
- Rate of pregnancies and repeat pregnancies among teens[43]
- Pregnancy rate per 1,000 females aged 10-14, 15-17 and 18-19[45]
- Pregnancy rate among school-age girls[46]
- Number of estimated pregnancies, abortions and births per 1,000 teenage women, by age (10-14, 15-19)[50]
- Pregnancy rate among females ages 14-17[51]
- Number of pregnancies/year in women aged less than 19 years per 1,000 women aged less than 19 years[52]
- Teen pregnancy (per 1,000 females ages 15-17)[53]

TELEVISION VIEWING

Related domains:
Child health and lifestyle behaviours; condition manifested in childhood; daily interactions (family rules about television); education and childcare (behavioural characteristic); education and skills (behaviour affecting learning); health (health-related behaviour); parent-child interaction; social and emotional development (emotional/personal development: productive use of non-school); social development, behavioural health and teen fertility (social development).

Recommended measures:
- Hours spent watching television each day[9]
- Percentage of students in Grades 8, 10 and 12 who report watching television for: a) 1 hour or less; and b) 4 hours or more on week days[10]
- Percentage of students in the USA who watch 6 or more hours of television per day (ages 9 , 13 and 17)[20]
- Excessive television viewing[21]
- Percentage of students watching 6+ hours of television per day (4th, 8th and 12th Grade)[21]
- Percentage of children who watch between 2-3 hours of television each day, by male, female and in total[27]
- Percentage of children who watch television daily, by male, female and in total[27]
- Percentage of children who watch between 3 hours of television each day, by male, female and in total[27]
- Percentage of youth who do not watch 3 or more hours of television on an average school day[43]
- TV rules by age group of child and race/ethnic group of parents[49]
- Percentage of children aged 3-5, 6-11, 12-17 living in households with at least one type of family TV rule: type of programme watched, time of day, number of hours[54]

TOBACCO USE AMONG ADULTS [INCLUDING PARENTS]

Related domains:
Community and school environment deficits (negative adult behaviour); development and behaviour measures; family and community (family); health (drugs, alcohol, tobacco).

Recommended measures:
- Percentage of parents who are current smokers. Current smokers are defined as those who have ever smoked 100 cigarettes and currently smoke every day or some days[10]
- Percentage of persons most knowledgeable about the child and the percentage of their spouses who are non-smokers[19]
- Number of smoking or substance-abusing women/primary care-givers accessing cessation, substance/alcohol abuse treatment services[23]
- Percentage of adults (aged 18+) who report they are current smokers[31]

TOBACCO USE AMONG YOUTH, AGE OF FIRST TOBACCO USE

Related domains:
Health (healthy lifestyles); health and safety (youth health: good health and health habits among youth).

Recommended measures:

- Average age children in Grades 6, 8, 10 and 12 first smoked cigarettes, as reported by students[41]
- Early initiation of alcohol, tobacco and other drugs (Grades 6, 8 and 11)[42]
- Percentage of high school students who reported initiating smoking by ages 11, 13 and 15[51]

TOBACCO USE AMONG YOUTH, APPROVAL OF PEER USE AND PERCEPTION OF PEER ACCEPTANCE OF TOBACCO USE

Related domains:

Health and safety (youth health: good health and health habits among youth); problem behaviour; social development, behavioural health and teen fertility (smoking, alcohol and substance abuse); substance misuse.

Recommended measures:

- Attitudes towards smoking, alcohol and illegal substances[7]
- Percentage of 12th Grade students in the USA who report that peers would not approve of their using alcohol, marijuana, cocaine or cigarettes[20]
- Percentage of teens who report peer approval of smoking tobacco, drinking alcohol[21]
- Perceived acceptability of cigarette use, percentage of students in Grades 6, 8, 10 and 12 who answered 'very good chance' to the question 'what are the chances you would be seen as cool if you smoked cigarettes?'[41]
- Approval of cigarette use by peers, percentage of students in Grades 6, 8, 10 and 12 who answered 'not wrong at all' to the question 'how wrong do you think it is for someone your age to smoke cigarettes?'[41]
- Attitudes of friends towards alcohol, tobacco and other drug use (Grades 6, 8 and 11)[42]

TOBACCO USE AMONG YOUTH, DAILY TOBACCO USE

Related domains:

Health; health (health-related behaviour); health status (adolescents).

Recommended measures:

- Percentage of children aged 15 smoking daily, by male, female and in total[6]
- Percentage of children by age (11, 13, 15) and gender who report smoking daily[16]
- Percentage of teens who smoke daily (or regularly)[21]
- Current smoking, daily smoking, current half pack a day, smoking in past 30 days[25]
- Percentage of 14-15 year-olds/Year 10 secondary school students who smoke daily or at least weekly[29]

TOBACCO USE AMONG YOUTH, LIFETIME TOBACCO USE

Related domains:

Child health and lifestyle behaviours; condition manifested in childhood; health; health status (adolescents); safety and physical status; substance misuse; tobacco, alcohol and drug use.

Recommended measures:

- Substance (tobacco, alcohol and drugs) abuse by age[5]
- Smoking cigarettes[7]
- Percentage who have ever smoked[9]
- Percentage of 16 year-olds who reported ever smoking[16]
- Percentage of children who have smoked at least once in their lifetime[27]
- Tobacco-smoking trends, adults and youth aged 15-19 years[38]
- Percentage of seniors reporting cigarette, alcohol and drug use by substance (cigarettes, alcohol, marijuana/hashish, cocaine) and frequency of use (ever used, used in the previous 30 days)[50]

TOBACCO USE AMONG YOUTH, PARENTAL GUIDANCE AND PERCEIVED PARENTAL APPROVAL OF TOBACCO USE

Related domains:
Health and safety (youth health: good health and health habits among youth); social and emotional development (social community relationships: positive parent-child relationships: communication between parents and children: provision of parental guidance around acceptable behaviour); substance misuse.

Recommended measures:
- Attitudes towards smoking, alcohol and illegal substances[7]
- Percentage of students in Grades 6, 8, 10 and 12 who answered 'not wrong at all' to the question 'how wrong do your parents feel it would be for you to smoke cigarettes?'[41,42]
- Percentage of youths in Grades 8, 10 and 12 whose parents/guardians have talked to them about not using tobacco[43]

TOBACCO USE AMONG YOUTH, PERCEPTION OF AVAILABILITY OF TOBACCO

Related domains:
Community and school environment deficits (availability of illicit drugs, alcohol and tobacco in the community); health and safety: youth health: good health and health habits among youth.

Recommended measures:
- Perceived availability of cigarettes by youth, percentage of students in Grades 6, 8, 10 and 12 who answered 'very easy' to the question 'if you wanted to get some cigarettes, how easy would it be for you to get some?'[41]
- Tobacco access by youth[43]

TOBACCO USE AMONG YOUTH, PERCEPTION OF HARMFULNESS OF TOBACCO USE

Related domains:
Health and safety (youth health: good health and health habits among youth)

Recommended measures:
- Perceived harmfulness of smoking cigarettes, percentage of students in Grades 6, 8, 10 and 12 who answered 'no risk' to the question 'how much do you think people risk harming themselves (physically or other ways) if they smoke one or more packs of cigarettes per day?'[41]
- Perceived harmfulness of alcohol, tobacco and other drugs among students in Grades 6, 8 and 11[42]

TOBACCO USE AMONG YOUTH, PERCEPTION OF POLICE INTERVENTION FOR TOBACCO USE

Related domains:
Health and safety (youth health: good health and health habits among youth)

Recommended measures:
- Percentage of students in Grades 6, 8, 10 and 12 who answered 'no' to the question 'if a kid smoked cigarettes in your neighbourhood or in the area around where you live, would he or she be caught by the police?'[41]

TOBACCO USE AMONG YOUTH, SMOKELESS TOBACCO USE

Related domains:
Health (healthy lifestyles); health and safety (youth health: good health and health habits

among youth); social development, behavioural health and teen fertility (smoking, alcohol and substance abuse).

Recommended measures:

- Percentage of youth in Grades 9 through 12 in the USA who reported having used smokeless tobacco during the previous 30 days[20]
- Percentage of 8th, 10th and 12th Grade students in the USA who reported using smokeless tobacco over the previous 30 days[20]
- Current smokeless tobacco use among students in Grades 9-12[40]
- Percentage of high school students who reported using smokeless tobacco monthly[51]

TOBACCO USE AMONG YOUTH, TOBACCO USE IN THE PAST 30 DAYS

Related domains:

Adolescent risk behaviours; behaviour and social environment; child health and lifestyle behaviours; health; health (drugs, alcohol, tobacco); health (healthy lifestyles); health and safety (youth engaging in risky behaviour); health and safety (youth health: good health and health habits among youth); health status (adolescents); healthy children; social and emotional development (delinquency and crime); social development, behavioural health and teen fertility (smoking, alcohol and substance abuse); tobacco and alcohol use; youth choose healthy behaviour.

Recommended measures:

- Proportion of children aged 12-14 who are current smokers[2]
- Percentage of students in Grades 8, 10 and 12 who reported smoking one or more cigarette per day in the last 30 days[10]
- Proportion of 16-years-old boys and girls who were current smokers between 1995 and 1999[16]
- Percentage of 16 year-olds who reported having smoked in the last 30 days[16]
- Percentage of 8th, 10th and 12th Grade students who reported smoking cigarettes daily in the previous 30 days[18]
- Percentage of students in Grades 9 through 12 in the USA who reported current and frequent smoking. Current smoking is smoking on 1 or more of the previous 30 days. Frequent smoking is smoking on 20 or more of the previous 30 days[20]
- Percentage of 8th, 10th and 12th Grade students in the USA who reported smoking cigarettes daily over the previous 30 days[20]
- Percentage of public school students who report using alcohol, tobacco or illegal drugs in the last 30 days by type of substance (cigarettes, alcohol, marijuana, heroin, ecstasy, LSD) and by age/Grade (6th, 8th, 10th and 12th)[24]
- Current smoking, daily smoking, current half pack a day, smoking in past 30 days[25]
- Long-term trends in thirty-day prevalence of cigarette smoking for 8th, 10th and 12th Graders[25]
- Percentage of children who are current smokers[27]
- Percentage of students in Grades 8 and 12 reporting they smoked cigarettes within the past 30 days[31]
- Percentage of students in Grades 9-12 who reported using the following in the past 30 days: cigarettes, smokeless tobacco, marijuana, alcohol (beer), cocaine[33]
- Teen smoking in past 30 days among students in Grades 9-12[40]
- Percentage of students in Grades 6, 8, 10 and 12 who reported smoking cigarettes at least once within the past 30 days[41]
- Percentage of youth in Grades 9-12 smoking cigarettes on one or more of the past 30 days[45]
- Percentage of seniors reporting cigarette, alcohol and drug use by substance (cigarettes, alcohol, marijuana/hashish, cocaine) and frequency of use (ever used, used in the previous 30 days)[50]
- Percentage of high school students who reporting smoking cigarettes in the past 30 days[51]

TOBACCO USE AMONG YOUTH, TOBACCO USE IN THE PAST WEEK

Related domains:

Child lifestyle determinants of child health, risk and protective factors; condition manifested in childhood.

Recommended measures:

- Percentage who have smoked in the past week[9]
- Percentage of all children aged 11-15 smoking cigarettes regularly. Regular smokers are defined as those who smoke at least one cigarette per week on average[15]
- Percentage of 14-15 year-olds/Year 10 secondary school students who smoke daily or at least weekly[29]
- Percentage of children reporting that they smoke every week, by male, female and in total, at ages 11, 13 and 15, and by socio-economic group when available[48]

TOBACCO USE DURING PREGNANCY

Related domains:

Demographics (birth and related outcomes); family-related indicators; health; health (drugs, alcohol, tobacco); health (health conditions); health (health-related behaviour); health and safety (youth engaging in risky behaviour); health and safety (youth health: good health and health habits among youth); healthy children; infant well-being; maternal and neo-natal conditions; parental health; population characteristics or risk factors; pre-natal period (healthy babies); tobacco, alcohol and drug use.

Recommended measures:

- Percentage of women who smoke pre-natally[1]
- Proportion of women smoking during pregnancy[2]
- Percentage of women who reported smoking throughout their pregnancies[8]
- Percentage of mothers smoking during pregnancy[9]
- Percentage of total births to mothers who smoked during pregnancy. Women are considered to be smokers if they smoked one cigarette daily during their pregnancy[10]
- Mothers not smoking during pregnancy[14]
- Proportion of women who continued to smoke throughout pregnancy. This includes all women who smoke at all during their pregnancy or in the year before conception, and who were smokers at the time of the baby's birth[15]
- Percentage of mothers who continued to smoke during pregnancy[19]
- Maternal use of tobacco, alcohol and other drug use during pregnancy[21]
- Number of all infants exposed to tobacco during pregnancy[23]
- Number and percentage of women who smoked during pregnancy. Women who reported to smoke during at least some part of their pregnancy or were currently smoking while pregnant[23]
- Proportion of children aged 0-1 years whose mother smoked during her pregnancy with the child[28]
- Percentage of pregnant mothers who used tobacco[34]
- Percentage of women smoking at 20 weeks of pregnancy[36]
- Percentage of women aged 15-49 who smoked during pregnancy[38]
- Number of pregnant women receiving alcohol, tobacco and other drug treatment from State-supported treatment centres, per 1,000 live births[41]
- Percentage of mothers (broken down by age 0-65+) who smoked during pregnancy[42]
- Number of infants born to mothers who did not drink or smoke during pregnancy[46]
- Number of women who smoked during the 3rd trimester of pregnancy, expressed as a percentage of all women delivering live or stillborn babies[58]

VOLUNTEERING

Related domains:

Citizenship and values (volunteer work and community affairs); civic life skills; community and school environment strengths (positive adult behaviours contributing to strong communities); family and community (school and community); social and emotional development (pro-social activities and attitude); social and emotional development (social community relationships: civic engagement); youth choose healthy behaviour.

Recommended measures:

- Percentage of children who volunteer[5]
- Opportunities for voluntary work of children[5]
- Percentage of students in Grades 8, 10 and 12 who are reported to volunteer at least once a month[10]
- Percentage of students (Grades 8 and 12) volunteering in their community. Students who reported spending one or more hours per week in an average week helping other people without getting paid (such as helping out at a hospital, day care centre, food shelf, youth programme, community service agency or doing other things) to make their community a better place for people to live[31]
- Service to others (Grades 6, 8 and 11) – on the average during the school year, how many hours per week do you spend helping friends, neighbours or others (including volunteer activities)?[42]
- Number of youth trained in community outreach[43]
- Number of 4-H volunteerism[43]
- Number of 'Citizenship in Community' merit badges given to youth[43]
- Youth (ages 13-19) in community service – asked youth ages 13-19 the following, 'during the average week, do you spend time doing community service-related activities (such as helping out at a hospital, food shelf or doing other things)? If so, how many hours per week (1-5, 6-11, 11+)? Was this community service organised through your school as a service learning opportunity?'[45]
- Volunteerism – asked of respondents, 'in the past 12 months, have you devoted your time outside of your regular family and work schedule for: a) helping out in the public schools with academic or other school-related activities; b) community organisations that help young people, such as little league; c) organisations that assist the elderly, home-bound and people in poor health? d) organisations that assist the needy or under-privileged; and e) an activity sponsored by an environmental organisation?[45]
- Percentage of high school seniors who participate in community affairs or volunteer work at least once per week, by sex and race[50]

VOTING

Related domains:

Civil rights; families, youth, and individuals are engaged in their community's decisions and activities; pro-social behaviour; social and emotional development (social community relationships: civic engagement); social development, behavioural health and teen fertility (social development).

Recommended measures:

- Percentage of persons ages 18 through 24 in the USA who reported that they had registered to vote[20]
- Percentage of persons ages 18 through 24 in the USA who reported that they had voted in the presidential election year[20]
- Percentage of persons ages 18 through 24 in the USA who reported that they had voted in the non-presidential election years[20]

- Percentage of youth age 18 who are registered to vote[21]
- Proportion of young people aged 18-24 years who indicated that they cast a vote in a New Zealand election, and the proportion of young people who are registered on the electoral roll and are eligible to vote[29]
- Percentage of the eligible population (ages 18+) voting in general elections[31]
- Percentage of people 18 and older who voted for the Office of President of the United States[45]

WASTING

Related domains:
Healthy children; nutrition.

Recommended measures:
- Child's height/weight for age is below the 5th percentile[1]
- Percentage of under-5 girls with moderate wasting[17]
- Percentage of under-5 boys with moderate wasting[17]
- Moderate and severe – below minus two standard deviations from median weight for height of reference population[56]

WATER

Related domains:
Community; development indicators.

Recommended measures:
- Percentage of households with access to safe water[17]
- Share of the population with reasonable access to an adequate amount of safe water[35]
- Access to safe water[57]

WEAPONS, AGE AT FIRST CARRYING A WEAPON

Related domains:
Health and safety (youth engaging in risky behaviour: youth use of violence and weapons).

Recommended measures:
- Average age children in Grades 6, 8, 10 and 12 first carried a handgun, as reported by students[41]

WEAPONS, APPROVAL OF PEER USE AND PERCEPTION OF PEER ACCEPTANCE OF WEAPON-CARRYING

Related domains:
Health and safety (youth engaging in risky behaviour: youth use of violence and weapons)

Recommended measures:
- Percentage of students in Grades 6, 8, 10 and 12 who answered 'not wrong at all' to the question 'how wrong do you think it is for someone your age to take a handgun to school?'[41]
- Percentage of students in Grades 6, 8, 10 and 12 who answered 'very good chance' to the question 'what are the chances you would be seen as cool if you carried a hand gun?'[41]

WEAPONS, CARRYING WEAPONS IN THE PAST 30 DAYS

Related domains:
Crime; health (health-related behaviour); health (violence); health and safety (youth engaging in risky behaviour: youth use of violence and weapons); health status (adolescents); problem behaviour; social and emotional development (delinquency and crime); social development, behavioural health and teen fertility (physical health and safety).

Recommended measures:

- Carrying of weapons[7]
- Percentage of students in Grades 9-12 who reported carrying weapons such as a gun, knife or club on one or more occasions in the last 30 days[10]
- Percentage of students in Grades 9 through 12 in the USA who reported having carried a weapon (such as a gun, knife or club) at least once within the past 30 days[20]
- Percentage of students in Grades 9 through 12 in the USA who reported having carried a gun at least once within the past 30 days[20]
- Percentage of teens who have carried a weapon to school in last month[21]
- Percentage of 9th to 12th Graders who have carried weapons (knife, gun, club) in last 30 days[21]
- Percentage of high school students who carried a weapon to school in the past 30 days, by gender[25]
- Percentage of high school students who carried a gun in the past 30 days, by sex and race[25]
- Percentage of students in Grades 9-12 who reported carrying a weapon onto school property in the past 30 days[40]

WEAPONS, CARRYING WEAPONS IN THE PAST 12 MONTHS

Related domains:

Health and safety (youth engaging in risky behaviour: youth use of violence and weapons).

Recommended measures:

- Percentage of students in Grades 6, 8, 10 and 12 who reported having carried a handgun at least once in the past 12 months[41]
- Annual rate of students in Grades 6, 8, 10 and 12 taking a handgun to school in the past 12 months[41]

WEAPONS, PARENTAL GUIDANCE AND PERCEIVED PARENTAL APPROVAL OF CARRYING WEAPONS

Related domains:

Health and safety (youth engaging in risky behaviour: youth use of violence and weapons).

Recommended measures:

- How wrong would your parents/guardians feel it would be for you to carry a gun, knife, club or other weapon to school? (Grade 6, 8 and 11)[42]

WEAPONS, PERCEPTION OF AVAILABILITY OF WEAPONS

Related domains:

Health (health-related behaviour); health and safety (youth engaging in risky behaviour: youth use of violence and weapons).

Recommended measures:

- Percentage of homes containing unlocked and loaded guns[21]
- Percentage of students in Grades 6, 8, 10 and 12 who answered 'very easy' to the question 'if you wanted to get a handgun, how easy would it be for you to get one?'[41]

WEAPONS, PERCEPTION OF POLICE INTERVENTION FOR CARRYING WEAPONS

Related domains:

Health and safety (youth engaging in risky behaviour: youth use of violence and weapons).

Recommended measures:

- Percentage of students in Grades 6, 8, 10 and 12 who answered 'no' to the question 'if a kid carried a hand gun in your neighbourhood or in the area where you live, would he or she be caught by the police?'[41]

WEAPONS, WEAPON RELATED INCIDENTS

Related domains:
Health and safety (youth engaging in risky behaviour: youth use of violence and weapons); health status (adolescents).

Recommended measures:

- Percentage of high school students who were threatened or injured with a weapon on school property, by race[25]
- Number of weapon-related incidents reported in school, per 1,000 students[34]

WEIGHT, OVERWEIGHT AND OBESITY

Related domains:
Child health and development (health); child protection; health; health (health status and disability); health (healthy lifestyles); health and safety (youth health: good health and health habits among youth); health conditions and health care (health conditions); health status (adolescents); healthy children; healthy weight; nutrition, physical activity and obesity; other determinant factors of child health, risk and protective factors; safety and physical status.

Recommended measures:

- Regular exercise or overweight children[1]
- Proportion of children aged 2-14 years whose body weight is at an acceptable/unacceptable level, as measured by BMI scores[2]
- Height, weight and body mass index measures[5]
- Overweight (BMI)[7]
- Percentage of children who are overweight. Overweight is defined as body mass index (BMI) at or above sex- and age-specific 95th percentile BMI cut-off points[10]
- Percentage of overweight children and adolescents in the USA. Overweight is defined as body mass index (BMI) at or above the sex- and age-specific 95th percentile BMI cut-off points calculated at 6-month age intervals for children ages 6 through 11 and for adolescents ages 12 through 17[20]
- Percentage of children ages 0-5 who are overweight[23]
- Percentage of high school students who thought they were overweight[25]
- Proportion of children aged 5-14 whose body mass index (BMI) met an international definition of obesity in the 2002 National Children's Nutrition Survey[29]
- Percentage of low-income children who are overweight[33]
- Percentage of prevalence of obesity (Body Mass Index) in children ages 0-19, by gender[36]
- Prevalence of overweight and obese children aged 7-13 years by sex[38]
- Percentage of youth with body mass index (BMI) at or above the 95th percentile of sex-specific BMI growth charts[45]
- Percentage of middle and high school youth who say they are slightly or very overweight[45]
- Percentage of children at school entry who are overweight or obese, as measured by the age- and sex-specific international reference standards for body mass index (BMI); optionally also at 10 and 15 years[48]
- Percentage of high school students who reported to be overweight[51]

WEIGHT, PRE-NATAL WEIGHT GAIN

Related domains:
Health (health conditions); pre-natal period (healthy babies).

Recommended measures:

- Low maternal weight gain during pregnancy (under 16 pounds)[21]
- Percentage of weight gain (0-24, 25-29, 40 or more pounds) experienced by women during pregnancy[36]

WEIGHT, UNDERWEIGHT

Related domains:
Development indicators; nutrition.

Recommended measures:

- Percentage of under-5 girls who are moderately underweight[17]
- Percentage of under-5 boys who are moderately underweight[17]
- Prevalence of underweight children measures the proportion of underweight children under-5 as a percentage of child population under-5. A child is considered underweight if his/her weight-for-age ratio is more than 2 standard deviations below the median weight for the healthy reference population[35]
- Moderate and severe – moderate is below minus two standard deviations from median weight for age of reference population; severe is below minus three standard deviations from median weight for age of reference population[56]

WEIGHT, WEIGHT CONTROL AND DISORDERED EATING

Related domains:
Health; health (health status and disability); health (healthy lifestyles); health (mental health); health status (adolescents).

Recommended measures:

- Eating disorders[7]
- Percentage of students in Grades 9-12 who reported vomiting or taking laxatives to lose weight or to keep from gaining weight in the last 30 days[10]
- Percentage of high school students who reported to be trying to lose weight[25]
- Percentage of high school students who reported unhealthy weight control[25]
- Percentage of high school students who reported they were trying to lose weight[51]

YOUTH EMPLOYMENT/UNEMPLOYMENT AND SOURCES OF INCOME

Related domains:
Child health and lifestyle behaviours; child protection; economic indicators; economic resources and contribution; economic security; economic security (employment); economic security indicators; education and childcare (enrolment); future; material well-being; school (out-of-school experiences); social inclusion; youth self-sufficiency (work).

Recommended measures:

- Percentage of family resources contributed by children[5]
- Children's perception of their contribution to the family resources[5]
- Percentage of family expenditures (spent by or on) by children[5]
- Measures of children's share of the family's material and economic resources[5]
- Average costs of children (for the household and society) by age group[5]
- Sources of income of children[5]
- Participation in the labour force[12]
- Percentage of boys aged 12-14 currently in paid employment[17]
- Youth attitudes towards work[21]
- Percentage of youth ages 16-19 who are unemployed[21]
- Average annual earnings foregone by students ages 18-24 attending college[21]
- Percentage of all 20-24 year-olds unemployed[26]
- Percentage of children engaged in part-time work of up to 6 hours per week, by male, female and in total[27]
- Number of 15-24 year-olds in the labour force who are not employed but are actively seeking and available for paid work, expressed as a percentage of 15-24 year-olds in the labour force[29]

- Median hourly earnings from all wage and salary jobs for employees aged 15-24 years and earning wage and salary income, as measured by the New Zealand Income Survey[29]
- Youth unemployment (ages 16-19)[31]
- Number of youth, 16 years of age and older who obtain employment[43]
- Unemployment rates of 16-24 year-olds, by sex, race/ethnicity and age (16-19, 20-24)[50]
- Labour force participation of persons 16 years-old and over, by sex and age (16-19, 20-24, 25-34)[50]
- Employment status of 16-24 year-olds who dropped out of school (employed, not employed but looking for work, not employed and not looking for work)[50]
- Employment status of 16-17 year-olds enrolled in school, by sex and race[50]
- Percentage of employed high school seniors spending 'most' or 'all or almost all' of their earnings on selected expenses (education savings, long-range savings, car expenses, personal items, family expenses), by race and college plans (planning to go to 4-year college, not planning to go to 4-year college)[50]
- Average annual expenditures of urban households, by age of head[50]
- Employment of 16-24 year-old college students, by attendance status (full-time or part-time), and hours worked per week (20 or more hours per week, 35 or more hours per week)[50]
- Employment and unemployment of high school graduates in year of graduation, by college enrolment status (in college, not in college)[50]
- Unemployment for youth ages 16-19 (per cent)[53]
- Age 15-24 registered unemployed (per cent of total year average unemployed)[55]
- Percentage of children aged 5 to 14 years involved in child labour activities at the moment of the survey. A child is considered to be involved in child labour activities under the following classification: (a) children 5 to 11 years of age that during the week preceding the survey did at least one hour of economic activity or at least 28 hours of domestic work; and (b) children 12 to 14 years of age that during the week preceding the survey did at least 14 hours of economic activity or at least 42 hours of domestic work combined[56]
- Child labour background variables: sex of the child; urban or rural place of residence; poorest 20% or richest 20% of the population constructed from household assets (a more detailed description of the household wealth estimation procedure can be found at www.childinfo.org); mother's education, reflecting mothers with and without some level of education[56]

YOUTH NEITHER ENROLLED IN SCHOOL NOR WORKING

Related domains:

Adolescent risk behaviours; detached youth; disconnectedness; economic security (employment); education; idle teens; social development, behavioural health and teen fertility (social development); youth self-sufficiency (work).

Recommended measures:

- Percentage of teens ages 16-19 not attending school and not working[3]
- Percentage of teens between ages 16 and 19 who are not enrolled in school (full- or part-time) and are not employed (full- or part-time)[4]
- Percentage of youth ages 16 to 19 who are neither enrolled in school nor working[18]
- Percentage of 16 through 19 year-olds in the USA who are neither enrolled in school nor working[20]
- Percentage of youth ages 16-19 who are idle in a given week (not in school and not at work)[21]
- Teens not attending school and not working[31]
- Estimated percentage of youth aged 16-19 who are not in school full-time or part-time, and are also not employed full-time or part-time over a 3-year period[45]
- Number of children aged 16-19 neither working any hours nor enrolled in school[51]

KEY DOMAINS OF CHILD WELL-BEING

DEMOGRAPHIC CHARACTERISTICS

- Child population and population projections[27]
- Demographic and socio-economic determinants of child health[48]
- Demographic indicators[56]
- Demographics[1, 8, 10, 32, 51]
- Family formation[55]
- Natality[55]
- Population[21, 55]
- Population and family characteristics[18]
- Population characteristics or risk factors[58]
- Population characteristics[25]
- Women[56]

ECONOMIC STATUS

- Access to housing[13]
- Children's economic well-being[32]
- Deprivation[12]
- Economic indicators[55, 56]
- Economic resources and contribution[5]
- Economic security[18, 20, 21, 47, 53]
- Economic status[51]
- General economic well-being[32]
- Income, assets and work[10]
- Material well-being[12, 26]
- Poverty[7]
- Rate of progress[56]
- Stable and economically independent families[24]
- Youth self-sufficiency[31, 39, 41, 42, 43, 45]

EDUCATION

- Academic achievement[54]
- Achievement[51]
- Child well-being within education[14]
- Children completing school[24]
- Children enter school ready to learn[24]
- Children ready for school and vice versa[1]
- Children succeeding in school[1]
- Children successful in school[24]
- Children's academic experiences[49]
- Early childhood experience[49]
- Education and achievement[20]
- Education and childcare[13, 21]
- Education and development[26]

- Education and personal development[12]
- Education and skills[10]
- Education outcome[7]
- Education[9, 18, 53, 55, 56]
- Educational development[30]
- Educational expectations[54]
- Educational well-being[32]
- Readiness and early school performance[51]
- School-age enrichment activities[49]

FAMILY, SCHOOL AND COMMUNITY CONTEXT

- Child well-being relating to the family[14]
- Child well-being within community[14]
- Children in strong, stable families[1]
- Children safe in their families and communities[24]
- Communities which support family life[24]
- Community and school environment deficits[31, 39, 41, 42, 43, 44, 45]
- Community and school environment strengths[31, 41, 42, 43, 44, 45, 46]
- Community[57]
- Community-related indicators[28]
- Family and community[10]
- Family and community context[38]
- Family and social functioning[9]
- Family environment[31, 39, 41, 42, 44, 45, 46]
- Family-related indicators[28]
- Family well-being[30]
- Family[51, 57]
- Family and household[21]
- Home[50]
- Neighbourhood[21]
- Parental determinants of child health, risk and protective factors[48]
- Permanency for children[30]
- Population, family and neighbourhood[20]
- School[50]

HEALTH AND SAFETY

- Abuse and neglect[29]
- Accidents in childhood[27]
- Babies born healthy[24]
- Care and protection[29]
- Child and maternal mortality[55]
- Child health and development[36]
- Child health and lifestyle behaviours[27]
- Child health status and well-being[48]
- Child protection[55, 56]
- Child safety[30]
- Childhood morbidity and mortality[27]
- Children's health and well-being[32]
- Communicable disease[38]
- Condition manifested in childhood[9]
- Conditions[22]
- Deaths[29]
- Dental health[38]

- Disability in childhood[27]
- Disability[9]
- Health and safety[24, 31, 39, 40, 41, 42, 43, 45, 46]
- Health and survival[2, 26]
- Healthcare services[58]
- Health conditions and health care[20]
- Health services utilisation[25]
- Health status[25]
- Health system[48]
- Health[7, 8, 10, 13, 16, 18, 21, 30, 33, 36, 47, 50, 51, 55, 56]
- Healthy children[1]
- HIV/AIDS[56]
- Illness and injury[29]
- Immunisation[9]
- Infant, child and teen health indicators[53]
- Infant health[38]
- Infant well-being[14]
- Injuries and violence[38]
- Injuries to children[48]
- Maternal and neo-natal conditions[9]
- Maternal health[58]
- Mortality[9]
- Neo-natal health[58]
- Physical health[28]
- Pre-natal period[36]
- Quality of care[8]
- Safety[47]
- Safety and physical status[5]
- Safety and security[2, 28]
- Survival and health[26]
- Youth health[31, 41, 45, 46]

SOCIAL, EMOTIONAL, BEHAVIOURAL DEVELOPMENT

- Access to developmental opportunities[47]
- Activity[30]
- Adolescent risk behaviours[51]
- Behaviour and social environment[18]
- Child lifestyle determinants of child health, risk and protective factors[48]
- Children's activities[5]
- Citizenship and values[50]
- Civic life skills[5]
- Crime indicators[55]
- Crime[7, 9]
- Development indicators[35]
- Development and behavioural measures[29]
- Early development[28]
- Future[50]
- Mental health of children[48]
- Mental health[7, 38]
- Nutrition[56]
- Nutrition, physical activity and obesity[38]
- Other determinant factors of child health, risk and protective factors[48]
- Participation in extra-curricular activities[54]

- Participation[29]
- Participation, quality of life and social inclusion[12]
- Personal life skills[5]
- Problem behaviour[21]
- Pro-social behaviour[21]
- Reproductive health[8, 29]
- Risk and enabling factors[7]
- Sexual health[38]
- Social adjustment[30]
- Social and emotional development[10, 31, 39, 40, 41, 42, 43, 45, 46]
- Social determinants of health[8, 27]
- Social development, behavioural health and teen fertility[20]
- Social inclusion[26]
- Social policy indicators[48]
- Social well-being[32]
- Substance misuse[7]
- Teenage fertility[7]
- Tobacco, alcohol and drug use[38]
- Youth engaging in risky behaviour[31, 39, 41, 42, 45, 46]

KEY INDICATOR SELECTION CRITERIA

IMPORTANCE

- All major infant, child and adolescent health events should be covered, as well as public health interventions relevant to this age group[52]
- Balanced so that no single area of children's lives dominates the reports[18]
- Challenge the stereotypes that were obstacles to action[5]
- Children of all ages[21, 22]
- Compelling to media and advocacy groups[5]
- Comprehensive coverage[21, 22]
- Depth, breadth and duration[21, 22]
- Evidenced-based, underpinned by research[58]
- Forward-looking[21, 22]
- Has clear links with improvement in health outcomes[2]
- Interpretable[29]
- National in scope or applicable to a regional or sub-population scope of national importance[2]
- Nationally significant[29]
- Objectively based on substantial research connecting them to child well-being and based on reliable data[18]
- Persuasive to policy-makers[5]
- Provides a basis for appreciating consequences[5]
- Recognised in the literature as important in understanding children and young people's well-being[13]
- Reflective of social goals[21, 22]
- Relate to sources and outcomes[5]
- Relevant to policy variables[5]
- Relevant[29]
- Representative of large segments of the population rather than one particular group[18]
- Representative of significant population groups[58]
- Responsive to change[2]
- Significance for the well-being of children[5]
- Significant burden to family[58]
- Significant burden to individual[58]
- Significant burden to society[58]
- The indicator is directly related to the well-being of children, families and communities[24]
- The indicator is well measured. It applies to all or most of the relevant population[24]
- Topic amenable to effective action[58]

PRACTICAL

- Able to be disaggregated[29]
- Adjusted for demographic trends[21, 22]
- Allow for repeated comparisons on an annual basis, in terms of providing annual report on the status of children and young people[13]
- As aggregate as possible[2]

- As retrievable as possible from routine data collection systems[52]
- Available and accessible[13]
- Available on a State level[13]
- Capable of being monitored easily and in a way that will provide a statistically verifiable time series[2]
- Capable of disaggregation by, for example, sex and gender[13]
- Collectable and assessable by operational units[5]
- Cost efficient[21, 22]
- Data availability[20, 58]
- Data on the indicator is available at State and local level[24]
- Data on the indicator is readily available from public sources[24]
- Feasibility[52]
- Geographically detailed[21, 22]
- Internationally comparable[29]
- Measured regularly so that they can be updated and show trends over time[18]
- Regularity and repeatability to enable trend analysis[58]
- Replicable[29]
- Timeliness[20]

TECHNICAL

- Accurate[5]
- Clear and comprehensible[21, 22]
- Clearly interpretable and understandable[5]
- Common interpretation[21, 22]
- Conceptually valid[5]
- Consistency over time[21, 22]
- Consistent and comparable with other indicators used in the States and Territories[2]
- Easy to understand by broad audiences[18]
- Easy to understand[2]
- Face validity (clearly understandable and interpretable)[5]
- Positive outcomes[21, 22]
- Post-dictive validity (constructed in such a way that changes in social, economic and/or policies factors would predict changes in the measured indicator)[5]
- Predictive validity (constructed in such a way that changes in the indicators measurements could be used to discuss changes in the well-being of children)[5]
- Provide clues for action by helping to define targets and determine policies and interventions[52]
- Quality and consistency[20]
- Reliability and validity[52]
- Reliable and valid with values that are meaningful to child health and well-being[2]
- Rigorous methods[21, 22]
- Robust to criticism[5]
- Statistically sound[29]
- The indicator is well measured. It is collected in ways that support data reliability and validity[24]
- Understandable to broad audience[58]
- Valid[29]

BIBLIOGRAPHY

Al-Yaman, F., Bryant, M. and Sargeant, H. (2002) *Australia's Children: Their Health and Well-Being 2002.* Canberra: Australian Institute of Health and Welfare. Available at: http://www.aihw.gov.au/publications/phe/ac02/ac02.pdf [Accessed: 14th January 2005].

Ben-Arieh, A., Hevener-Kaufman, N., Bowers-Andrews, A., Goerge, R.M., Joo-Lee, B. and Aber, J.L. (2001) *Measuring and Monitoring Children's Well-Being.* Dordrecht, the Netherlands: Kluwer Academic Publishers.

Bradshaw, J. and Barnes, H. (1999) *How do Nations Monitor the Well-Being of Their Children?* Florence: UNICEF, International Child Development Centre.

Carroll, E. (2002) *The Well-Being of Children: Four Papers Exploring Conceptual, Ethical and Measurement Issues.* Dublin: Irish Youth Foundation.

Combat Poverty Agency (2000) *Submission on the National Children's Strategy.* Dublin: Combat Poverty Agency.

Costello, L. (1999) *A Literature Review of Children's Well-Being.* Dublin: Combat Poverty Agency.

Department of Health and Children (2000) *Child Care Interim Minimum Dataset.* Dublin: Department of Health and Children.

Department of Health and Children (2001) *The Health of Our Children: The Second Annual Report of the Chief Medical Officer.* Dublin: Stationery Office.

Department of Health and Children (2002a) *Traveller Health: A National Strategy 2002-2005.* Dublin: Stationery Office.

Department of Health and Children (2002b) *Health Services National Performance Indicators.* Dublin: Department of Health and Children.

Federal Interagency Programme on Child and Family Statistics (2002) *America's Children – Key National Indicators of Child Well-Being.* Washington, DC: US Government Printing Office. Available at: http://www.childstats.gov/ac2002/pdf/ac2002.pdf [Accessed: 10th February 2003].

Government of Canada (2002) *The Well-Being of Canada's Young Children.* Ottawa: Human Resources Development Canada and Health Canada. Available at: http://www.socialunion.gc.ca/ecd/2002/reportb-e.pdf [Accessed: 10th February 2003].

Gutmann, B. and Hamilton, J. (2001) *Trends in the Well-Being of America's Children and Youth 2001.* Washington, DC: Office of the Assistant Secretary for Planning and Evaluation, US Department of Health and Human Services.
Available at: http://www.aspe.hhs.gov/hsp/01trends/ [Accessed: 10th February 2003].

Hauser, R.M., Brown, B.V. and Prosser, W.R. (eds.) (1997) *Indicators of Children's Well-Being.* New York: Russell Sage Foundation.

Jensen, W., Myers, J., Sidorova, M., Duerr, M., Cragle, S., Brisolara, S., Berryhill, M., Lapp, B., Kehoe, D.A., Reed, B., Skillman, D.R., Englesby-Smith, J. and Wayda, M. (2002) *Indicators of Well-Being Report: Shasta County Children Pre-Natal to Five and their Families.* Shasta County: First 5 Shasta, the Shasta Children and Family First Commission. Available at: http://www.ccfc.ca.gov/shasta/PDFs/Well-BeingRpt.pdf

McKeown K., Haasse, T. and Pratschke, J. (2001) *Springboard: Promoting Family Well-Being Through Family Support Services.* Dublin: Department of Health and Children.

McKeown, K., Pratschke, J. and Haase, T. (2003) *Family Well-Being: What Makes a Difference.* Shannon: The Ceifin Centre.

Mid-Western Health Board (2001) *Health and Well-Being of Children in the Mid-West: Report of the Director of Public Health.* Limerick: Mid-Western Health Board.

National Children's Strategy (2000) *Our Children – Their Lives.* Dublin: Stationery Office.

New Policy Institute (2001) *Poverty Reduction Indicators: A Discussion Paper.* Dublin: Combat Poverty Agency.

Nolan, B. (2000) *Child Poverty in Ireland.* Dublin: Combat Poverty Agency.

Pollard, E.L. and Lee, P. (2002) 'Child Well-Being: A Systematic Review of the Literature'. *Social Indicators Research*, 61: 59-78.

Quinlan, A., Greally, T., Heslin, J., Nicholson, A., O'Reilly, C., O'Sullivan, M., Pelly, H. and Thornton, L. (2001) *Towards the Development of Health Indicators for Irish Children.* Dublin: Best Health for Children.

Rigby, K. and Kohler, L. (eds.) (2002) *Child Health Indicators of Life and Development.* Luxembourg: European Commission. Available at: http://www.europa.eu.int/comm/health/ph_projects/2000/monitoring/fp_monitoring_2000_exs_08_en.pdf [Accessed: 10th February 2003].

UNICEF (2005) *The State of the World's Children.* New York: UNICEF.

United Nations (1989) *Convention on the Rights of the Child.* Geneva: United Nations.

United Nations Educational, Scientific and Cultural Organisation (UNESCO) (1995) *Early Childhood Care and Education: Basic Indicators on Young Children* Paris: UNESCO. Available at: http://www.unesdoc.unesco.org/images/0010/001036/103655e.pdf

Zeitlin, J. and Wildman, K. (2003) *PERISTAT: Indicators for Monitoring and Evaluating Perinatal Health in Europe.* Luxembourg: European Commission. Available at: http://www.europa.eu.int/comm/health/ph_projects/2000/monitoring/fp_monitoring_2000_frep_07_en.pdf

Zeitlin, J., Wildman, K., Bréart, G., Alexander, S., Barros, H., Blondel, B., Buitendijk, S., Gissler, M., and MacFarlane, A. (2003a) 'Selecting an Indicator Set for Monitoring and Evaluating Perinatal Health in Europe: Criteria, Methods and Results from the PERISTAT Project'. *European Journal of Obstetrics and Gynaecology,* 111: S5-S14.

Zeitlin, J., Wildman, K. and Bréart, G. (2003b) 'Editorial: Perinatal Health Indicators for Europe: An Introduction to the PERISTAT Project'. *European Journal of Obstetrics and Gynaecology,* 203: S1-S4.

APPENDIX

LIST OF REPORTS IN THE INVENTORY

1. **Alaska Department of Health and Human Services (2000)** *Building Blocks: The Next Steps for Supporting Alaska's Young Children and Their Families.* Available at: http://www.gov.state.ak.us/children/nominations.html [Accessed: 4th March 2003].

2. **Al-Yaman, F., Bryant, M. and Sargeant, H. (2002)** *Australia's Children: Their Health and Well-Being 2002.* Canberra: Australian Institute of Health and Welfare. Available at: http://www.aihw.gov.au/publications/phe/ac02/ac02.pdf [Accessed: 14th January 2005].

3. **Annie E. Casey Foundation (2002)** *Children at Risk: State Trends 1990-2000: A PRB/ KIDS COUNT Special Report.* Baltimore, Maryland: Annie E. Casey Foundation. Available at: http://www.aecf.org/kidscount/c2ss/pdfs/entire_book.pdf [Accessed: 10th February 2003].

4. **Annie E. Casey Foundation (2003)** *Kidscount Data Book.* Baltimore, Maryland: Annie E. Casey Foundation. Available at: http://www.aecf.org/kidscount/databook/ [Accessed: 10th February 2003].

5. **Ben-Arieh, A., Hevener-Kaufman, N., Bowers-Andrews, A., Goerge, R.M., Joo-Lee, B. and Aber, J.L. (2001)** *Measuring and Monitoring Children's Well-Being.* Dordrecht, the Netherlands: Kluwer Academic Publishers.

6. **Bradshaw, J. (ed.) (2002)** *The Well-Being of Children in the UK.* London: Save the Children.

7. **Bradshaw, J. and Barnes, H. (1999)** *How do Nations Monitor the Well-Being of their Children? Paper to the LIS Child Poverty Conference, Luxembourg, 30th September - 2nd October 1999.* Heslington, York: Social Policy Research Unit, University of York. Available at: http://www.lisproject.org/links/cpconf/ bradshaw.pdf [Accessed: 10th February 2003].

8. **Brownell, M., Martens, P., Kozyrskyj, A., Fergusson, P., Lerfald, J., Mayer, T., Derksen, S. and Friesen, D. (2001)** *Assessing the Health of Children in Manitoba: A Population-based Study.* Manitoba: Manitoba Centre for Health Policy and Evaluation, Department of Community Health Sciences Faculty of Medicine, University of Manitoba. Available at: http://www.umanitoba.ca/centres/mchp/reports/child_pdfs.htm [Accessed: 3rd August 2004].

9. **Centre for Epidemiology, Indicators, Research and Evaluation (2000)** *The Health Status and Well-being of Children and Youth in Western Sydney.* Western Sydney: Western Sydney Area Health Service. Available at: http://www.203.32.142.101/ services/dsdph/EIRE/Publicat/HEALTH_S.PDF [Accessed: 21st May 2003].

10. **Child Trends (2003)** *Child Trends Data Bank.* Washington, DC: Child Trends. Available from: http://www.childtrendsdatabank.org/ [Accessed: 14th April 2003].

11. **Children's Defence Fund (2003)** *Minnesota Kids A Closer Look: 2003 Data Book.* Minnesota: Children's Defence Fund. Available at: http://www.cdf-mn.org/PDF/KidsCountData_03/DataBook_2003.pdf [Accessed: 3rd August 2004].

12. **Combat Poverty Agency (2000)** *Submission on the National Children's Strategy.* Dublin: Combat Poverty Agency.

13. **Commission for Children and Young People (2002)** *Children and Young People in Queensland - A Snap Shot.* Queensland: Commission for Children and Young People. Available at: http://www.childcomm.qld.gov.au/publications/reports.htm [Accessed: 21st May 2003].

14. **Costello, L. (1999)** *A Literature Review of Children's Well-being.* Dublin: Combat Poverty Agency.

15. **Department for Work and Pensions (2002)** *Opportunity for All: Fourth Annual Report.* London: HMSO. Available at: http://www.dwp.gov.uk/ofa/reports/2003/ pdf/report.pdf [Accessed: 10th February 2003].

16. **Department of Health and Children (2001)** *The Health of Our Children: The Second Annual Report of the Chief Medical Officer.* Dublin: Stationery Office.

17. **El Tawila, S. (1997)** *Child Well-Being in Egypt.* Cairo: Social Research Centre, American University. Available at: http://www.childinfo.org/mics/Cntry_files/ Egyintro.pdf [Accessed: 10th February 2003].

18. **Federal Interagency Programme on Child and Family Statistics (2002)** *America's Children – Key National Indicators of Child Well-Being.* Washington, DC: US Government Printing Office. Available at: http://www.childstats.gov/ac2002/ pdf/ac2002.pdf [Accessed: 10th February 2003].

19. **Government of Canada (2002)** *The Well-Being of Canada's Young Children.* Ottawa: Human Resources Development Canada and Health Canada. Available at: http://www.socialunion.gc.ca/ecd/2002/reportb-e.pdf [Accessed: 10th February 2003].

20. **Gutmann, B. and Hamilton, J. (2001)** *Trends in the Well-Being of America's Children and Youth 2001.* Washington, DC: Office of the Assistant Secretary for Planning and Evaluation, US Department of Health and Human Services. Available at: http://www.aspe.hhs.gov/hsp/01trends/ [Accessed: 10th February 2003].

21. **Hauser, R.M., Brown, B.V. and Prosser, W.R. (eds.) (1997)** *Indicators of Children's Well-Being.* New York: Russell Sage Foundation.

22. **Howell, F., Howell, P.R. and Gipson Wells, J. (1998)** *Indicators of the Well-Being of Mississippi Children.* Mississippi: Social Science Research Centre, Mississippi State University. Available at: http://www.ssrc.msstate.edu/publications/srrs98-1.pdf [Accessed: 3rd August 2003].

23. **Jensen, W., Myers, J., Sidorova, M., Duerr, M., Cragle, S., Brisolara, S., Berryhill, M., Lapp, B., Kehoe, D.A., Reed, B., Skillman, D.R., Englesby-Smith, J. and Wayda, M. (2002)** *Indicators of Well-Being Report: Shasta County Children Pre-Natal to Five and their Families.* Shasta County: First 5 Shasta, the Shasta Children and Family First Commission. Available at: http://www.ccfc.ca.gov/ shasta/PDFs/Well-BeingRpt.pdf [Accessed: 3rd August 2003].

24. **Maryland Partnership for Children, Youth and Families (2002)** *Maryland's Results for Well-Being.* Baltimore, Maryland: Maryland Partnership for Children, Youth and Families. Available at: http://www.ocyf.state.md.us/ [Accessed: 10th February 2003].

25. **Maternal and Child Health Bureau (2002)** *Child Health USA: 2002.* Washington, DC: Maternal and Child Health Bureau, US Department of Health and Human Services. Available at: http://www.mchb.hrsa.gov/chusa02/index.htm [Accessed: 3rd August 2003].

26. **Micklewright, J. and Stewart, K. (1999)** *Is the Well-Being of Children Converging in the European Union? Paper to the LIS Child Poverty Conference, Luxembourg, 30th September - 2nd October 1999.* Florence: UNICEF International Child Development Centre. Available at: http://www.lisproject.org/links/cpconf/ micklewright.pdf [Accessed: 10th February 2003].

27. **Mid-Western Health Board (2001)** *Health and Well-Being of Children in the Mid-West: Report of the Director of Public Health.* Limerick: Mid-Western Health Board.

28. **Ministry of Children and Family Development (2000)** *Indicators of Early Childhood Health and Well-Being in British Columbia: A Baseline Report.* British Columbia: Ministry of Children and Family Development. Available at: http://www.mcf.gov.bc.ca/publications/measure_success/final_indicators_document.pdf [Accessed: 10th February 2003].

29. **Ministry of Social Development (2004)** *Children and Young People: Indicators of Well-Being in New Zealand.* Available at: http://www.msd.govt.nz/documents/work-areas/csre/children-young-people-indicators-wellbeing-nz.pdf [Accessed: 14th January 2005].

30. **Minnesota Department of Human Services (2000)** *Measuring Our Performance and the Well-Being of Children: Indicators to Help Strengthen Minnesota's Child Welfare System.* Minnesota: Department of Human Services. Available at: http://www.dhs.state.mn.us/main/groups/children/documents/pub/DHS_id_007125.pdf [Accessed: 10th February 2003].

31. **Murphey, D. (2004)** *The Social Well-Being of Vermonters: A Report on Outcomes for Vermont Citizens.* Waterbury, Vermont: Vermont Agency of Human Services, Planning Division. Available at: http://www.ahs.state.vt.us/publs/docs/04swb/ 04SWB.pdf [Accessed: 14th January 2005].

32. **North Carolina Child Advocacy Institute (2002)** *NC Children's Index: A Profile of Leading Indicators on the Health and Well-Being of North Carolina's Children.* Raleigh, North Carolina: North Carolina Child Advocacy Institute. Available at: http://www.ncchild.org/CI2004/INDEX_02_WEB.pdf [Accessed: 10th February 2003].

33. **North Carolina Child Advocacy Institute and North Carolina Institute of Medicine (2002)** *North Carolina Child Health Report Card.* Raleigh, North Carolina: North Carolina Child Advocacy Institute and Durham, North Carolina: North Carolina Institute of Medicine. Available at: http://www.nciom.org/docs/ card2002.pdf [Accessed: 10th February 2003].

34. **Olivier, D.J. (2004)** *The State of the Child in Pennsylvania – 2004: State of the Child in Pennsylvania Fact Book Series.* Harrisburg, Pennsylvania: Pennsylvania KIDS COUNT. Available at: http://www.papartnerships.org/stateofthechild.asp [Accessed: 14th January 2005].

35. **Organisation for Economic Co-operation and Development (OECD) (1998)** *Methodology Sheets for Development Indicators: Methodological Notes and Indicator Sheets.* Paris: OECD. Available at: http://www.oecd.org/dataoecd/3/45/ 1896978.pdf [Accessed: 10th February 2003].

36. **Peterborough County – City Health Unit (2003)** *The First Nine Years: A Profile of Perinatal and Child Health in Peterborough County and City.* Peterborough: Peterborough County, City Health Unit. Available at: http://www.pcchu.peterborough.on.ca/First_Nine_Years_Second_Edition.pdf [Accessed: 3rd August 2004].

37. **Rahman, M., Palmer, G. and Kenway, P. (2001)** *Monitoring Poverty and Social Exclusion.* York, North Yorkshire: Joseph Rowntree Foundation. Available at: http://www.jrf.org.uk/knowledge/findings/socialpolicy/d31.asp [Accessed: 10th February 2003].

38. **Region of Peel Health Department (2002)** *Child Health Report: A Peel Health Status Report.* Peel: Region of Peel Health Department. Available at: http://www.region.peel.on.ca/health/health-status-report/pdfs-child/CH_report.pdf [Accessed: 3rd August 2004].

39. **Reidy, M. and Winje, C. (2002)** *Youth Indicators in Use in States as of September 2002: New York.* Chicago: Chapin Hall Centre for Children, University of Chicago. Available at: http://www.chapinhall.org/PDFDownload_new.asp?tk=1229292&ar= 1343&L2=65&L3=120 [Accessed: 13th May 2003].

40. **Reidy, M. and Winje, C. (2002)** *Youth Indicators in Use in States as of September 2002: Wyoming.* Chicago: Chapin Hall Centre for Children, University of Chicago. Available at: http://www.chapinhall.org/PDFDownload_new.asp?tk=1229292&ar= 1343&L2=65&L3=120 [Accessed: 13th May 2003].

41. **Reidy, M. and Winje, C. (2002)** *Youth Indicators in Use in States as of September 2002: Kansas.* Chicago: Chapin Hall Centre for Children, University of Chicago. Available at: http://www.chapinhall.org/PDFDownload_new.asp?tk=1229292&ar= 1343&L2=65&L3=120 [Accessed: 13th May 2003].

42. **Reidy, M. and Winje, C. (2002)** *Youth Indicators in Use in States as of September 2002: Iowa.* Chicago: Chapin Hall Centre for Children, University of Chicago. Available at: http://www.chapinhall.org/PDFDownload_new.asp?tk=1229292&ar= 1343&L2=65&L3=120 [Accessed: 13th May 2003].

43. **Reidy, M. and Winje, C. (2002)** *Youth Indicators in Use in States as of September 2002: Illinois.* Chicago: Chapin Hall Centre for Children, University of Chicago. Available at: http://www.chapinhall.org/PDFDownload_new.asp?tk=1229292&ar= 1343&L2=65&L3=120 [Accessed: 13th May 2003].

44. **Reidy, M. and Winje, C. (2002)** *Youth Indicators in Use in States as of September 2002: Missouri.* Chicago: Chapin Hall Centre for Children, University of Chicago.. Available at: http://www.chapinhall.org/PDFDownload_new.asp?tk=1229292&ar= 1343&L2=65&L3=120 [Accessed: 13th May 2003].

45. **Reidy, M. and Winje, C. (2002)** *Youth Indicators in Use in States as of September 2002: Maine.* Chicago: Chapin Hall Centre for Children, University of Chicago. Available at: http://www.chapinhall.org/PDFDownload_new.asp?tk=1229292&ar= 1343&L2=65&L3=120 [Accessed: 13th May 2003].

46. **Reidy, M. and Winje, C. (2002)** *Youth Indicators in Use in States as of September 2002: Georgia.* Chicago: Chapin Hall Centre for Children, University of Chicago. Available at: http://www.chapinhall.org/PDFDownload_new.asp?tk=1229292&ar= 1343&L2=65&L3=120 [Accessed: 13th May 2003].

47. **Report Card Working Group (2003)** *Toronto Report Card on Children: Volume 5.* Toronto: Report Card Working Group. Available at: http://www.city.toronto.on.ca/children/report/repcard5/repcard5.htm [Accessed: 3rd August 2004].

48. **Rigby, K. and Kohler, L. (eds.) (2002)** *Child Health Indicators of Life and Development.* Luxembourg: European Commission. Available at: http://www.europa.eu.int/comm/health/ph_ projects/000/monitoring/fp_monitoring_2000_exs_08_en.pdf [Accessed: 10th February 2003].

49. **Smith, K.E., Bass, L.E. and Fields, J.M. (1998)** *Child Well-Being Indicators From the Survey of Income and Program Participation (SIPP): Working Paper 24.* Washington, DC: Population Division, US Bureau of the Census. Available at: http://www.census.gov/population/www/documentation/twps0024/twps0024.html [Accessed: 13th May 2003].

50. **Snyder, T. and Shafer, L. (1996)** *Youth Indicators 1996: Trends in the Well-Being of American Youth.* Washington, DC: US Department of Education, National Centre for Education Statistics. Available at: http://www.nces.ed.gov/pubs98/yi/youth.pdf [Accessed: 10th February 2003].

51. ***South Carolina KIDSCOUNT Report (2003)*** Available at: http://www.sckidscount.org/report03/SC_kc03.pdf [Accessed: 3rd August 2004].

52. **Tamburlini, G., Ronfani, L. and Buzzetti, R. (2001)** 'Development of a Child Health Indicator System in Italy'. *European Journal of Public Health,* 11 (1): 11-17.

53. **Tennessee Commission on Children and Youth (2002)** *The State of the Child in Tennessee.* Nashville, Tennessee: Tennessee Commission on Children and Youth. Available at: http://www.state.tn.us/tccy/kc02.pdf [Accessed: 13th May 2003].

54. **US Department of Commerce (2003)** *A Child's Day: 2000 (Selected Indicators of Child Well-Being).* Washington, DC: US Department of Commerce, US Census Bureau. Available at: http://www.census.gov/prod/2003pubs/p70-89.pdf [Accessed: 3rd August 2004].

55. **UNICEF (2001)** *A Decade of Transition: Regional Monitoring Report No. 8.* Florence: UNICEF Innocenti Research Centre. Available at: http://www.unicef-icdc.org/publications/pdf/monee8/eng/monee8_annex.pdf [Accessed: 14th April 2003].

i **Amanniyazova, L. (2000)** *Family Welfare in Turkmenistan: Trends and Indicators.* Ashgabat: National Institute of Statistics and Prognosis. Available at: http://www.unicef-icdc.org/research/ESP/CountryReports2000_01/Turkmen00.pdf [Accessed: 14th April 2003].

ii **Banovec, T. (2000)** *Trends and Indicators on Child and Family Well-Being in Slovenia, 1989-1999.* Ljubljana: Statistical Office. Available at: http://www.uniceficdc.org/research/ESP/CountryReports2000_01/Slovenia00.pdf [Accessed: 14th April 2003].

iii **Chirca, C. (2000)** *Trends and Indicators on Child and Family Well-Being in Romania.* Bucharest: National Institute for Statistics and Economic Studies. Available at: http://www.unicef-icdc.org/research/ESP/CountryReports2000_01/Romania00.pdf [Accessed: 14th April 2003].

iv **Eidukiene, V. (2000)** *Child and Family Well-Being in Lithuania.* Lithuania: Department of Statistics. Available at: http://www.unicef-icdc.org/research/ESP/CountryReports 2000_01/Lithuania00.pdf [Accessed: 14th April 2003].

v **Galazka, Z. (2000)** *Trends and Indicators on Child and Family Well-Being in Poland.* Warsaw: Central Statistical Office. Available at: http://www.unicef-icdc.org/research/ESP/CountryReports2000_01/Poland00.pdf [Accessed: 14th April 2003].

vi **Gardashkhanova, M. (2000)** *Trends and Indicators on Family and Children Well-Being in Azerbaijan.* Baku: State Statistical Committee. Available at: http://www.unicef-icdc.org/research/ESP/CountryReports2000_01/Azerbaijan00.pdf [Accessed: 14th April 2003].

vii **Gasyuk, G. (2000)** *Trends and Indicators of the Child and Family Welfare in the Republic of Belarus (1990-1999).* Minsk: Ministry of Statistics and Analysis. Available at: http://www.unicef-icdc.org/research/ESP/CountryReports2000_01/Belarus00eng.pdf [Accessed: 14th April 2003].

viii **Gogishvili, T. (2000)** *Trends and Family Well-Being in Georgia.* Georgia: State Department for Statistics of Georgia. Available at: http://www.unicef-icdc.org/research/ESP/CountryReports2000_01/Georgia00fam.pdf [Accessed: 14th April 2003].

ix **Kalachova, I. (2000)** *Child and Family Welfare in Ukraine: Trends and Indicators.* Kiev: State Committee for Statistics. Available at: http://www.unicef-icdc.org/research/ESP/CountryReports2000_01/Ukraine00.pdf [Accessed: 14th April 2003].

x **Kask, U. (2000)** *Trends and Indicators on Child Well-Being in Estonia.* Estonia: Statistical Office. Available at: http://www.unicef-icdc.org/research/ESP/Country Reports2000_01/Estonia00.pdf [Accessed: 14th April 2003].

xi **Koichumanova, K. (2000)** *Family and Child Welfare Trends in the Transition Period in Kyrgyzstan.* Bishkek: National Statistical Committee. Available at: http://www.unicef-icdc.org/research/ESP/CountryReports2000_01/Kyrgyz00eng.pdf [Accessed: 14th April 2003].

xii Lakatos, J. (2000) *Poverty and Welfare Trends Over the 1990s in Hungary.* Budapest: Hungarian Central Statistical Office. Available at: http://www.unicef-icdc.org/research/ESP/CountryReports2000_01/Hungary00.pdf [Accessed: 14th April 2003].

xiii Magloutchiants, J. (2000) *Trends and Indicators on Child and Family Well-Being in Armenia.* Yerevan: Department of Statistics State Register and Analysis. Available at: http://www.unicef-icdc.org/research/ESP/CountryReports2000_01/Armenia00.pdf [Accessed: 14th April 2003].

xiv Mukhammadieva, B. (2000) *Child and Family Welfare in Tajikistan: The Main Trends and Indicators.* Dushanbe: State Statistics Agency. Available at: http://www.unicef-icdc.org/research/ESP/CountryReports2000_01/Tajik00.pdf [Accessed: 14th April 2003].

xv Musabekov, E. (2000) *Child and Family Welfare: Trends and Indicators in the Republic of Kazakhstan.* Almaty: National Statistics Agency. Available at: http://www.unicef-icdc.org/research/ESP/CountryReports2000_01/Kazak00.pdf [Accessed: 14th April 2003].

xvi Novak, J. (2000) *Trends and Indicators on Child and Family Well-Being in the Czech Republic.* Prague: Czech Statistical Office. Available at: http://www.unicef-icdc.org/research/ESP/CountryReports2000_01/CzechRep00.pdf [Accessed: 14th April 2003].

xvii Placintar, E. (2000) *Trends and Indicators on Child and Family Well-Being in Slovakia.* Bratislava: Statistical Office. Available at: http://www.unicef-icdc.org/research/ESP/CountryReports2000_01/Slovakia00.pdf [Accessed: 14th April 2003].

xviii Puskovic, D. (2000) *Poverty and Welfare Trends Over the 1990s in the FR Yugoslavia.* Belgrade: Federal Statistical Office. Available at: http:// www.unicef-icdc.org/research/ESP/CountryReports2000_01/FRYugos00.pdf [Accessed: 14th April 2003].

xix Tafi, J. (2000) *Poverty and Welfare Over the 1990s in the Republic of Moldova: Indicators of Status and Trends.* Chisinau: Department for Statistical and Sociological Analysis. Available at: http://www.unicef-icdc.org/research/ESP/CountryReports2000_01/Moldova00.pdf [Accessed: 14th April 2003].

xx Tzvetkova-Anguelova, J. (2000) *Trends and Indicators on Child and Family Well-Being in Bulgaria.* Sofia: National Statistical Institute. Available at: http://www.unicef-icdc.org/research/ESP/CountryReports2000_01/Bulgaria00.pdf [Accessed: 14th April 2003].

xxi Vaskis, E. (2000) *Trends and Indicators on Child and Family Well-Being in Latvia.* Riga: Central Statistical Bureau. Available at: http://www.unicef-icdc.org/research/ESP/CountryReports2000_01/Latvia00.pdf [Accessed: 14th April 2003].

xxii Zbarskaya, I. (2000) *Child and Family Welfare in Russia: Trends and Indicators.* Goskomstat of Russia: State Committee of the Russian Federation on Statistics. Available at: http://www.unicef-icdc.org/research/ESP/CountryReports2000_01/Russia00.pdf [Accessed: 14th April 2003].

56. **UNICEF (2005)** *The State of the World's Children.* New York: UNICEF. Available at: http://www.unicef.org/sowc05/english/index.html [Accessed: 14th January 2005].

57. **United Nations Educational, Scientific and Cultural Organisation (UNESCO) (1995)** *Early Childhood Care and Education: Basic Indicators on Young Children.* Paris: UNESCO. Available at: http://www.unesdoc.unesco.org/images/0010/001036/ 103655e.pdf [Accessed: 14th April 2003].

58. **Zeitlin, J. and Wildman, K. (2003)** *PERISTAT: Indicators for Monitoring and Evaluating Perinatal Health in Europe.* Luxembourg: European Commission. Available at: http://www.europa.eu.int/comm/health/ph_projects/2000/monitoring/ fp_monitoring_2000_frep_07_en.pdf [Accessed: 3rd August 2004].